OTHER BONE BOOKS BY JEFF SMITH

THE FIRST TRILOGY

BONE VOLUME ONE: OUT FROM BONEVILLE

BONE VOLUME TWO: THE GREAT COW RACE

BONE VOLUME THREE: EYES OF THE STORM

THE SECOND TRILOGY

BONE VOLUME FOUR: THE DRAGONSLAYER

BONE VOLUME FIVE: ROCK JAW, MASTER OF THE EASTERN BORDER

BONE VOLUME SIX: OLD MAN'S CAVE

(WITH TOM SNIEGOSKI AND STAN SAKAI)

*STUPID, STUPID RAT-TAILS: THE ADVENTURES OF BIG JOHNSON BONE,
FRONTIER HERO*

(COMING SOON)

BONE VOLUME SEVEN: GHOST CIRCLES

Stupid, Stupid Rat-Tails

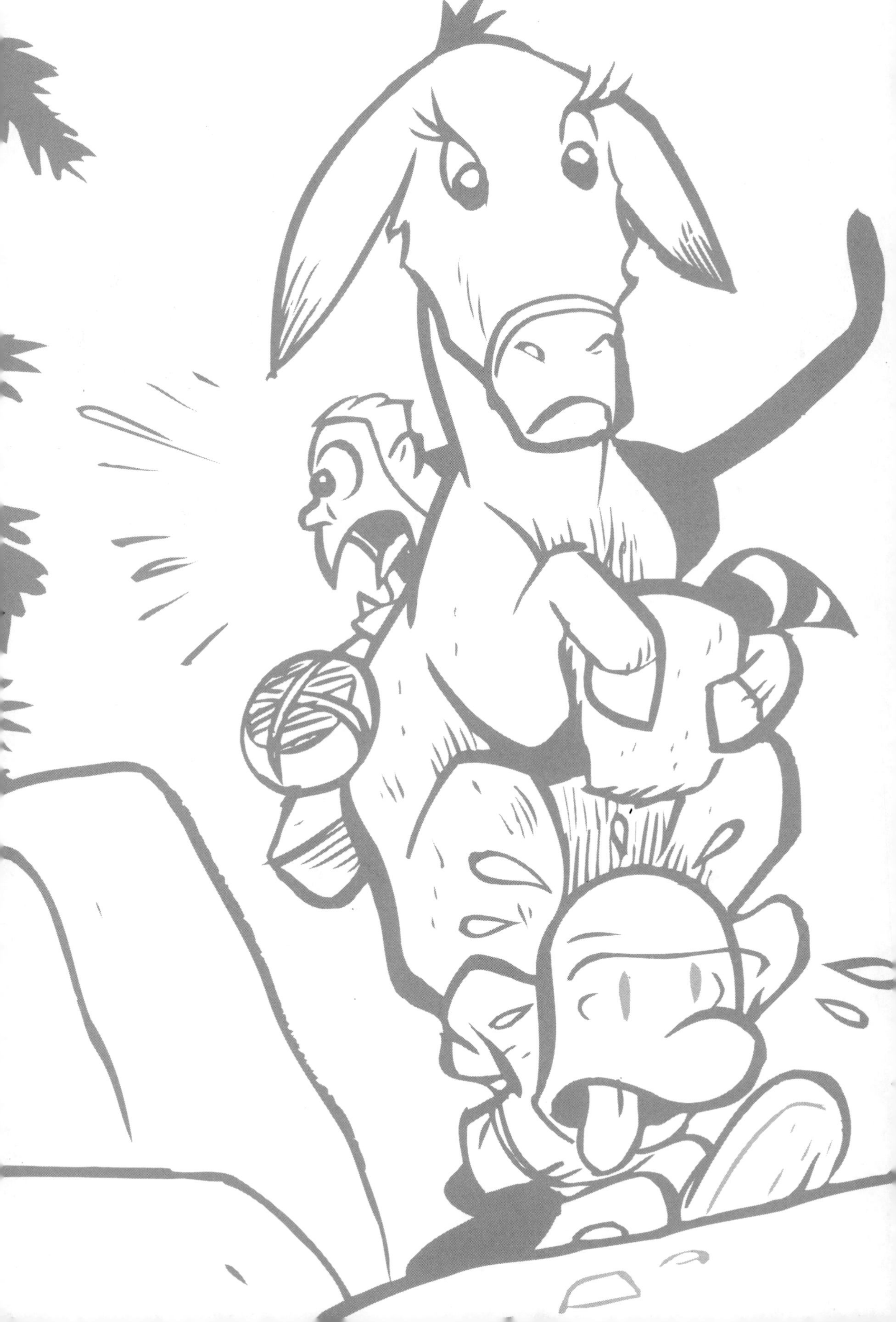

STUPID, STUPID Rat-tails

The Adventures Of Big Johnson Bone, Frontier Hero

written by Tom Sniegoski and
drawn by Jeff Smith

Riblet

written by Tom Sniegoski and
drawn by Stan Sakai

Series Editor
Jeff Smith

A  Book

CARTOON BOOKS
COLUMBUS, OHIO

Artwork on cover by: Jeff Smith and Elizabeth Lewis.
For information write:
Cartoon Books
P.O. Box 16973
Columbus, OH 43216

ISBN: 1-888963-06-9

10 9 8 7 6 5 4 3 2

Printed in Canada

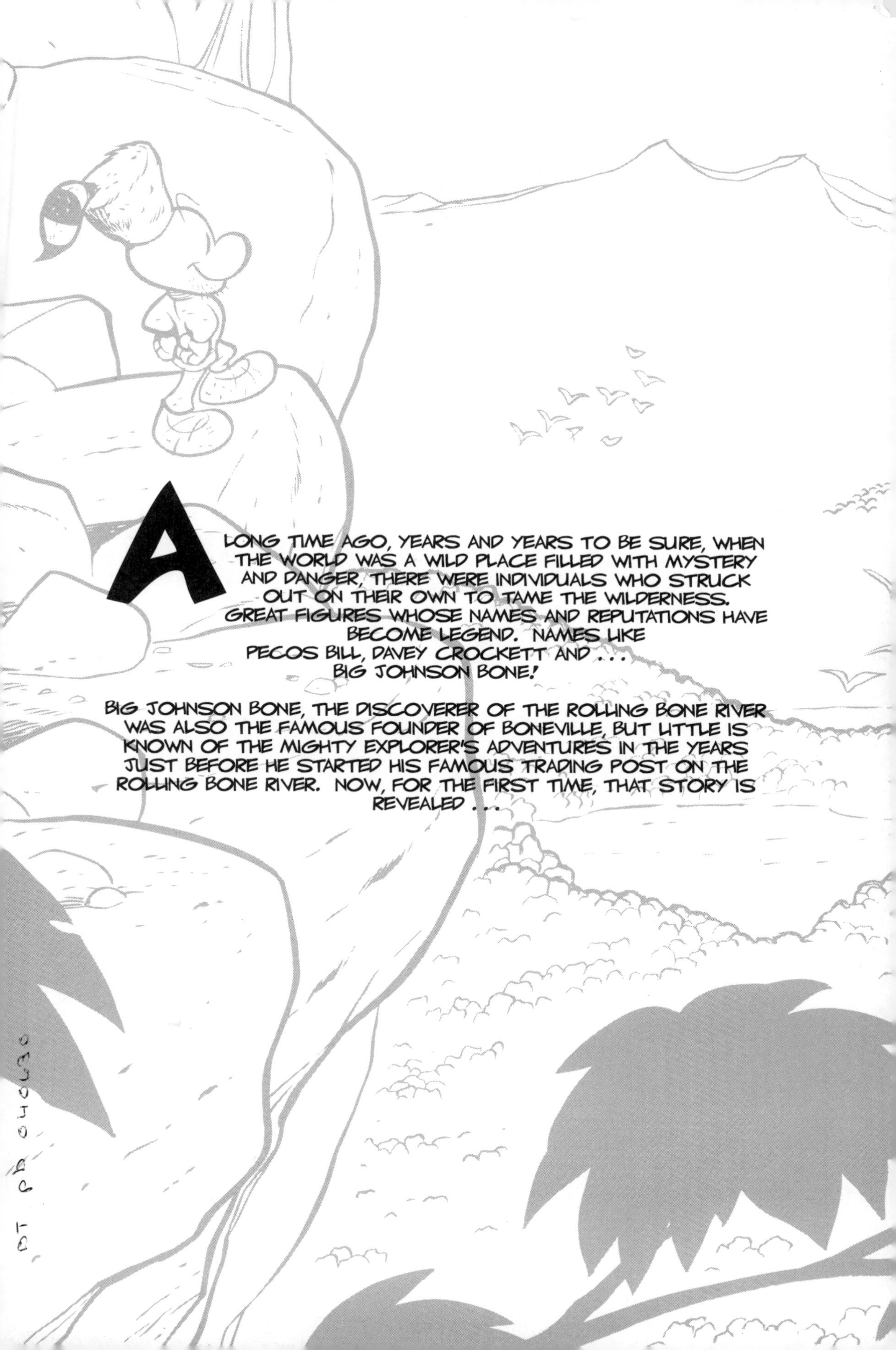

A LONG TIME AGO, YEARS AND YEARS TO BE SURE, WHEN THE WORLD WAS A WILD PLACE FILLED WITH MYSTERY AND DANGER, THERE WERE INDIVIDUALS WHO STRUCK OUT ON THEIR OWN TO TAME THE WILDERNESS. GREAT FIGURES WHOSE NAMES AND REPUTATIONS HAVE BECOME LEGEND. NAMES LIKE PECOS BILL, DAVEY CROCKETT AND . . . BIG JOHNSON BONE!

BIG JOHNSON BONE, THE DISCOVERER OF THE ROLLING BONE RIVER WAS ALSO THE FAMOUS FOUNDER OF BONEVILLE, BUT LITTLE IS KNOWN OF THE MIGHTY EXPLORER'S ADVENTURES IN THE YEARS JUST BEFORE HE STARTED HIS FAMOUS TRADING POST ON THE ROLLING BONE RIVER. NOW, FOR THE FIRST TIME, THAT STORY IS REVEALED . . .

Stupid, Stupid Rat-tails

The Adventures of Big Johnson Bone, Frontier Hero

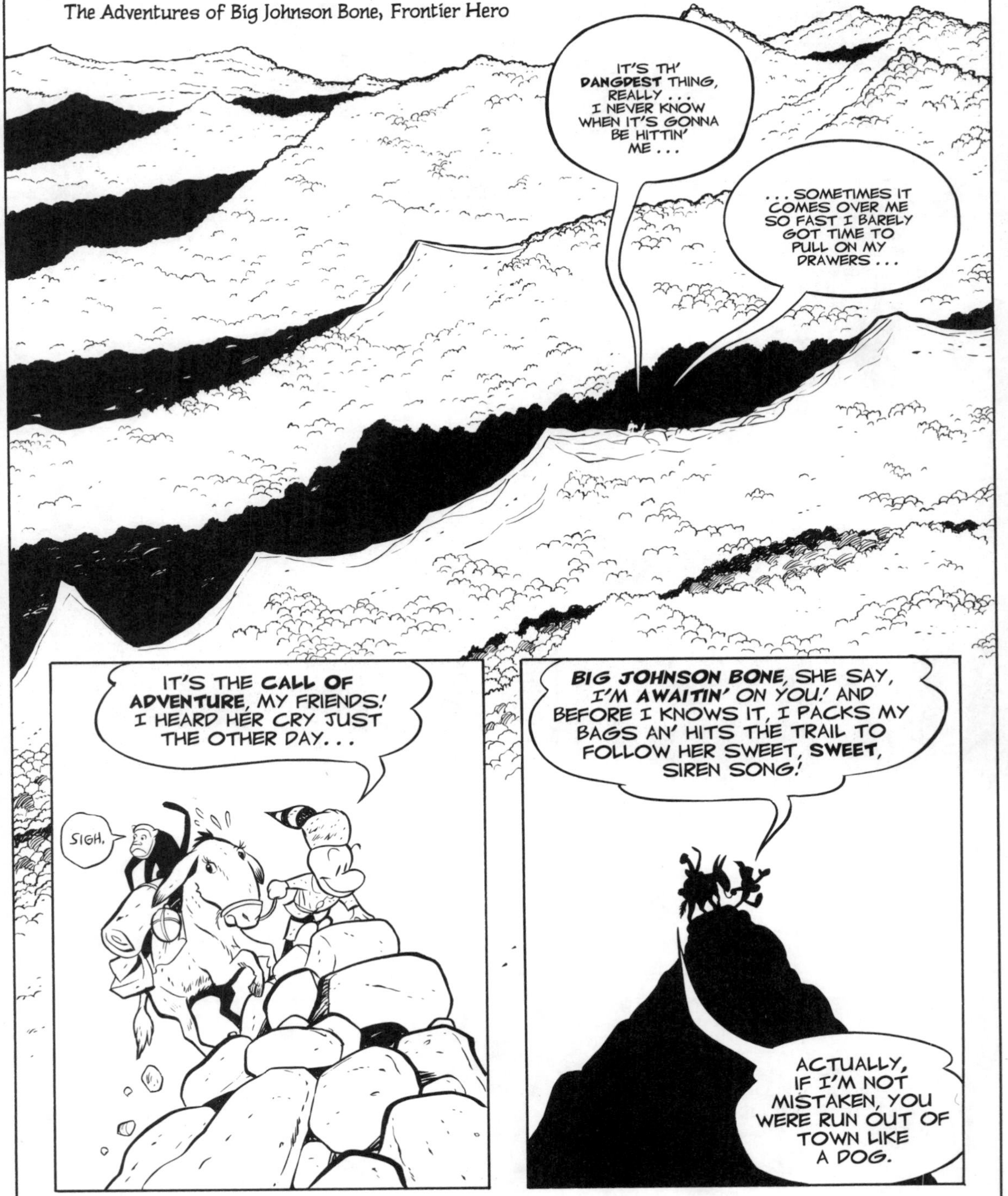
IT'S TH' DANGDEST THING, REALLY . . . I NEVER KNOW WHEN IT'S GONNA BE HITTIN' ME . . .
. . . SOMETIMES IT COMES OVER ME SO FAST I BARELY GOT TIME TO PULL ON MY DRAWERS . . .
IT'S THE CALL OF ADVENTURE, MY FRIENDS! I HEARD HER CRY JUST THE OTHER DAY. . .
SIGH.
BIG JOHNSON BONE, SHE SAY, I'M AWAITIN' ON YOU! AND BEFORE I KNOWS IT, I PACKS MY BAGS AN' HITS THE TRAIL TO FOLLOW HER SWEET, SWEET, SIREN SONG!
ACTUALLY, IF I'M NOT MISTAKEN, YOU WERE RUN OUT OF TOWN LIKE A DOG.

WELL, WHO'D A THUNK THEY'D GET SO GOSH DARNED FIRED UP OVER A GAME OF **CARDS**?

ALL'S I WON WAS A **MONKEY**, FOR CRYIN' OUT LOUD.

AHEM, YES, A MONKEY. LET ME AGAIN REMIND YOU THAT THIS MONKEY HAS A **NAME** -- MR. PIP. AND YOU **CHEATED!**

WON YOU FAIR AND SQUARE, MR. POOP--

IT'S PIP! **PIP!**

WHATEVER. LADYLUCK WAS LOOKIN' DOWN AN' BLESSED ME WITH A **WINNIN'** HAND. SIMPLE AS THAT.

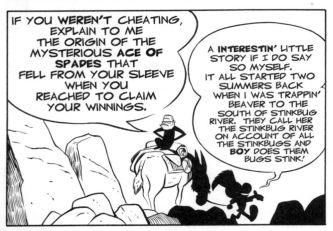

IF YOU **WEREN'T** CHEATING, EXPLAIN TO ME THE ORIGIN OF THE MYSTERIOUS **ACE OF SPADES** THAT FELL FROM YOUR SLEEVE WHEN YOU REACHED TO CLAIM YOUR WINNINGS.

A **INTERESTIN'** LITTLE STORY IF I DO SAY SO MYSELF. IT ALL STARTED TWO SUMMERS BACK WHEN I WAS TRAPPIN' BEAVER TO THE SOUTH OF STINKBUG RIVER. THEY CALL HER THE STINKBUG RIVER ON ACCOUNT OF ALL THE STINKBUGS AND **BOY** DOES THEM BUGS STINK!

-- BUT BY THEN I'D ALREADY GONE TWO MONTHS WITHOUT A BITE TO EAT AND WAS FEELIN' A MIGHT CRANKY --

--AFTERWARDS, THEY DECLARED ME THE **WINNER**, BUT I KNEW TH' **JIG WAS UP!** SO I GRABBED TH' STUFFED POSSUM --

-- THEN **WHAT DID I SEE** AT MY FEET? COMPLETELY UNTOUCHED BY THE EXPLOSION THAT LEVELED A GOOD HUNDRED MILES OF FOREST -- YES SIR, THAT'S RIGHT, A SINGLE PLAYING CARD -- AN **ACE OF SPADES** TO BE PRECISE.

SO I PICKED IT UP AND PUT IT INSIDE MY COAT IN CASE WHOEVER **LOST** IT CAME **LOOKIN'.**

DOES THAT ANSWER YOUR QUESTION?

HUMPH! NO APPRECIATION FOR THE ART OF STORYTELLIN'. LAST TIME I WASTE A PERFECTLY GOOD YARN ON THE LIKES A **THEM!**

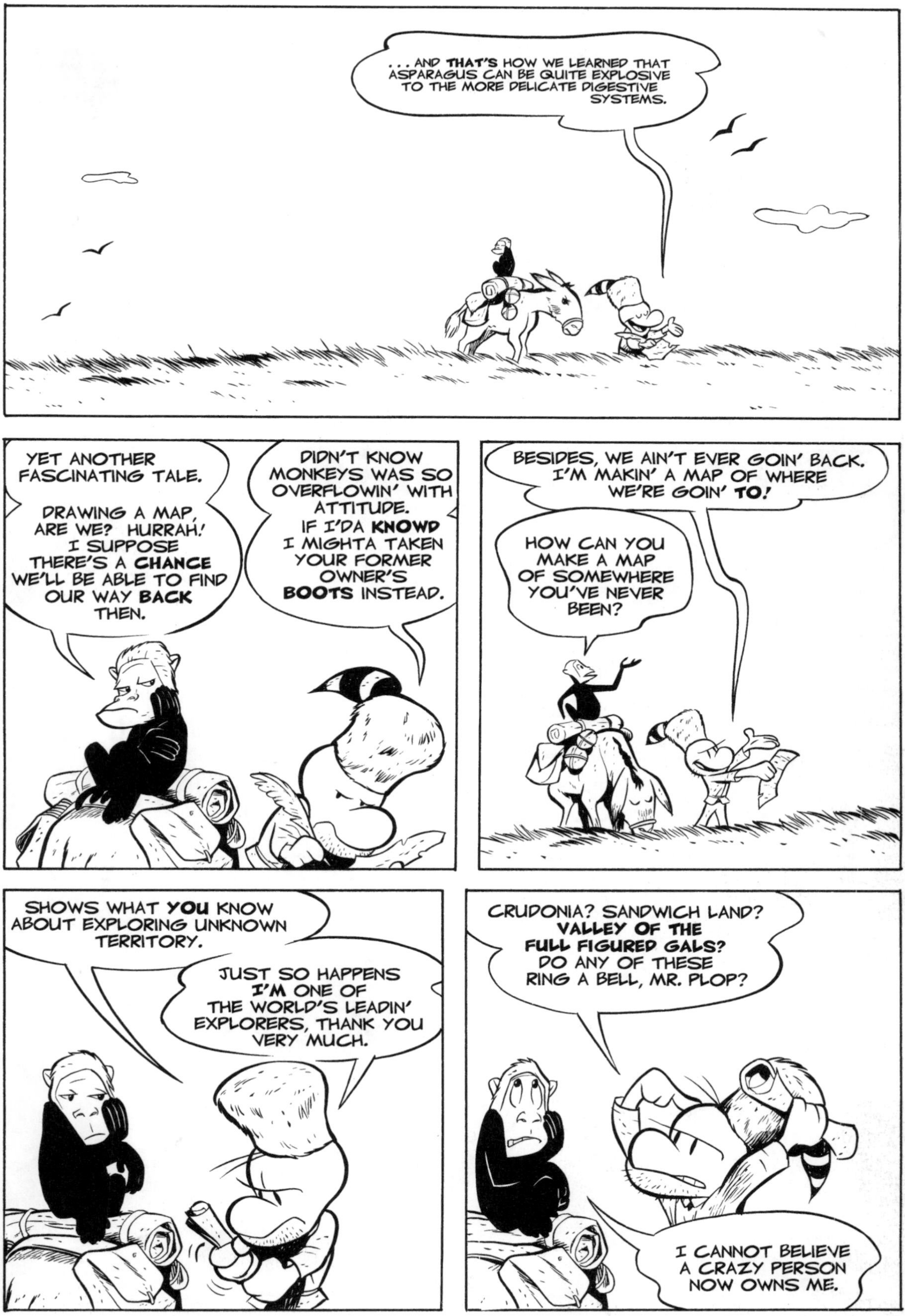
. . . AND **THAT'S** HOW WE LEARNED THAT ASPARAGUS CAN BE QUITE EXPLOSIVE TO THE MORE DELICATE DIGESTIVE SYSTEMS.
YET ANOTHER FASCINATING TALE.
DRAWING A MAP, ARE WE? HURRAH! I SUPPOSE THERE'S A **CHANCE** WE'LL BE ABLE TO FIND OUR WAY **BACK** THEN.
DIDN'T KNOW MONKEYS WAS SO OVERFLOWIN' WITH ATTITUDE.
IF I'DA **KNOWD** I MIGHTA TAKEN YOUR FORMER OWNER'S **BOOTS** INSTEAD.
BESIDES, WE AIN'T EVER GOIN' BACK. I'M MAKIN' A MAP OF WHERE WE'RE GOIN' **TO!**
HOW CAN YOU MAKE A MAP OF SOMEWHERE YOU'VE NEVER BEEN?
SHOWS WHAT **YOU** KNOW ABOUT EXPLORING UNKNOWN TERRITORY.
JUST SO HAPPENS **I'M** ONE OF THE WORLD'S LEADIN' EXPLORERS, THANK YOU VERY MUCH.
CRUDONIA? SANDWICH LAND? **VALLEY OF THE FULL FIGURED GALS?** DO ANY OF THESE RING A BELL, MR. PLOP?
I CANNOT BELIEVE A CRAZY PERSON NOW OWNS ME.

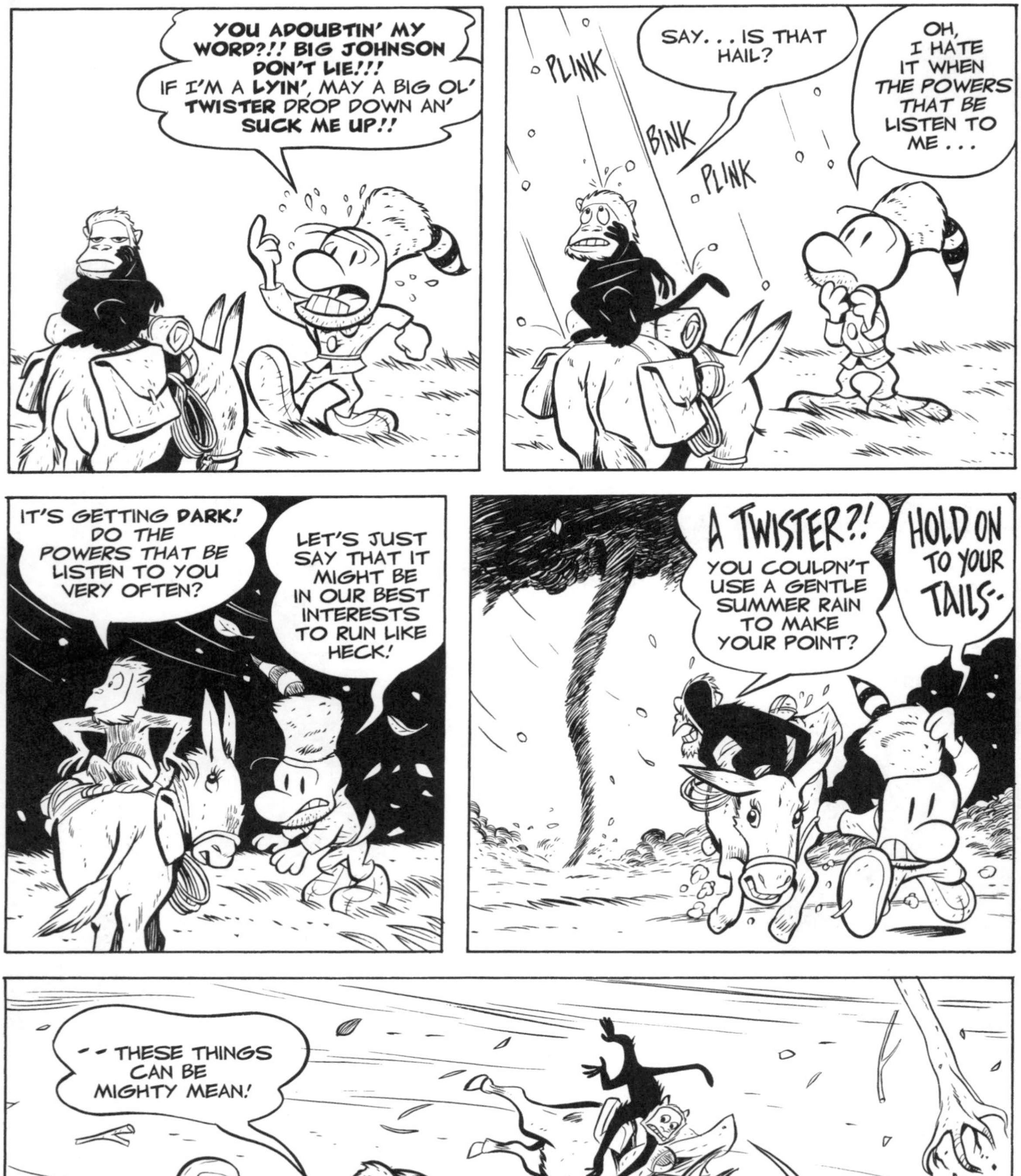

YOU ADOUBTIN' MY WORD?!! BIG JOHNSON DON'T LIE!!! IF I'M A LYIN', MAY A BIG OL' TWISTER DROP DOWN AN' SUCK ME UP!!
PLINK
BINK
PLINK
SAY. . . IS THAT HAIL?
OH, I HATE IT WHEN THE POWERS THAT BE LISTEN TO ME . . .
IT'S GETTING DARK! DO THE POWERS THAT BE LISTEN TO YOU VERY OFTEN?
LET'S JUST SAY THAT IT MIGHT BE IN OUR BEST INTERESTS TO RUN LIKE HECK!
A TWISTER?! YOU COULDN'T USE A GENTLE SUMMER RAIN TO MAKE YOUR POINT?
HOLD ON TO YOUR TAILS--
--THESE THINGS CAN BE MIGHTY MEAN!
LET ME GUESS, YOU'VE HAD EXPERIENCE WITH TWISTERS BEFORE?

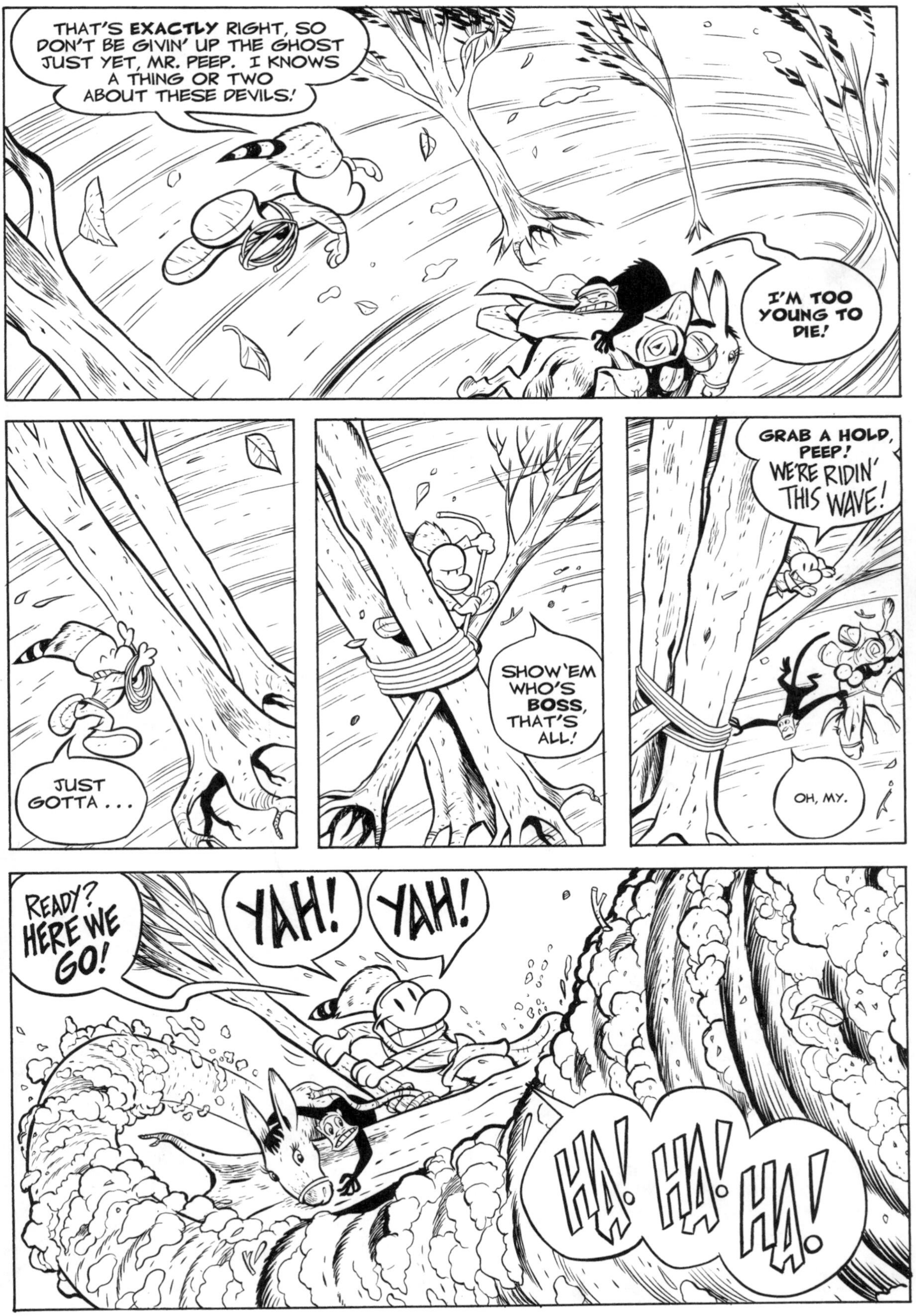

THAT'S EXACTLY RIGHT, SO DON'T BE GIVIN' UP THE GHOST JUST YET, MR. PEEP. I KNOWS A THING OR TWO ABOUT THESE DEVILS!
I'M TOO YOUNG TO DIE!
JUST GOTTA . . .
SHOW 'EM WHO'S BOSS, THAT'S ALL!
GRAB A HOLD, PEEP! WE'RE RIDIN' THIS WAVE!
OH, MY.
READY? HERE WE GO!
YAH!
YAH!
HA! HA! HA!

Oh, YEAH!
YEAH!
SHE'S FIGHTIN'!
SHE'S FIGHTIN'!
I LOVE THAT!
I'M JUST A VERY SMALL MONKEY AND I'D LIKE TO GET DOWN NOW.
YAH! GO ON! I WAS DONE WITH YA ANYWAY!
PLEASE . . . I DON'T WANT TO GO ROUND AND ROUND ANYMORE.
HA! HA! JUST LIKE OLD TIMES, EH, BLOSSOM, OL' GIRL?
NOW THAT'S ADVENTURE! YOU CAN SMELL IT IN THE AIR!
IS THAT WHAT I SMELL? I THOUGHT SOMETHING HAD GONE BAD.
NUTHIN' BAD ABOUT THAT SMELL, NO SIR. GETS THE BLOOD PUMPIN'!
NOW, LET'S HAVE A LOOK AROUND AND SEE WHERE WE ARE.
LOTS OF ROCKS AN' BUSHES -- I THINK THAT'S A DINGLEBERRY BUSH OVER THERE.
MONSTERS!
NOPE, NO MONSTERS. BELIEVE ME, I KNOW A MONSTER WHEN I SEE ONE.

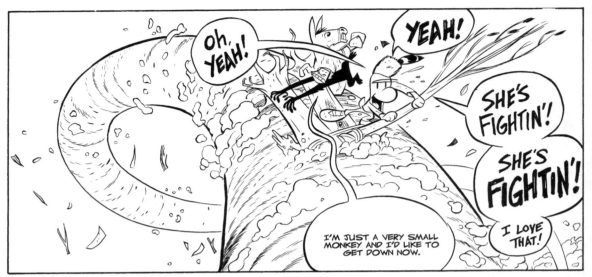

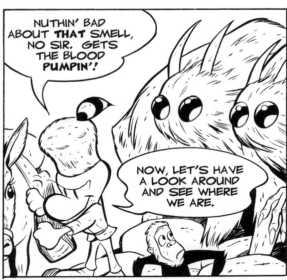

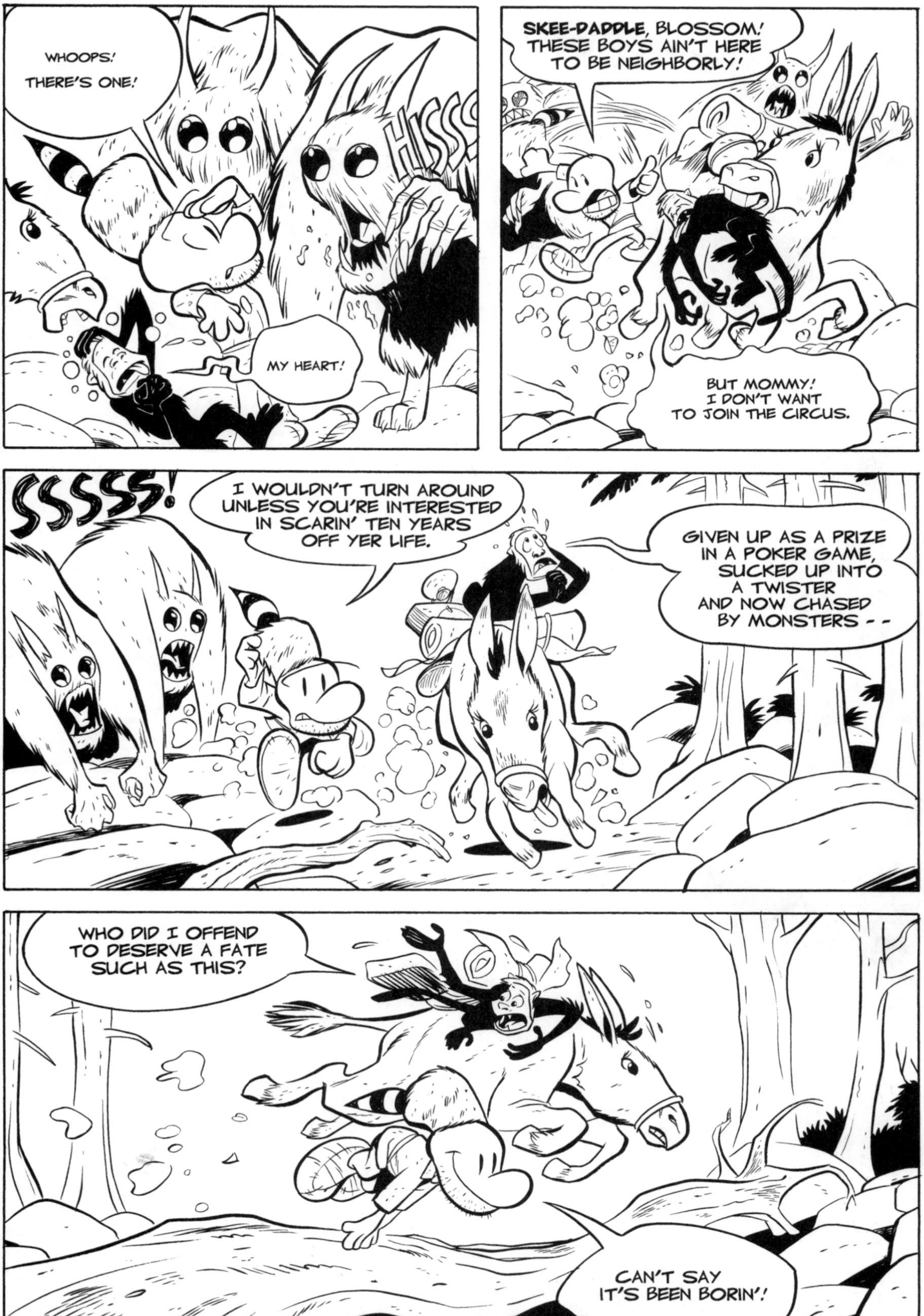
WHOOPS! THERE'S ONE!
HISSS
MY HEART!
SKEE-DADDLE, BLOSSOM! THESE BOYS AIN'T HERE TO BE NEIGHBORLY!
BUT MOMMY! I DON'T WANT TO JOIN THE CIRCUS.
SSSSS!
I WOULDN'T TURN AROUND UNLESS YOU'RE INTERESTED IN SCARIN' TEN YEARS OFF YER LIFE.
GIVEN UP AS A PRIZE IN A POKER GAME, SUCKED UP INTO A TWISTER AND NOW CHASED BY MONSTERS - -
WHO DID I OFFEND TO DESERVE A FATE SUCH AS THIS?
CAN'T SAY IT'S BEEN BORIN'!

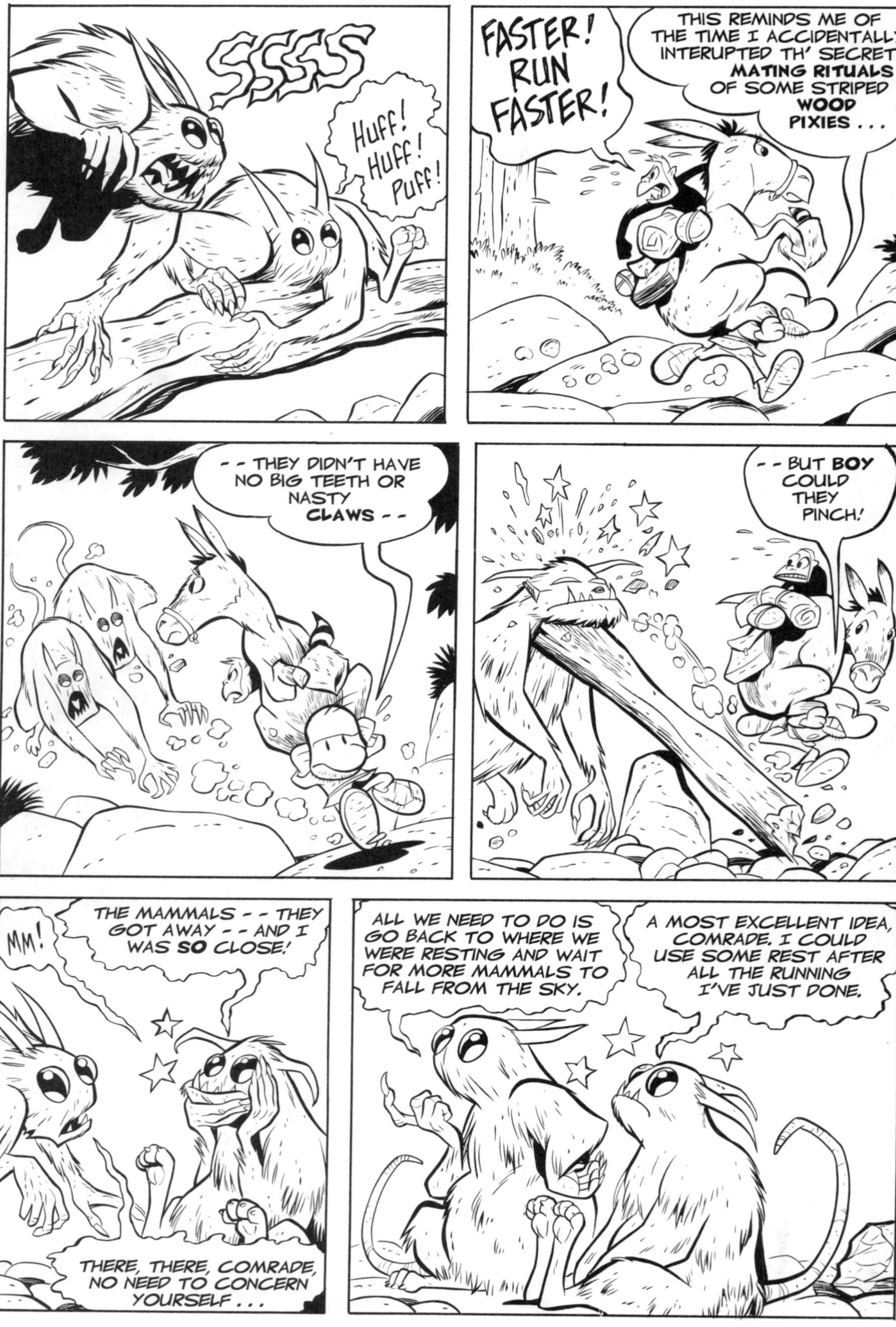
SSSSS
Huff! Huff! Puff!
FASTER! RUN FASTER!
THIS REMINDS ME OF THE TIME I ACCIDENTALLY INTERUPTED TH' SECRET MATING RITUALS OF SOME STRIPED WOOD PIXIES . . .
- - THEY DIDN'T HAVE NO BIG TEETH OR NASTY CLAWS - -
- - BUT BOY COULD THEY PINCH!
MM!
THE MAMMALS - - THEY GOT AWAY - - AND I WAS SO CLOSE!
THERE, THERE, COMRADE, NO NEED TO CONCERN YOURSELF . . .
ALL WE NEED TO DO IS GO BACK TO WHERE WE WERE RESTING AND WAIT FOR MORE MAMMALS TO FALL FROM THE SKY.
A MOST EXCELLENT IDEA, COMRADE. I COULD USE SOME REST AFTER ALL THE RUNNING I'VE JUST DONE.

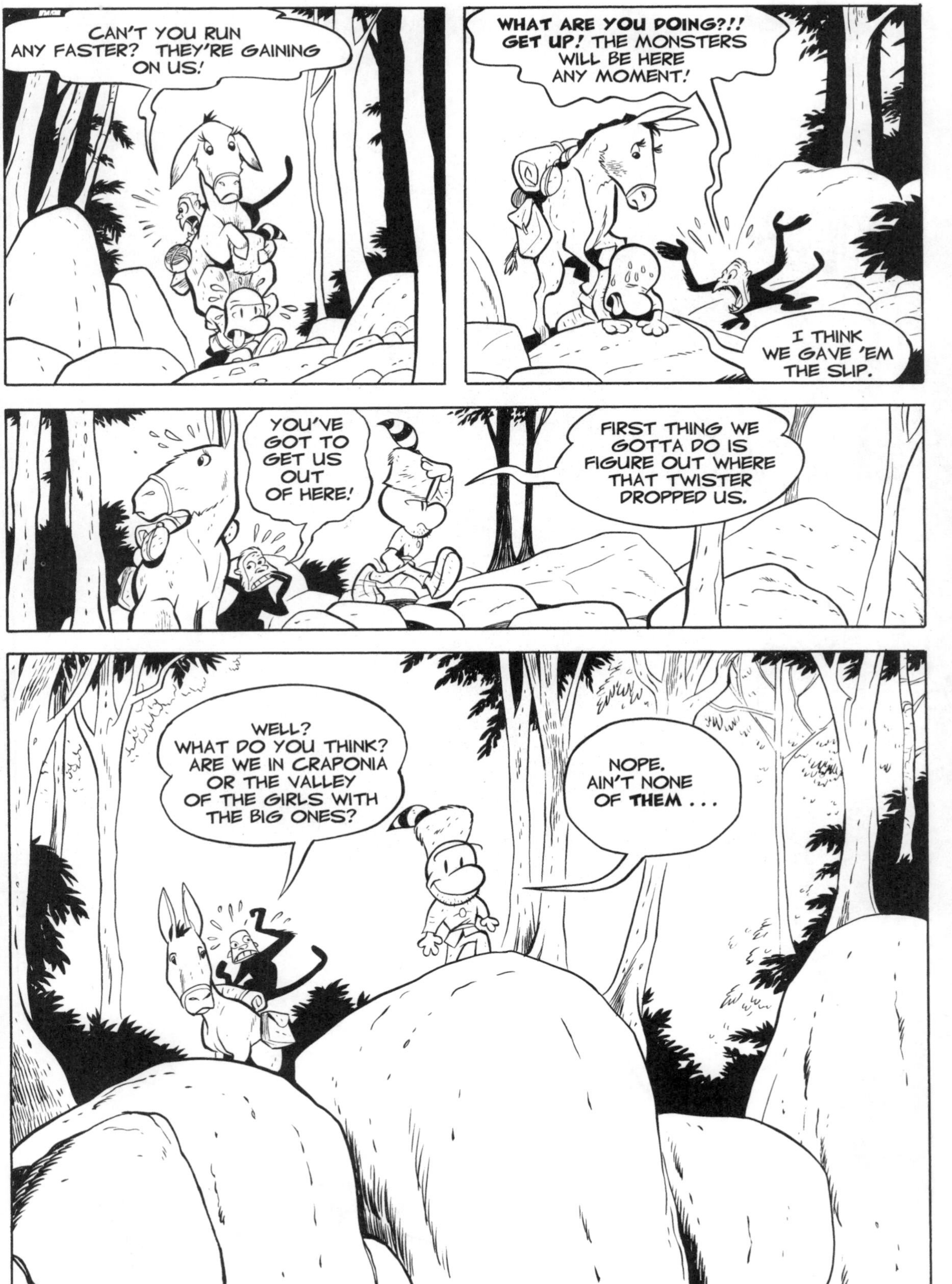
CAN'T YOU RUN ANY FASTER? THEY'RE GAINING ON US!
WHAT ARE YOU DOING?!! GET UP! THE MONSTERS WILL BE HERE ANY MOMENT!
I THINK WE GAVE 'EM THE SLIP.
YOU'VE GOT TO GET US OUT OF HERE!
FIRST THING WE GOTTA DO IS FIGURE OUT WHERE THAT TWISTER DROPPED US.
WELL? WHAT DO YOU THINK? ARE WE IN CRAPONIA OR THE VALLEY OF THE GIRLS WITH THE BIG ONES?
NOPE. AIN'T NONE OF **THEM** . . .

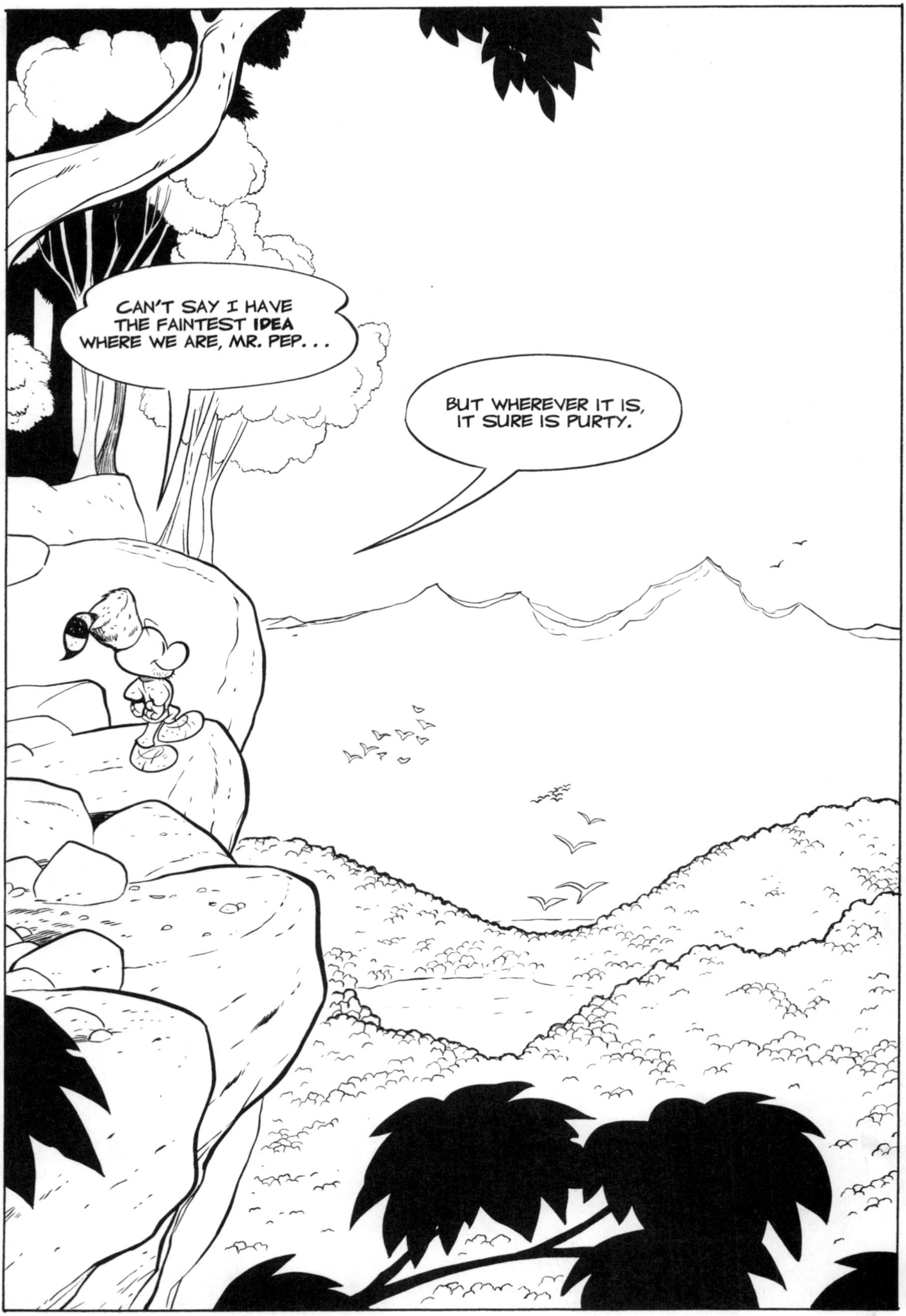
CAN'T SAY I HAVE THE FAINTEST **IDEA** WHERE WE ARE, MR. PEP...
BUT WHEREVER IT IS, IT SURE IS PURTY.

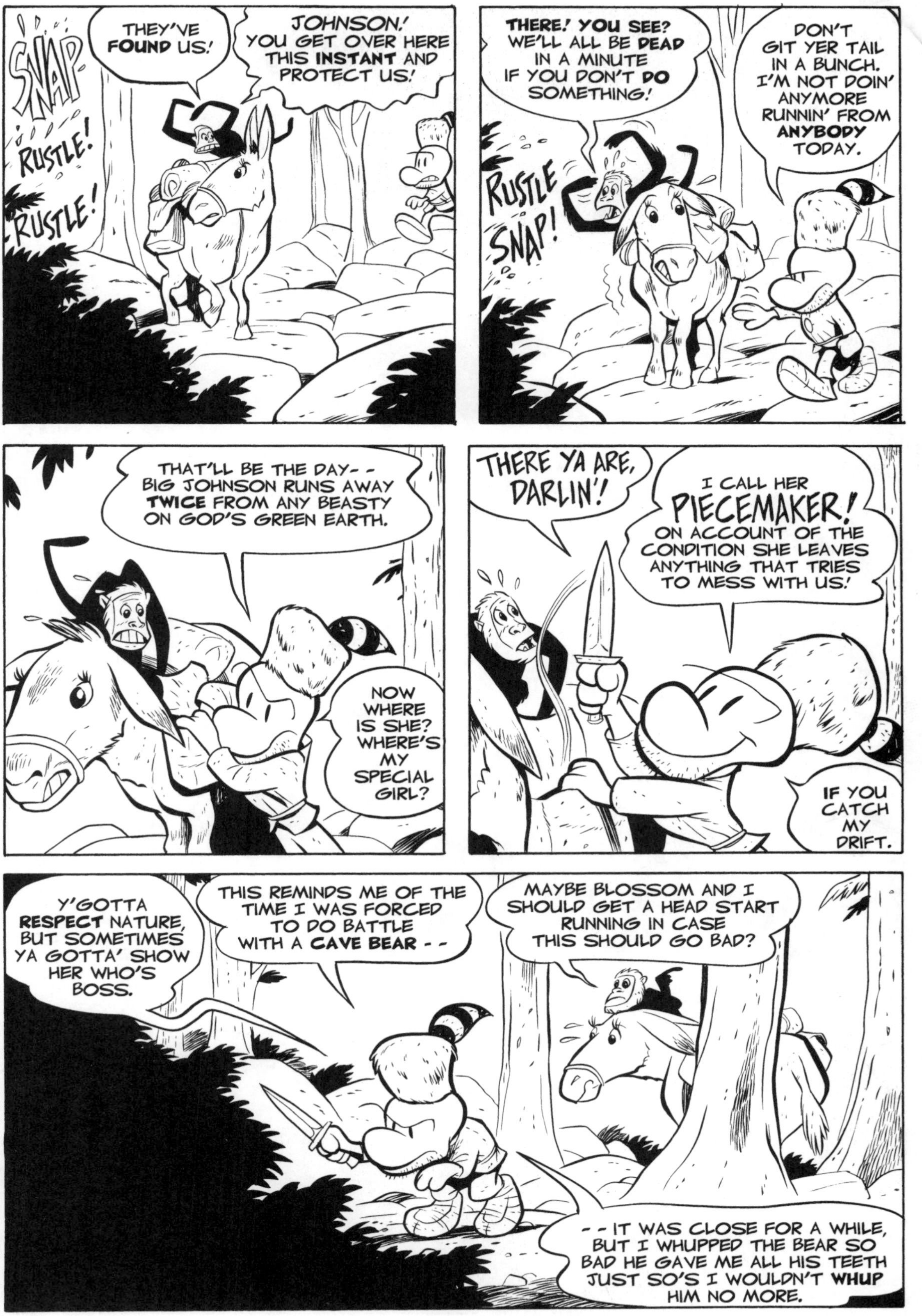
SNAP
THEY'VE FOUND US!
JOHNSON! YOU GET OVER HERE THIS INSTANT AND PROTECT US!
RUSTLE!
RUSTLE!
THERE! YOU SEE? WE'LL ALL BE DEAD IN A MINUTE IF YOU DON'T DO SOMETHING!
DON'T GIT YER TAIL IN A BUNCH. I'M NOT DOIN' ANYMORE RUNNIN' FROM ANYBODY TODAY.
RUSTLE
SNAP!
THAT'LL BE THE DAY- - BIG JOHNSON RUNS AWAY TWICE FROM ANY BEASTY ON GOD'S GREEN EARTH.
NOW WHERE IS SHE? WHERE'S MY SPECIAL GIRL?
THERE YA ARE, DARLIN'!
I CALL HER PIECEMAKER! ON ACCOUNT OF THE CONDITION SHE LEAVES ANYTHING THAT TRIES TO MESS WITH US!
IF YOU CATCH MY DRIFT.
Y'GOTTA RESPECT NATURE, BUT SOMETIMES YA GOTTA' SHOW HER WHO'S BOSS.
THIS REMINDS ME OF THE TIME I WAS FORCED TO DO BATTLE WITH A CAVE BEAR - -
MAYBE BLOSSOM AND I SHOULD GET A HEAD START RUNNING IN CASE THIS SHOULD GO BAD?
- - IT WAS CLOSE FOR A WHILE, BUT I WHUPPED THE BEAR SO BAD HE GAVE ME ALL HIS TEETH JUST SO'S I WOULDN'T WHUP HIM NO MORE.

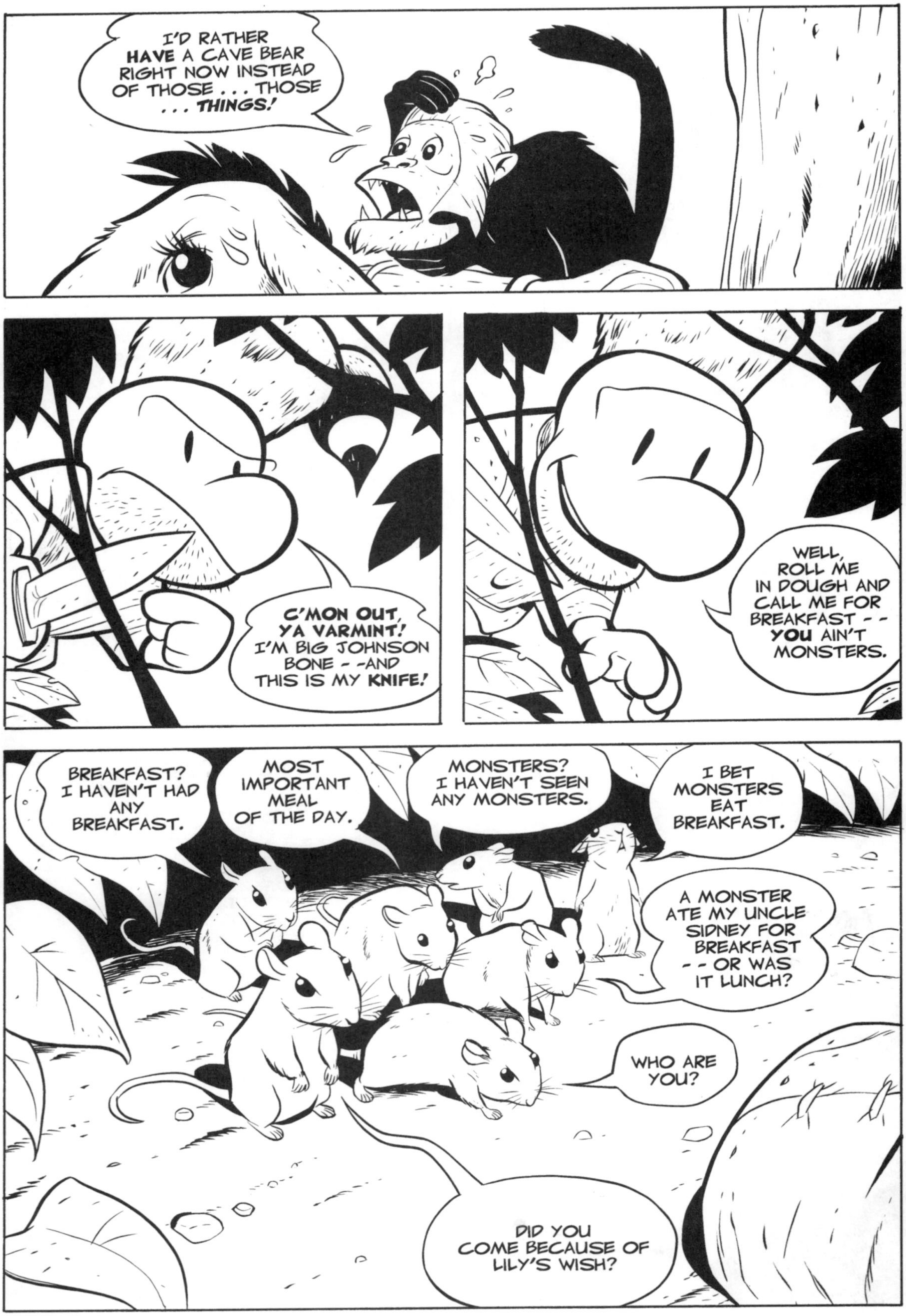
I'D RATHER HAVE A CAVE BEAR RIGHT NOW INSTEAD OF THOSE . . . THOSE . . . THINGS!
C'MON OUT, YA VARMINT! I'M BIG JOHNSON BONE - -AND THIS IS MY KNIFE!
WELL, ROLL ME IN DOUGH AND CALL ME FOR BREAKFAST - - YOU AIN'T MONSTERS.
BREAKFAST? I HAVEN'T HAD ANY BREAKFAST.
MOST IMPORTANT MEAL OF THE DAY.
MONSTERS? I HAVEN'T SEEN ANY MONSTERS.
I BET MONSTERS EAT BREAKFAST.
A MONSTER ATE MY UNCLE SIDNEY FOR BREAKFAST - - OR WAS IT LUNCH?
WHO ARE YOU?
DID YOU COME BECAUSE OF LILY'S WISH?

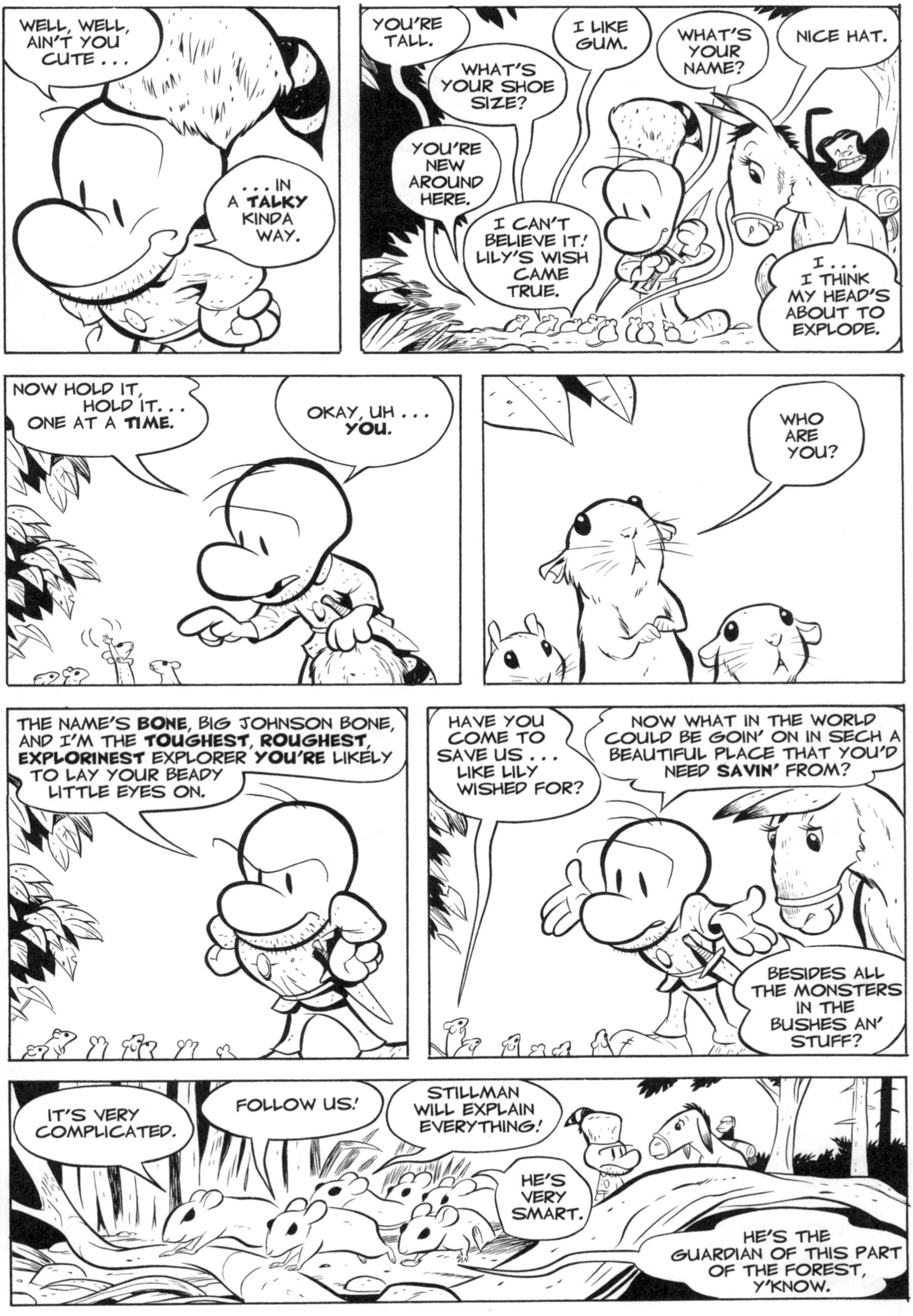
WELL, WELL, AIN'T YOU CUTE . . .
. . . IN A TALKY KINDA WAY.
YOU'RE TALL.
WHAT'S YOUR SHOE SIZE?
I LIKE GUM.
WHAT'S YOUR NAME?
NICE HAT.
YOU'RE NEW AROUND HERE.
I CAN'T BELIEVE IT! LILY'S WISH CAME TRUE.
I . . . I THINK MY HEAD'S ABOUT TO EXPLODE.
NOW HOLD IT, HOLD IT. . . ONE AT A TIME.
OKAY, UH . . . YOU.
WHO ARE YOU?
THE NAME'S BONE, BIG JOHNSON BONE, AND I'M THE TOUGHEST, ROUGHEST, EXPLORINEST EXPLORER YOU'RE LIKELY TO LAY YOUR BEADY LITTLE EYES ON.
HAVE YOU COME TO SAVE US . . . LIKE LILY WISHED FOR?
NOW WHAT IN THE WORLD COULD BE GOIN' ON IN SECH A BEAUTIFUL PLACE THAT YOU'D NEED SAVIN' FROM?
BESIDES ALL THE MONSTERS IN THE BUSHES AN' STUFF?
IT'S VERY COMPLICATED.
FOLLOW US!
STILLMAN WILL EXPLAIN EVERYTHING!
HE'S VERY SMART.
HE'S THE GUARDIAN OF THIS PART OF THE FOREST, Y'KNOW.

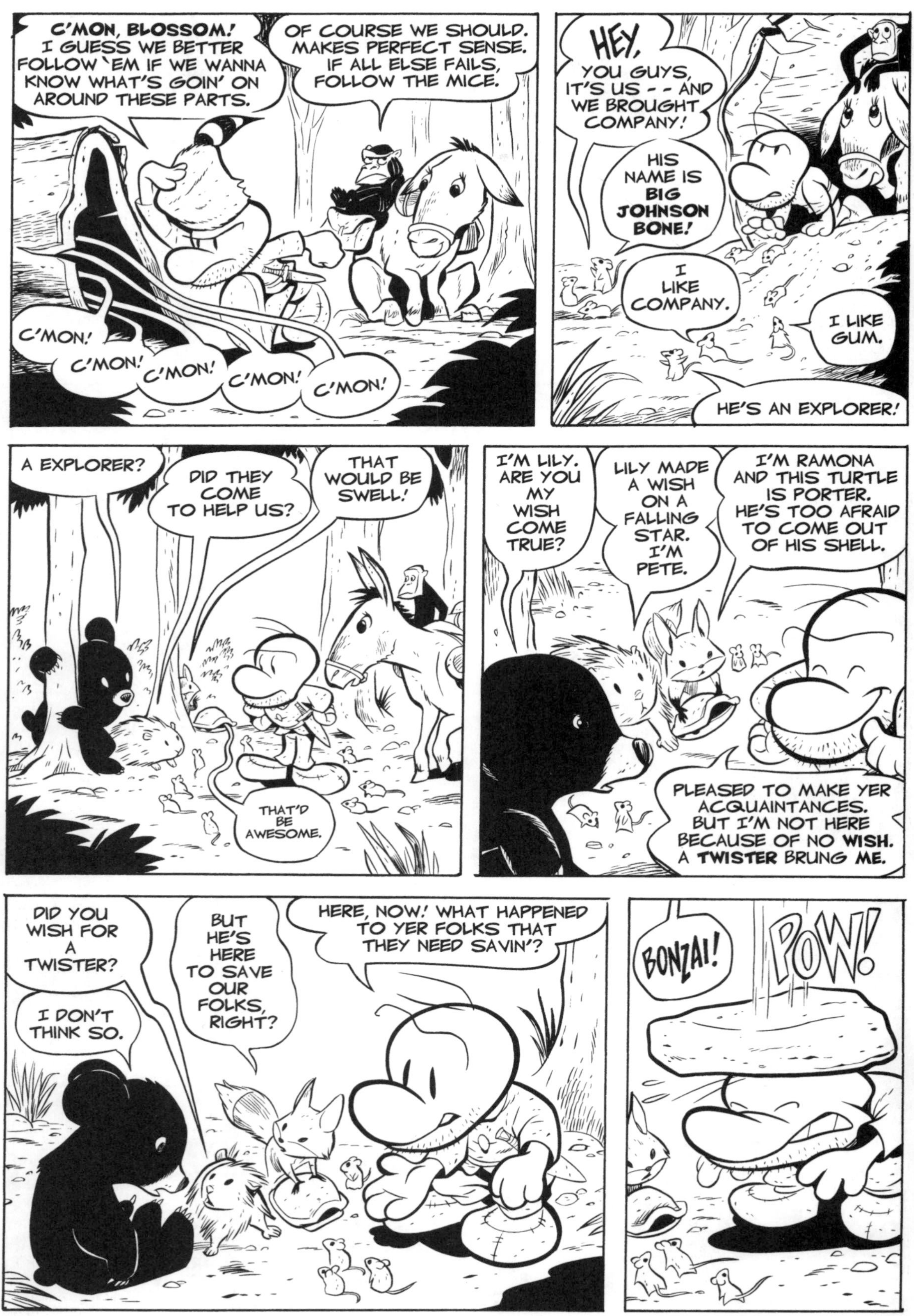
C'MON, BLOSSOM! I GUESS WE BETTER FOLLOW 'EM IF WE WANNA KNOW WHAT'S GOIN' ON AROUND THESE PARTS.
OF COURSE WE SHOULD. MAKES PERFECT SENSE. IF ALL ELSE FAILS, FOLLOW THE MICE.
C'MON!
C'MON!
C'MON!
C'MON!
C'MON!
HEY, YOU GUYS, IT'S US -- AND WE BROUGHT COMPANY!
HIS NAME IS BIG JOHNSON BONE!
I LIKE COMPANY.
I LIKE GUM.
HE'S AN EXPLORER!
A EXPLORER?
DID THEY COME TO HELP US?
THAT WOULD BE SWELL!
THAT'D BE AWESOME.
I'M LILY. ARE YOU MY WISH COME TRUE?
LILY MADE A WISH ON A FALLING STAR. I'M PETE.
I'M RAMONA AND THIS TURTLE IS PORTER. HE'S TOO AFRAID TO COME OUT OF HIS SHELL.
PLEASED TO MAKE YER ACQUAINTANCES. BUT I'M NOT HERE BECAUSE OF NO WISH. A TWISTER BRUNG ME.
DID YOU WISH FOR A TWISTER?
I DON'T THINK SO.
BUT HE'S HERE TO SAVE OUR FOLKS, RIGHT?
HERE, NOW! WHAT HAPPENED TO YER FOLKS THAT THEY NEED SAVIN'?
BONZAI!
POW!

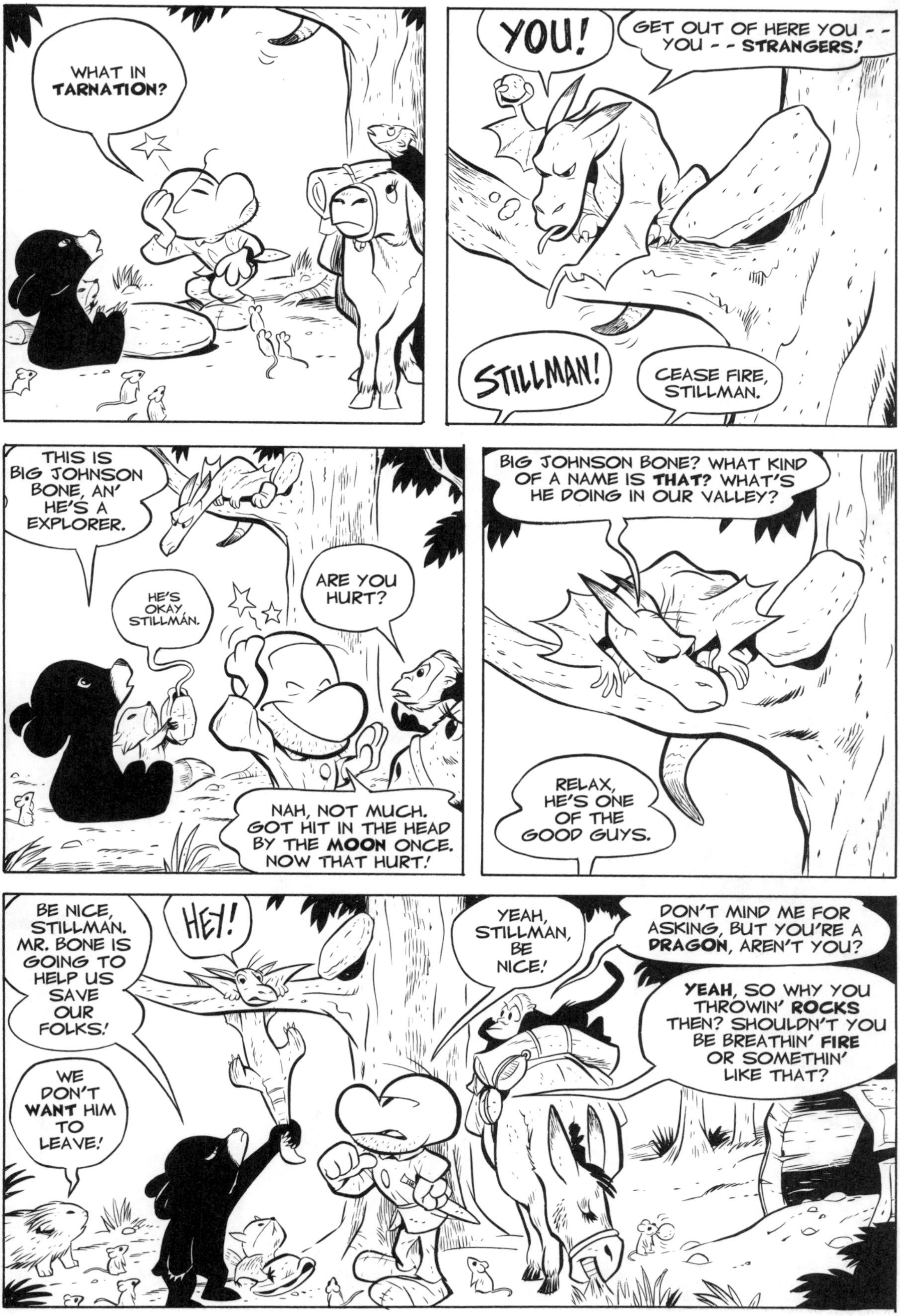
WHAT IN TARNATION?
YOU!
GET OUT OF HERE YOU - - YOU - - STRANGERS!
STILLMAN!
CEASE FIRE, STILLMAN.
THIS IS BIG JOHNSON BONE, AN' HE'S A EXPLORER.
HE'S OKAY STILLMAN.
ARE YOU HURT?
NAH, NOT MUCH. GOT HIT IN THE HEAD BY THE MOON ONCE. NOW THAT HURT!
BIG JOHNSON BONE? WHAT KIND OF A NAME IS THAT? WHAT'S HE DOING IN OUR VALLEY?
RELAX, HE'S ONE OF THE GOOD GUYS.
BE NICE, STILLMAN. MR. BONE IS GOING TO HELP US SAVE OUR FOLKS!
HEY!
WE DON'T WANT HIM TO LEAVE!
YEAH, STILLMAN, BE NICE!
DON'T MIND ME FOR ASKING, BUT YOU'RE A DRAGON, AREN'T YOU?
YEAH, SO WHY YOU THROWIN' ROCKS THEN? SHOULDN'T YOU BE BREATHIN' FIRE OR SOMETHIN' LIKE THAT?

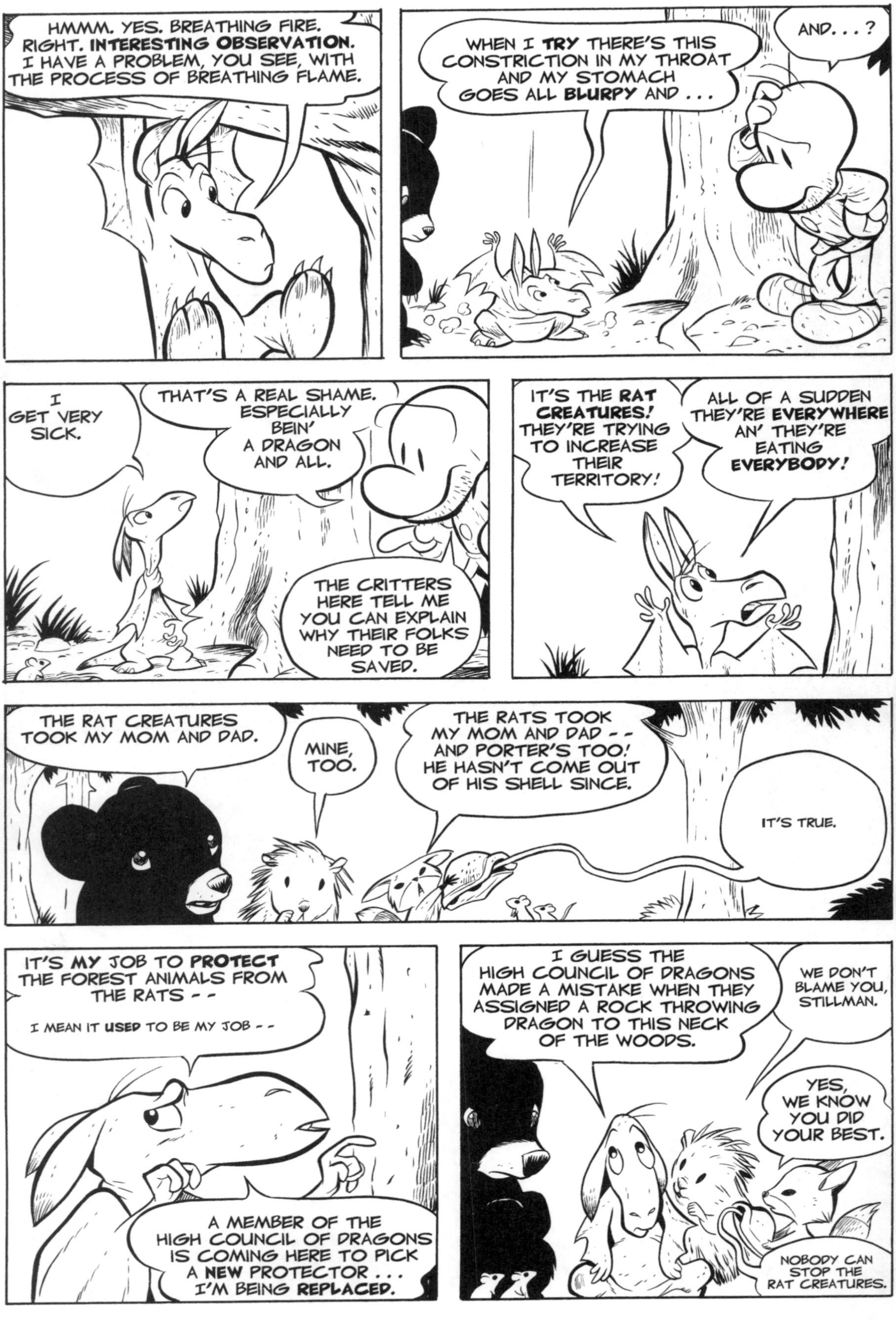
HMMM. YES. BREATHING FIRE. RIGHT. INTERESTING OBSERVATION. I HAVE A PROBLEM, YOU SEE, WITH THE PROCESS OF BREATHING FLAME.
WHEN I TRY THERE'S THIS CONSTRICTION IN MY THROAT AND MY STOMACH GOES ALL BLURPY AND . . .
AND. . . ?
I GET VERY SICK.
THAT'S A REAL SHAME. ESPECIALLY BEIN' A DRAGON AND ALL.
THE CRITTERS HERE TELL ME YOU CAN EXPLAIN WHY THEIR FOLKS NEED TO BE SAVED.
IT'S THE RAT CREATURES! THEY'RE TRYING TO INCREASE THEIR TERRITORY!
ALL OF A SUDDEN THEY'RE EVERYWHERE AN' THEY'RE EATING EVERYBODY!
THE RAT CREATURES TOOK MY MOM AND DAD.
MINE, TOO.
THE RATS TOOK MY MOM AND DAD -- AND PORTER'S TOO! HE HASN'T COME OUT OF HIS SHELL SINCE.
IT'S TRUE.
IT'S MY JOB TO PROTECT THE FOREST ANIMALS FROM THE RATS --
I MEAN IT USED TO BE MY JOB --
A MEMBER OF THE HIGH COUNCIL OF DRAGONS IS COMING HERE TO PICK A NEW PROTECTOR . . . I'M BEING REPLACED.
I GUESS THE HIGH COUNCIL OF DRAGONS MADE A MISTAKE WHEN THEY ASSIGNED A ROCK THROWING DRAGON TO THIS NECK OF THE WOODS.
WE DON'T BLAME YOU, STILLMAN.
YES, WE KNOW YOU DID YOUR BEST.
NOBODY CAN STOP THE RAT CREATURES.

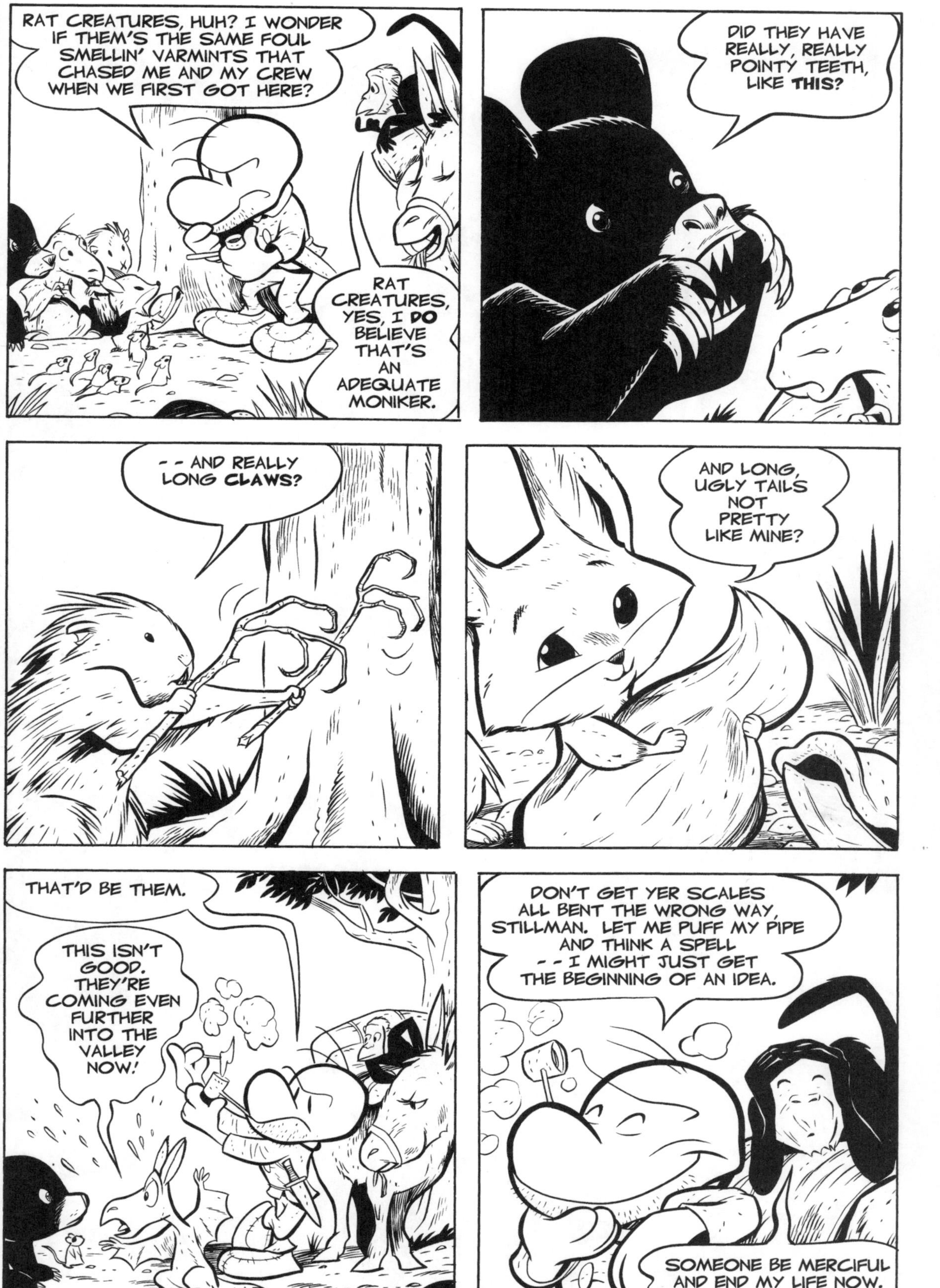
RAT CREATURES, HUH? I WONDER IF THEM'S THE SAME FOUL SMELLIN' VARMINTS THAT CHASED ME AND MY CREW WHEN WE FIRST GOT HERE?
RAT CREATURES, YES, I **DO** BELIEVE THAT'S AN ADEQUATE MONIKER.
DID THEY HAVE REALLY, REALLY POINTY TEETH, LIKE **THIS**?
- - AND REALLY LONG **CLAWS**?
AND LONG, UGLY TAILS NOT PRETTY LIKE MINE?
THAT'D BE THEM.
THIS ISN'T GOOD. THEY'RE COMING EVEN FURTHER INTO THE VALLEY NOW!
DON'T GET YER SCALES ALL BENT THE WRONG WAY, STILLMAN. LET ME PUFF MY PIPE AND THINK A SPELL - - I MIGHT JUST GET THE BEGINNING OF AN IDEA.
SOMEONE BE MERCIFUL AND END MY LIFE NOW.

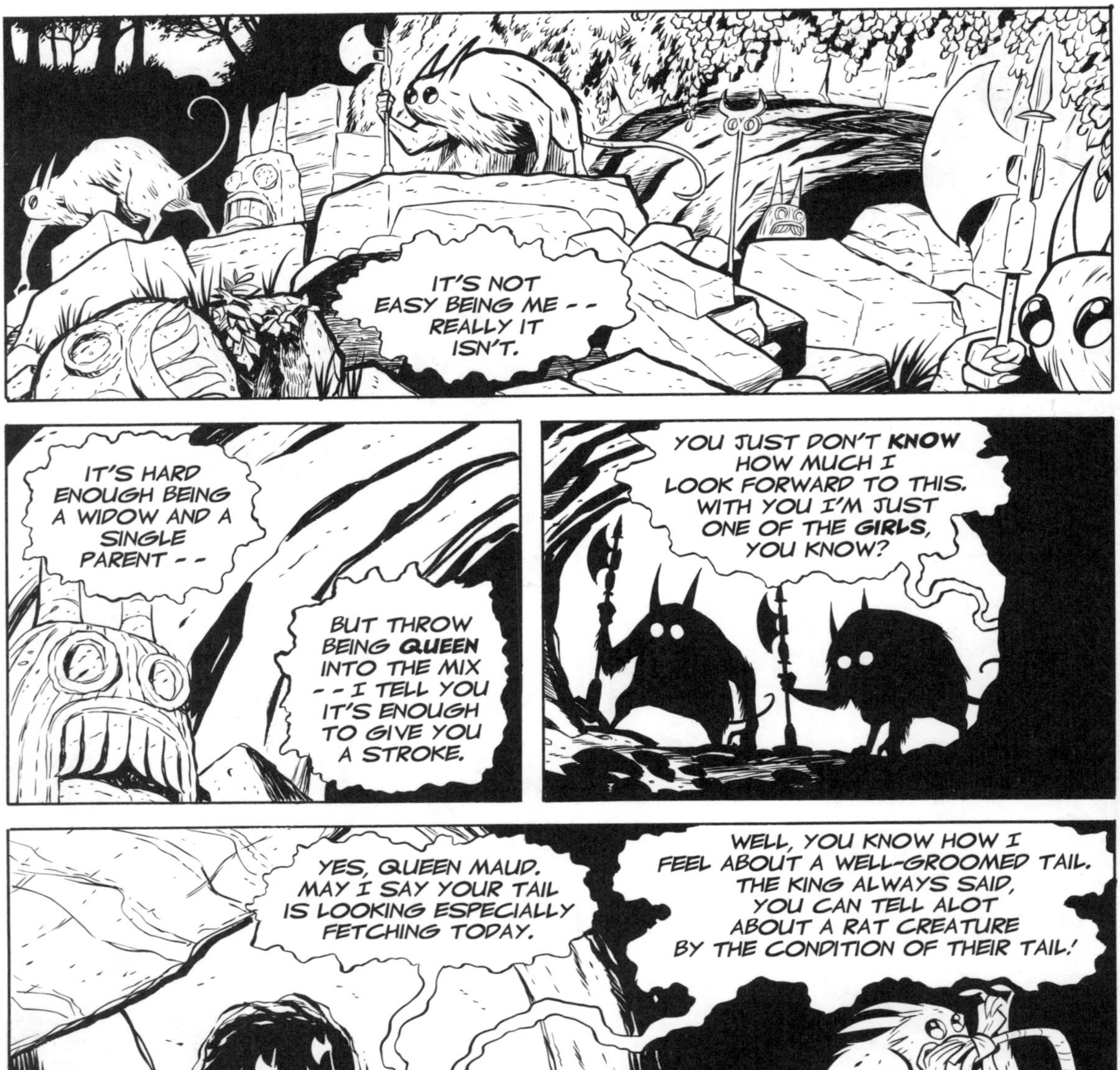
IT'S NOT EASY BEING ME - - REALLY IT ISN'T.
IT'S HARD ENOUGH BEING A WIDOW AND A SINGLE PARENT - -
BUT THROW BEING **QUEEN** INTO THE MIX - - I TELL YOU IT'S ENOUGH TO GIVE YOU A STROKE.
YOU JUST DON'T **KNOW** HOW MUCH I LOOK FORWARD TO THIS. WITH YOU I'M JUST ONE OF THE **GIRLS**, YOU KNOW?
YES, QUEEN MAUD. MAY I SAY YOUR TAIL IS LOOKING ESPECIALLY FETCHING TODAY.
WELL, YOU KNOW HOW I FEEL ABOUT A WELL-GROOMED TAIL. THE KING ALWAYS SAID, YOU CAN TELL ALOT ABOUT A RAT CREATURE BY THE CONDITION OF THEIR TAIL!
BOY I MISS HIM. WHO'D A THUNK THAT A BAD PIECE OF PORK COULD BE SO **DEVASTATING**?

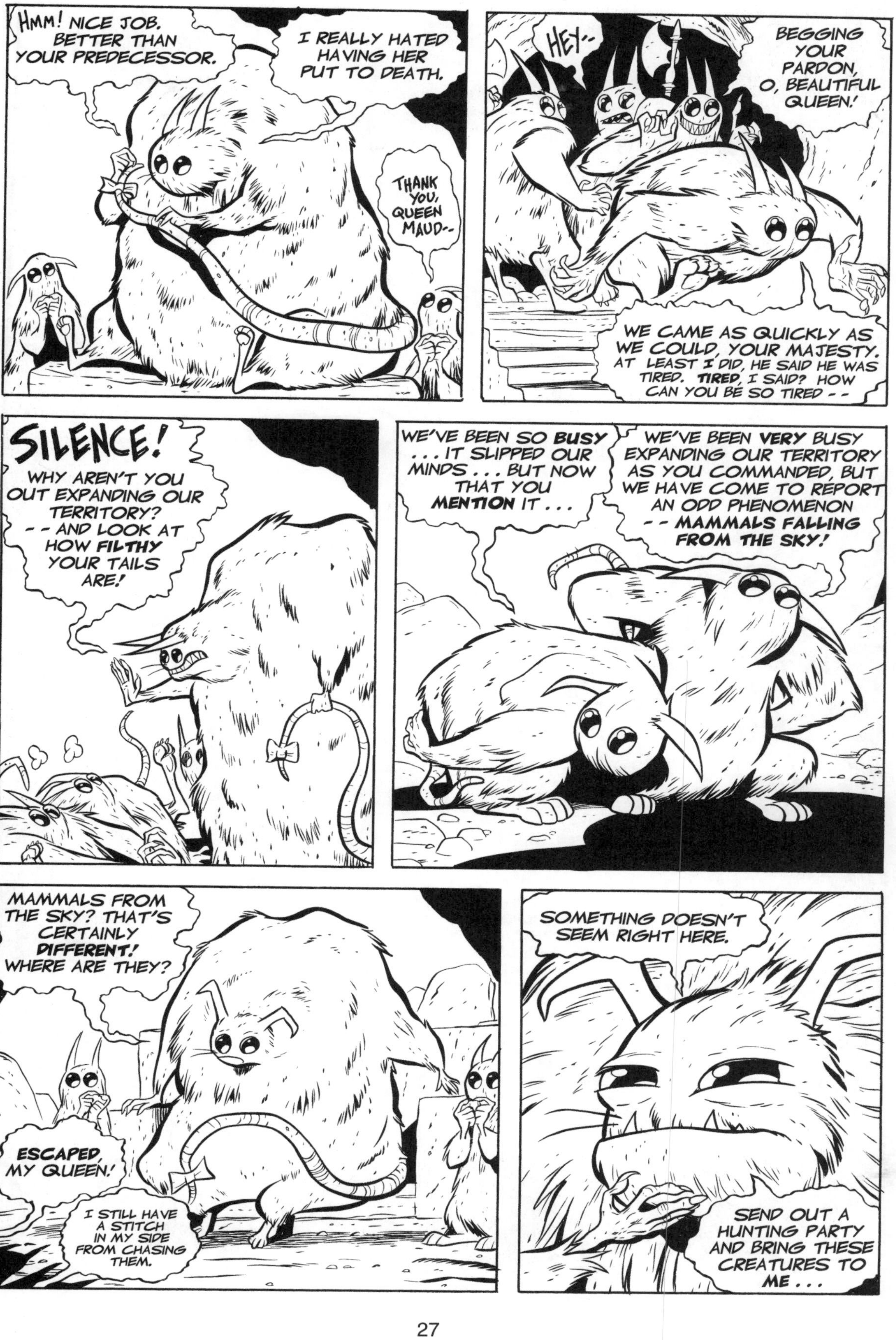
HMM! NICE JOB. BETTER THAN YOUR PREDECESSOR.
I REALLY HATED HAVING HER PUT TO DEATH.
THANK YOU, QUEEN MAUD--
HEY--
BEGGING YOUR PARDON, O, BEAUTIFUL QUEEN!
WE CAME AS QUICKLY AS WE COULD, YOUR MAJESTY. AT LEAST I DID, HE SAID HE WAS TIRED. TIRED, I SAID? HOW CAN YOU BE SO TIRED --
SILENCE!
WHY AREN'T YOU OUT EXPANDING OUR TERRITORY? -- AND LOOK AT HOW FILTHY YOUR TAILS ARE!
WE'VE BEEN SO BUSY ... IT SLIPPED OUR MINDS ... BUT NOW THAT YOU MENTION IT ...
WE'VE BEEN VERY BUSY EXPANDING OUR TERRITORY AS YOU COMMANDED, BUT WE HAVE COME TO REPORT AN ODD PHENOMENON -- MAMMALS FALLING FROM THE SKY!
MAMMALS FROM THE SKY? THAT'S CERTAINLY DIFFERENT! WHERE ARE THEY?
ESCAPED, MY QUEEN!
I STILL HAVE A STITCH IN MY SIDE FROM CHASING THEM.
SOMETHING DOESN'T SEEM RIGHT HERE.
SEND OUT A HUNTING PARTY AND BRING THESE CREATURES TO ME ...

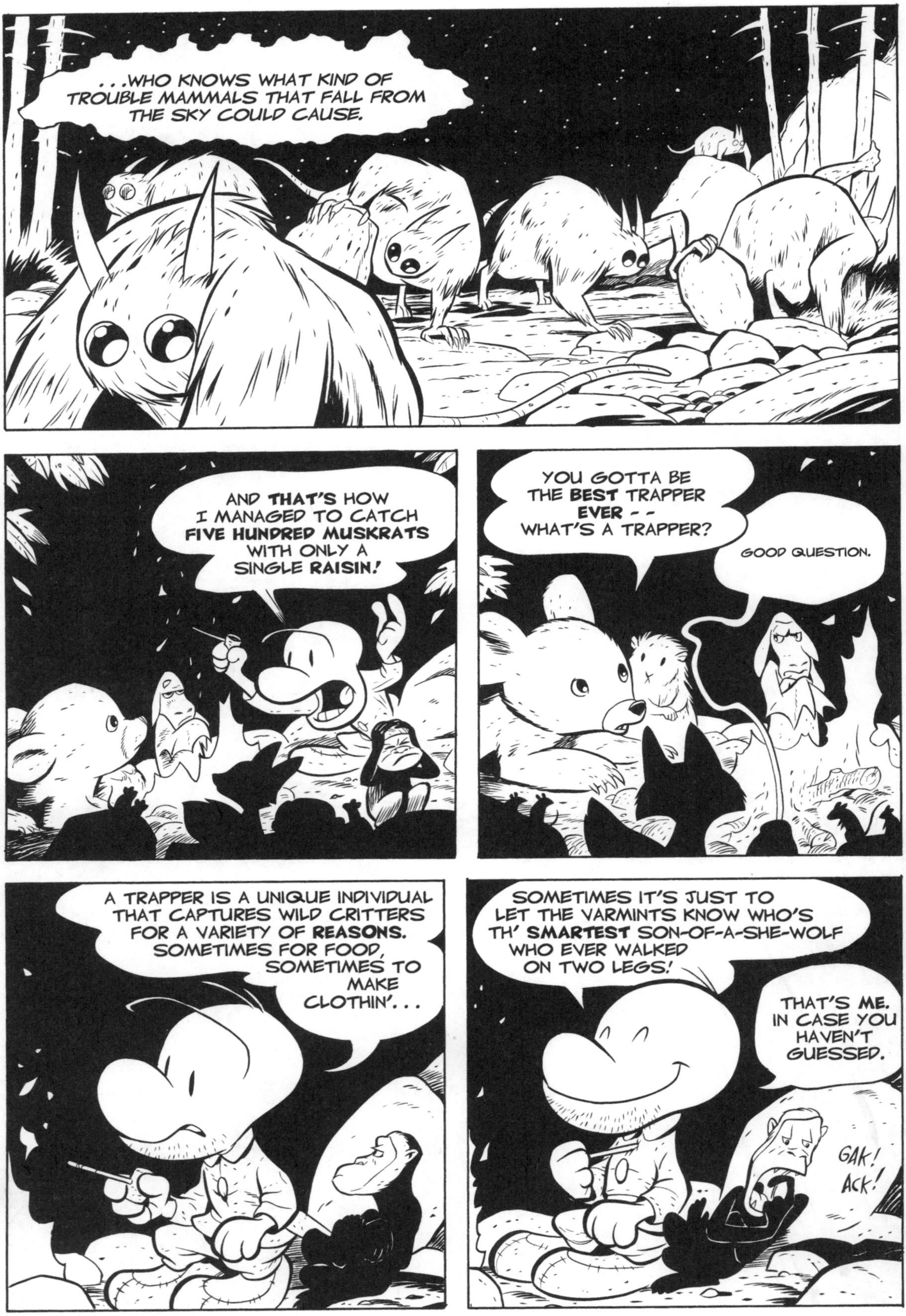

. . .WHO KNOWS WHAT KIND OF TROUBLE MAMMALS THAT FALL FROM THE SKY COULD CAUSE.
AND **THAT'S** HOW I MANAGED TO CATCH **FIVE HUNDRED MUSKRATS** WITH ONLY A SINGLE **RAISIN!**
YOU GOTTA BE THE **BEST** TRAPPER **EVER** - - WHAT'S A TRAPPER?
GOOD QUESTION.
A TRAPPER IS A UNIQUE INDIVIDUAL THAT CAPTURES WILD CRITTERS FOR A VARIETY OF **REASONS.** SOMETIMES FOR FOOD, SOMETIMES TO MAKE CLOTHIN'. . .
SOMETIMES IT'S JUST TO LET THE VARMINTS KNOW WHO'S TH' **SMARTEST** SON-OF-A-SHE-WOLF WHO EVER WALKED ON TWO LEGS!
THAT'S **ME.** IN CASE YOU HAVEN'T GUESSED.
GAK! ACK!

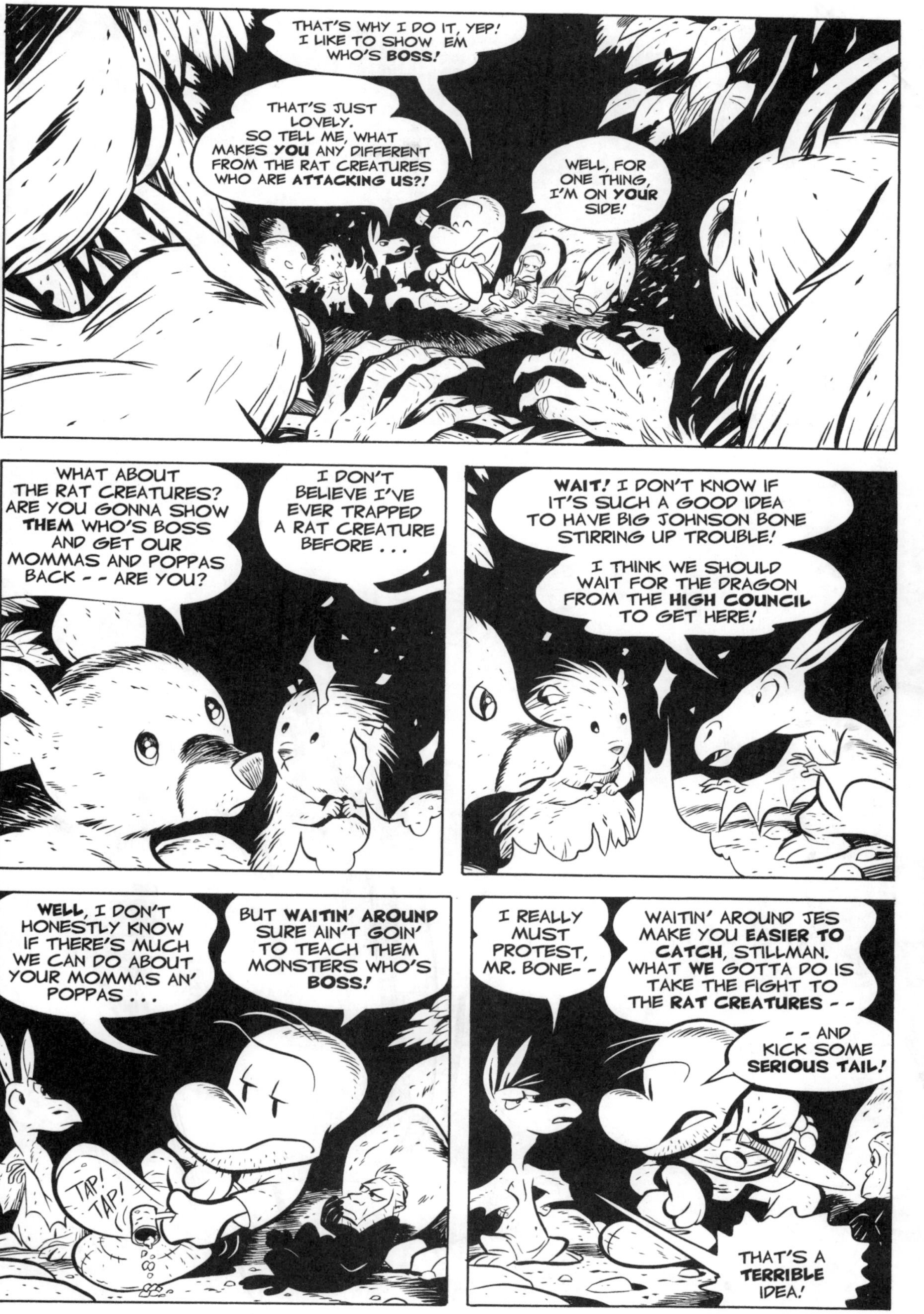
THAT'S WHY I DO IT, YEP! I LIKE TO SHOW EM WHO'S BOSS!
THAT'S JUST LOVELY. SO TELL ME, WHAT MAKES YOU ANY DIFFERENT FROM THE RAT CREATURES WHO ARE ATTACKING US?!
WELL, FOR ONE THING, I'M ON YOUR SIDE!
WHAT ABOUT THE RAT CREATURES? ARE YOU GONNA SHOW THEM WHO'S BOSS AND GET OUR MOMMAS AND POPPAS BACK - - ARE YOU?
I DON'T BELIEVE I'VE EVER TRAPPED A RAT CREATURE BEFORE . . .
WAIT! I DON'T KNOW IF IT'S SUCH A GOOD IDEA TO HAVE BIG JOHNSON BONE STIRRING UP TROUBLE!
I THINK WE SHOULD WAIT FOR THE DRAGON FROM THE HIGH COUNCIL TO GET HERE!
WELL, I DON'T HONESTLY KNOW IF THERE'S MUCH WE CAN DO ABOUT YOUR MOMMAS AN' POPPAS . . .
BUT WAITIN' AROUND SURE AIN'T GOIN' TO TEACH THEM MONSTERS WHO'S BOSS!
TAP! TAP!
I REALLY MUST PROTEST, MR. BONE- -
WAITIN' AROUND JES MAKE YOU EASIER TO CATCH, STILLMAN. WHAT WE GOTTA DO IS TAKE THE FIGHT TO THE RAT CREATURES - -
- - AND KICK SOME SERIOUS TAIL!
THAT'S A TERRIBLE IDEA!

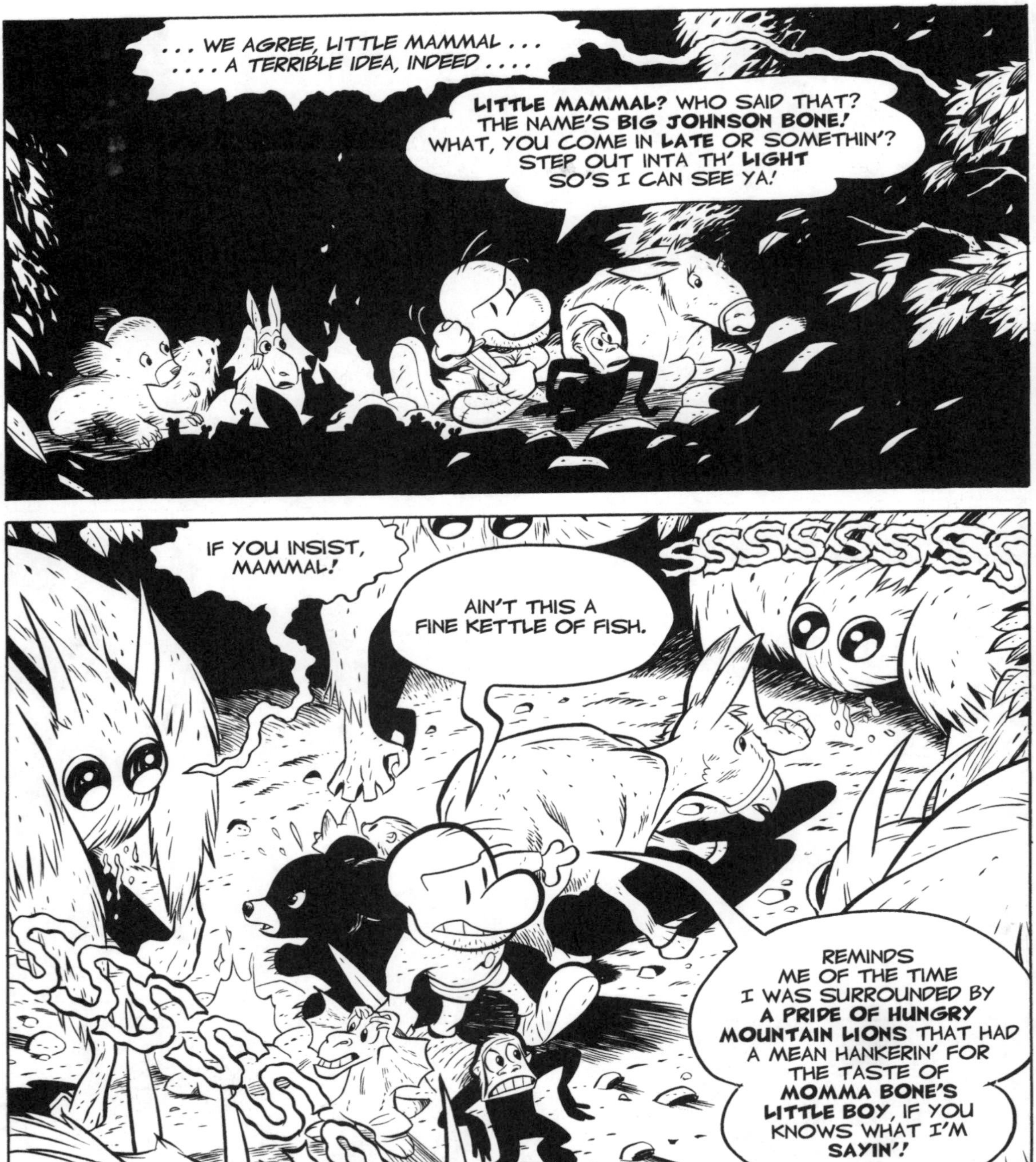
. . . WE AGREE, LITTLE MAMMAL . . . . A TERRIBLE IDEA, INDEED . . . .
LITTLE MAMMAL? WHO SAID THAT? THE NAME'S BIG JOHNSON BONE! WHAT, YOU COME IN LATE OR SOMETHIN'? STEP OUT INTA TH' LIGHT SO'S I CAN SEE YA!
IF YOU INSIST, MAMMAL!
SSSSSSSSS
AIN'T THIS A FINE KETTLE OF FISH.
REMINDS ME OF THE TIME I WAS SURROUNDED BY A PRIDE OF HUNGRY MOUNTAIN LIONS THAT HAD A MEAN HANKERIN' FOR THE TASTE OF MOMMA BONE'S LITTLE BOY, IF YOU KNOWS WHAT I'M SAYIN'!
MOTHER WAS RIGHT, I SHOULD HAVE JOINED THE CIRCUS!

NEXT: SCARY, SCARY RAT CREATURES

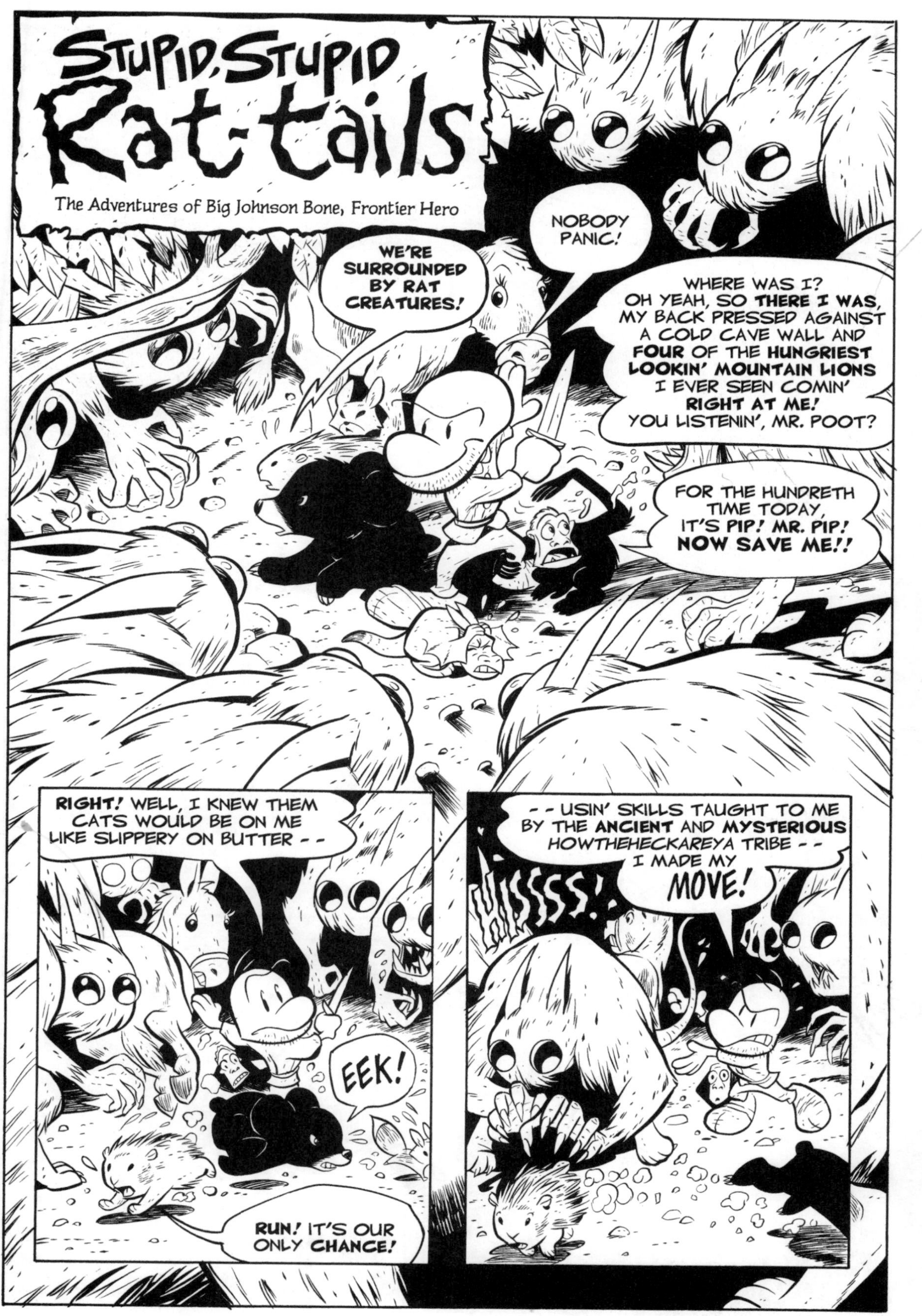
STUPID, STUPID Rat-tails
The Adventures of Big Johnson Bone, Frontier Hero
WE'RE SURROUNDED BY RAT CREATURES!
NOBODY PANIC!
WHERE WAS I? OH YEAH, SO THERE I WAS, MY BACK PRESSED AGAINST A COLD CAVE WALL AND FOUR OF THE HUNGRIEST LOOKIN' MOUNTAIN LIONS I EVER SEEN COMIN' RIGHT AT ME! YOU LISTENIN', MR. POOT?
FOR THE HUNDRETH TIME TODAY, IT'S PIP! MR. PIP! NOW SAVE ME!!
RIGHT! WELL, I KNEW THEM CATS WOULD BE ON ME LIKE SLIPPERY ON BUTTER - -
EEK!
RUN! IT'S OUR ONLY CHANCE!
- - USIN' SKILLS TAUGHT TO ME BY THE ANCIENT AND MYSTERIOUS HOWTHEHECKAREYA TRIBE - - I MADE MY MOVE!
HISSSS!

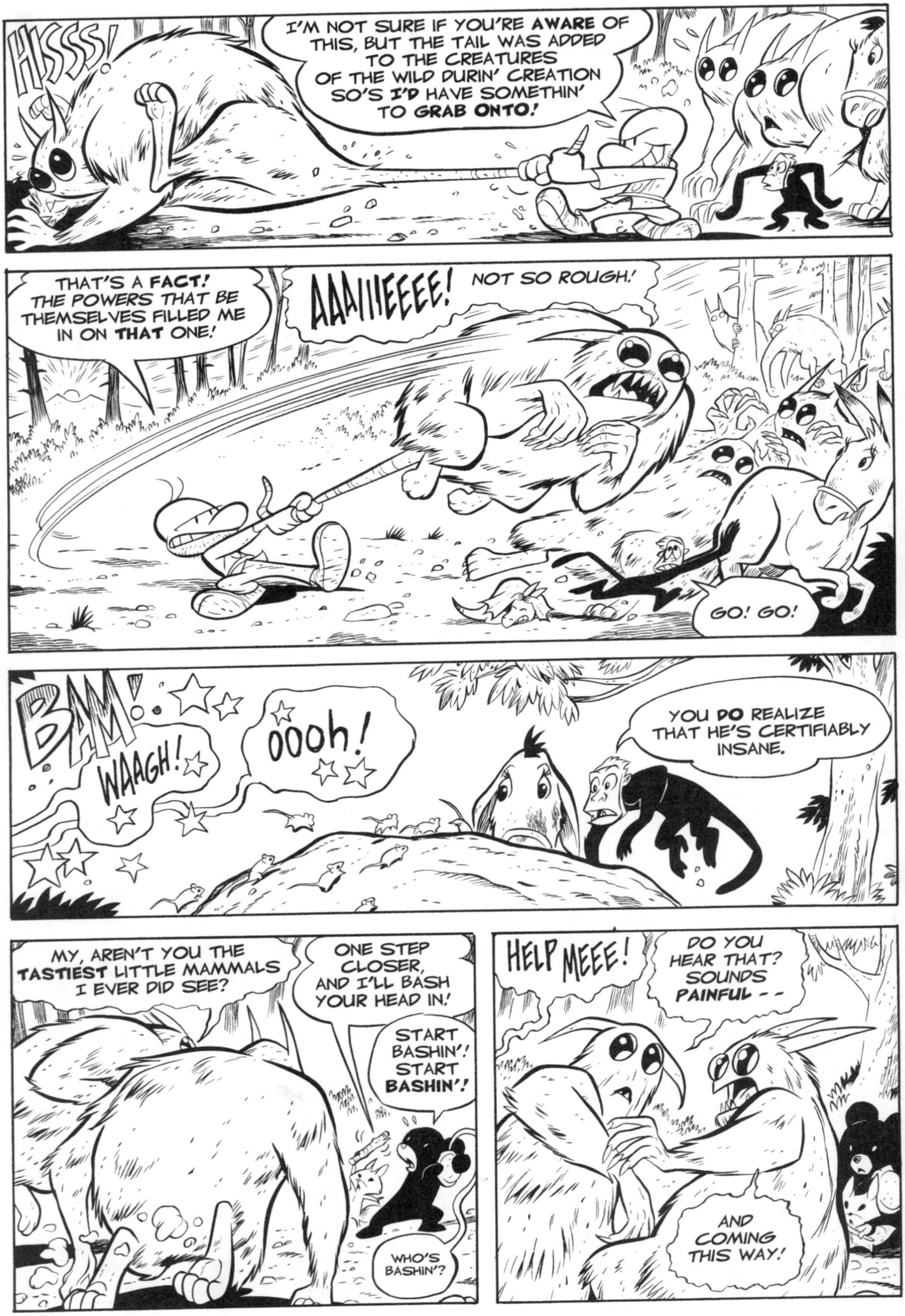
HISSS!
I'M NOT SURE IF YOU'RE AWARE OF THIS, BUT THE TAIL WAS ADDED TO THE CREATURES OF THE WILD DURIN' CREATION SO'S I'D HAVE SOMETHIN' TO GRAB ONTO!
THAT'S A FACT! THE POWERS THAT BE THEMSELVES FILLED ME IN ON THAT ONE!
AAAIIIEEEEE!
NOT SO ROUGH!
GO! GO!
BAM!
WAAGH!
oooh!
YOU DO REALIZE THAT HE'S CERTIFIABLY INSANE.
MY, AREN'T YOU THE TASTIEST LITTLE MAMMALS I EVER DID SEE?
ONE STEP CLOSER, AND I'LL BASH YOUR HEAD IN!
START BASHIN'! START BASHIN'!
WHO'S BASHIN'?
HELP MEEE!
DO YOU HEAR THAT? SOUNDS PAINFUL - -
AND COMING THIS WAY!

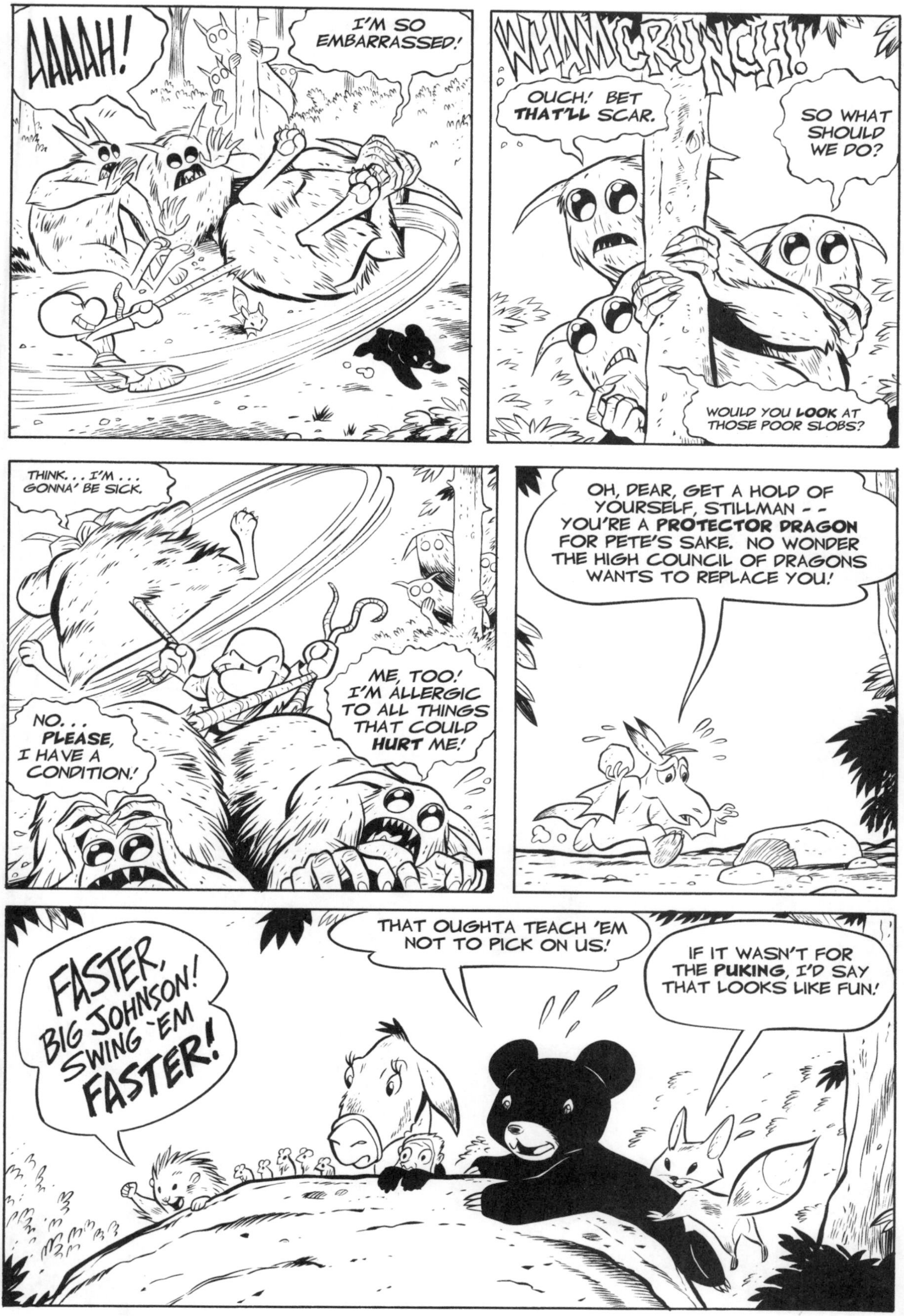
AAAAH!
I'M SO EMBARRASSED!
WHAMCRUNCH!
OUCH! BET THAT'LL SCAR.
SO WHAT SHOULD WE DO?
WOULD YOU LOOK AT THOSE POOR SLOBS?
THINK... I'M... GONNA' BE SICK.
NO... PLEASE, I HAVE A CONDITION!
ME, TOO! I'M ALLERGIC TO ALL THINGS THAT COULD HURT ME!
OH, DEAR, GET A HOLD OF YOURSELF, STILLMAN -- YOU'RE A PROTECTOR DRAGON FOR PETE'S SAKE. NO WONDER THE HIGH COUNCIL OF DRAGONS WANTS TO REPLACE YOU!
FASTER, BIG JOHNSON! SWING 'EM FASTER!
THAT OUGHTA TEACH 'EM NOT TO PICK ON US!
IF IT WASN'T FOR THE PUKING, I'D SAY THAT LOOKS LIKE FUN!

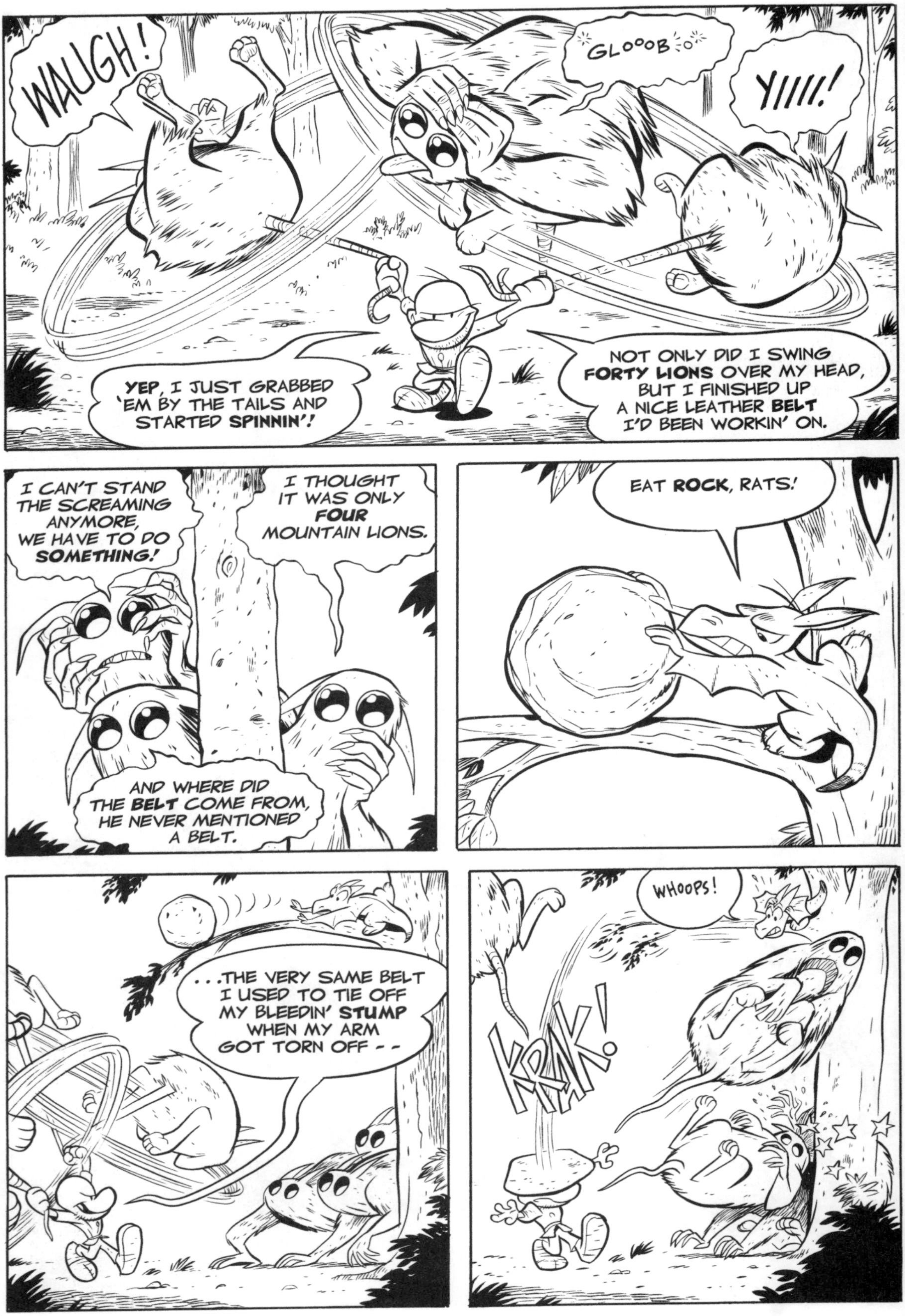
WAUGH!
GLOOOB
YIIII!
YEP, I JUST GRABBED 'EM BY THE TAILS AND STARTED SPINNIN'!
NOT ONLY DID I SWING FORTY LIONS OVER MY HEAD, BUT I FINISHED UP A NICE LEATHER BELT I'D BEEN WORKIN' ON.
I CAN'T STAND THE SCREAMING ANYMORE, WE HAVE TO DO SOMETHING!
I THOUGHT IT WAS ONLY FOUR MOUNTAIN LIONS.
AND WHERE DID THE BELT COME FROM, HE NEVER MENTIONED A BELT.
EAT ROCK, RATS!
...THE VERY SAME BELT I USED TO TIE OFF MY BLEEDIN' STUMP WHEN MY ARM GOT TORN OFF --
WHOOPS!
KRAK!

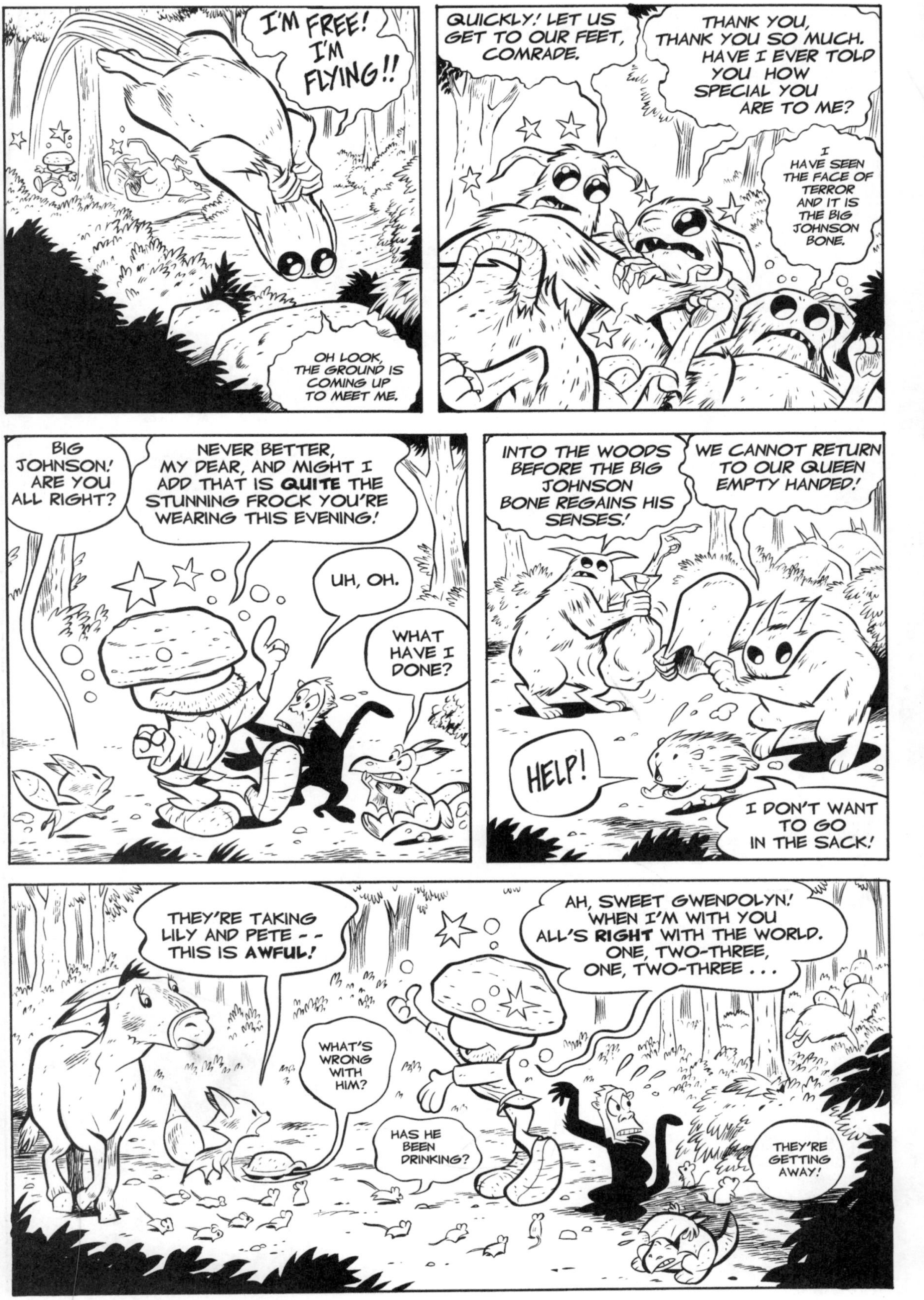

I'M FREE! I'M FLYING!!
OH LOOK, THE GROUND IS COMING UP TO MEET ME.
QUICKLY! LET US GET TO OUR FEET, COMRADE.
THANK YOU, THANK YOU SO MUCH. HAVE I EVER TOLD YOU HOW SPECIAL YOU ARE TO ME?
I HAVE SEEN THE FACE OF TERROR AND IT IS THE BIG JOHNSON BONE.
BIG JOHNSON! ARE YOU ALL RIGHT?
NEVER BETTER, MY DEAR, AND MIGHT I ADD THAT IS QUITE THE STUNNING FROCK YOU'RE WEARING THIS EVENING!
UH, OH.
WHAT HAVE I DONE?
INTO THE WOODS BEFORE THE BIG JOHNSON BONE REGAINS HIS SENSES!
WE CANNOT RETURN TO OUR QUEEN EMPTY HANDED!
HELP!
I DON'T WANT TO GO IN THE SACK!
THEY'RE TAKING LILY AND PETE -- THIS IS AWFUL!
AH, SWEET GWENDOLYN! WHEN I'M WITH YOU ALL'S RIGHT WITH THE WORLD. ONE, TWO-THREE, ONE, TWO-THREE . . .
WHAT'S WRONG WITH HIM?
HAS HE BEEN DRINKING?
THEY'RE GETTING AWAY!

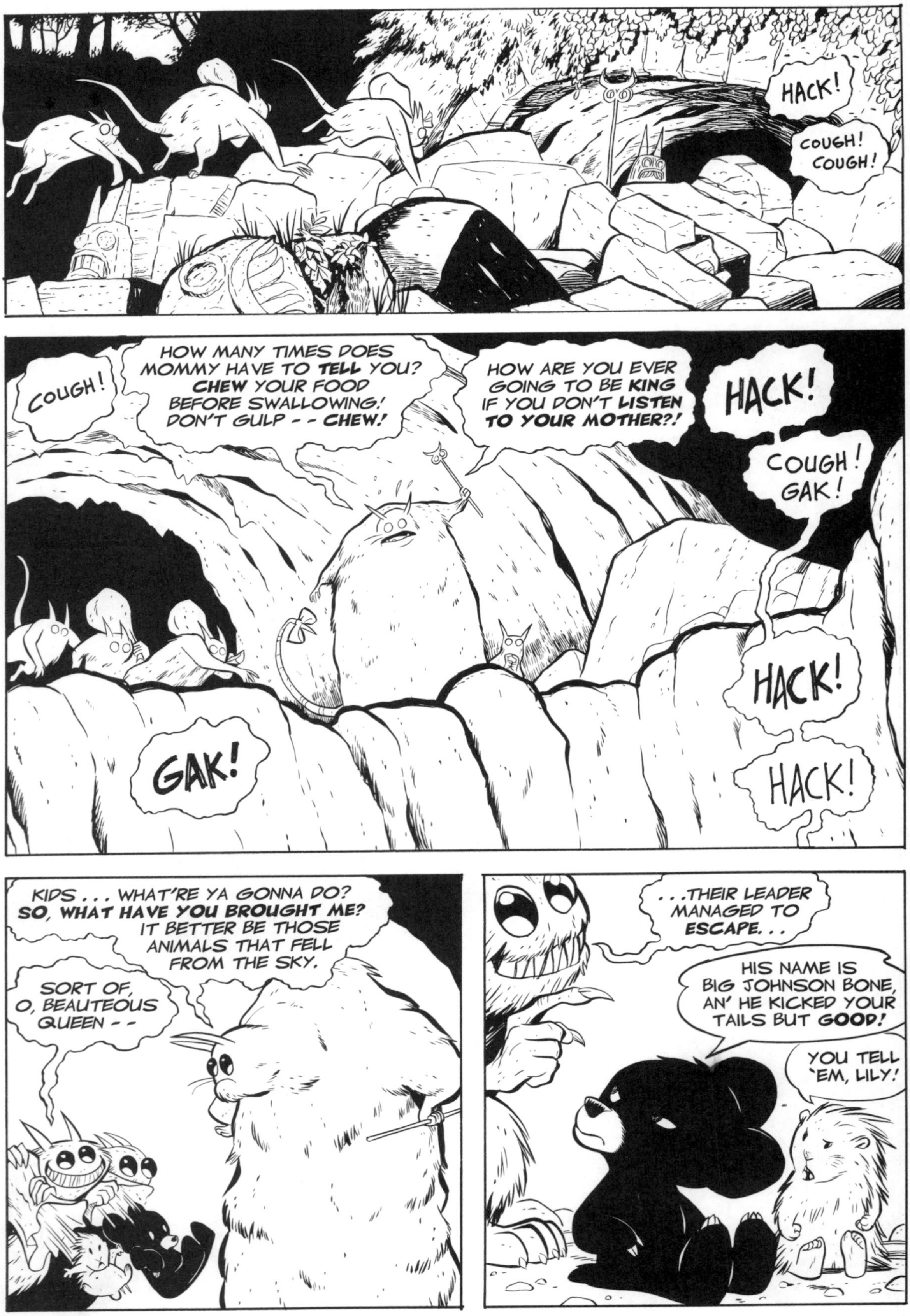
HACK!
COUGH! COUGH!
COUGH!
HOW MANY TIMES DOES MOMMY HAVE TO TELL YOU? CHEW YOUR FOOD BEFORE SWALLOWING! DON'T GULP - - CHEW!
HOW ARE YOU EVER GOING TO BE KING IF YOU DON'T LISTEN TO YOUR MOTHER?!
HACK!
COUGH! GAK!
HACK!
GAK!
HACK!
KIDS . . . WHAT'RE YA GONNA DO? SO, WHAT HAVE YOU BROUGHT ME? IT BETTER BE THOSE ANIMALS THAT FELL FROM THE SKY.
SORT OF, O, BEAUTEOUS QUEEN - -
. . .THEIR LEADER MANAGED TO ESCAPE. . .
HIS NAME IS BIG JOHNSON BONE, AN' HE KICKED YOUR TAILS BUT GOOD!
YOU TELL 'EM, LILY!

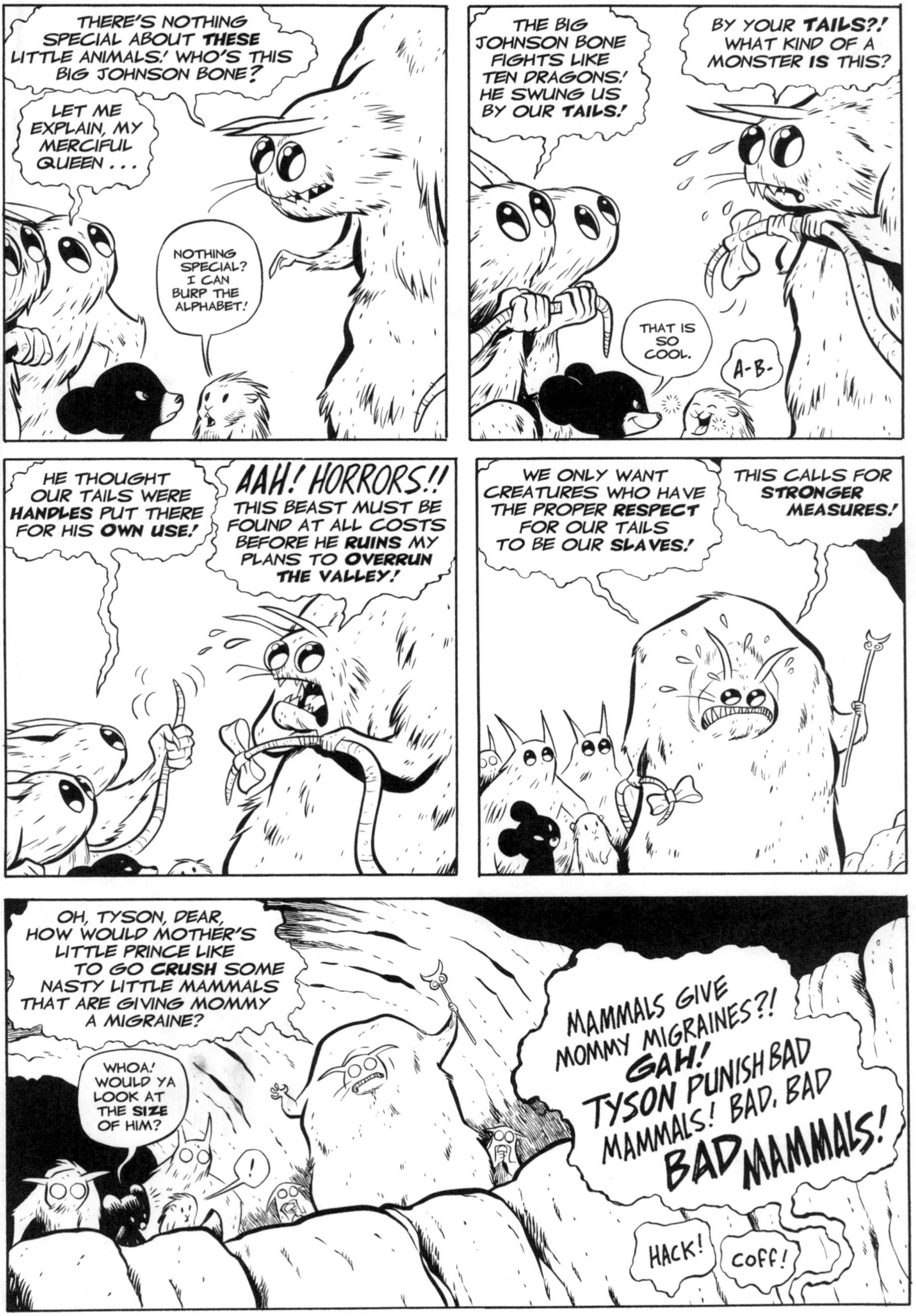
THERE'S NOTHING SPECIAL ABOUT **THESE** LITTLE ANIMALS! WHO'S THIS BIG JOHNSON BONE?
LET ME EXPLAIN, MY MERCIFUL QUEEN . . .
NOTHING SPECIAL? I CAN BURP THE ALPHABET!
THE BIG JOHNSON BONE FIGHTS LIKE TEN DRAGONS! HE SWUNG US BY OUR **TAILS!**
BY YOUR **TAILS?!** WHAT KIND OF A MONSTER **IS** THIS?
THAT IS SO COOL.
A-B-
HE THOUGHT OUR TAILS WERE **HANDLES** PUT THERE FOR HIS **OWN USE!**
AAH! HORRORS!! THIS BEAST MUST BE FOUND AT ALL COSTS BEFORE HE **RUINS** MY PLANS TO **OVERRUN THE VALLEY!**
WE ONLY WANT CREATURES WHO HAVE THE PROPER **RESPECT** FOR OUR TAILS TO BE OUR **SLAVES!**
THIS CALLS FOR **STRONGER MEASURES!**
OH, TYSON, DEAR, HOW WOULD MOTHER'S LITTLE PRINCE LIKE TO GO **CRUSH** SOME NASTY LITTLE MAMMALS THAT ARE GIVING MOMMY A MIGRAINE?
WHOA! WOULD YA LOOK AT THE **SIZE** OF HIM?
!
MAMMALS GIVE MOMMY MIGRAINES?! GAH! TYSON PUNISH BAD MAMMALS! BAD, BAD BAD MAMMALS!
HACK!
COFF!

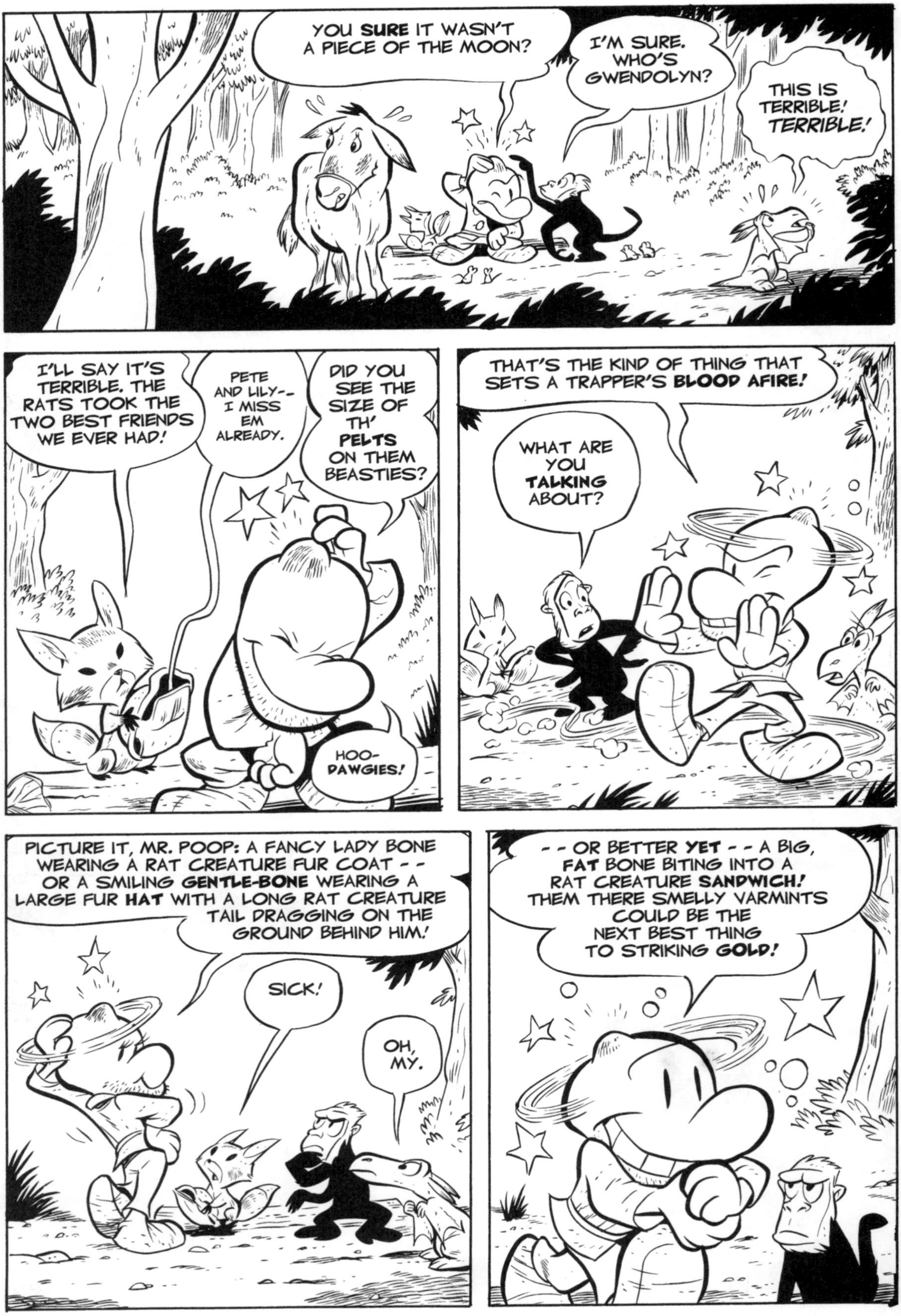
YOU **SURE** IT WASN'T A PIECE OF THE MOON?
I'M SURE. WHO'S GWENDOLYN?
THIS IS TERRIBLE! *TERRIBLE!*
I'LL SAY IT'S TERRIBLE. THE RATS TOOK THE TWO BEST FRIENDS WE EVER HAD!
PETE AND LILY-- I MISS EM ALREADY.
DID YOU SEE THE SIZE OF TH' **PELTS** ON THEM BEASTIES?
HOO-DAWGIES!
THAT'S THE KIND OF THING THAT SETS A TRAPPER'S **BLOOD AFIRE!**
WHAT ARE YOU **TALKING** ABOUT?
PICTURE IT, MR. POOP: A FANCY LADY BONE WEARING A RAT CREATURE FUR COAT -- OR A SMILING **GENTLE-BONE** WEARING A LARGE FUR **HAT** WITH A LONG RAT CREATURE TAIL DRAGGING ON THE GROUND BEHIND HIM!
SICK!
OH, MY.
-- OR BETTER **YET** -- A BIG, **FAT** BONE BITING INTO A RAT CREATURE **SANDWICH!** THEM THERE SMELLY VARMINTS COULD BE THE NEXT BEST THING TO STRIKING **GOLD!**

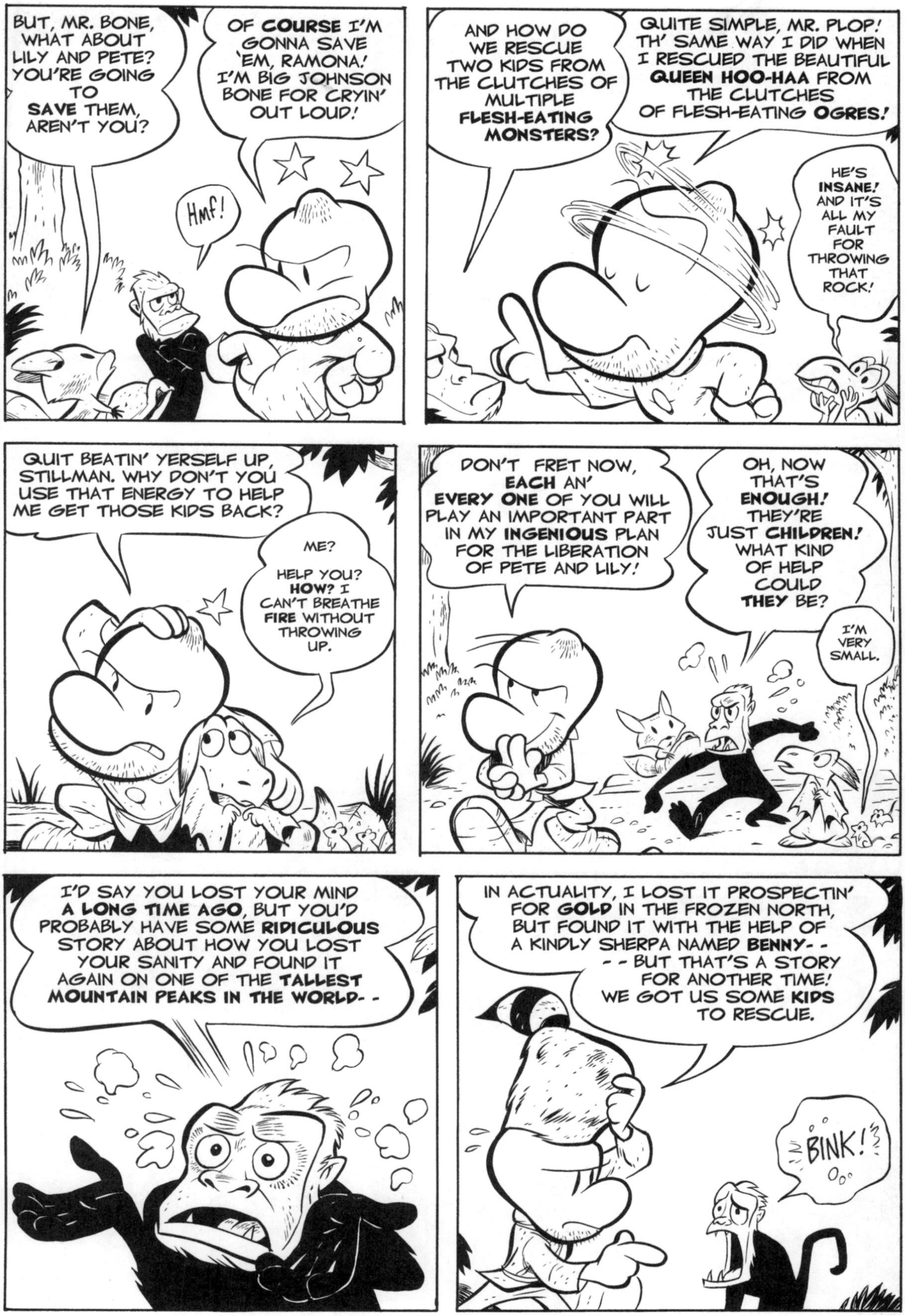
BUT, MR. BONE, WHAT ABOUT LILY AND PETE? YOU'RE GOING TO SAVE THEM, AREN'T YOU?
OF COURSE I'M GONNA SAVE 'EM, RAMONA! I'M BIG JOHNSON BONE FOR CRYIN' OUT LOUD!
Hmf!
AND HOW DO WE RESCUE TWO KIDS FROM THE CLUTCHES OF MULTIPLE FLESH-EATING MONSTERS?
QUITE SIMPLE, MR. PLOP! TH' SAME WAY I DID WHEN I RESCUED THE BEAUTIFUL QUEEN HOO-HAA FROM THE CLUTCHES OF FLESH-EATING OGRES!
HE'S INSANE! AND IT'S ALL MY FAULT FOR THROWING THAT ROCK!
QUIT BEATIN' YERSELF UP, STILLMAN. WHY DON'T YOU USE THAT ENERGY TO HELP ME GET THOSE KIDS BACK?
ME? HELP YOU? HOW? I CAN'T BREATHE FIRE WITHOUT THROWING UP.
DON'T FRET NOW, EACH AN' EVERY ONE OF YOU WILL PLAY AN IMPORTANT PART IN MY INGENIOUS PLAN FOR THE LIBERATION OF PETE AND LILY!
OH, NOW THAT'S ENOUGH! THEY'RE JUST CHILDREN! WHAT KIND OF HELP COULD THEY BE?
I'M VERY SMALL.
I'D SAY YOU LOST YOUR MIND A LONG TIME AGO, BUT YOU'D PROBABLY HAVE SOME RIDICULOUS STORY ABOUT HOW YOU LOST YOUR SANITY AND FOUND IT AGAIN ON ONE OF THE TALLEST MOUNTAIN PEAKS IN THE WORLD- -
IN ACTUALITY, I LOST IT PROSPECTIN' FOR GOLD IN THE FROZEN NORTH, BUT FOUND IT WITH THE HELP OF A KINDLY SHERPA NAMED BENNY- - - - BUT THAT'S A STORY FOR ANOTHER TIME! WE GOT US SOME KIDS TO RESCUE.
BINK!

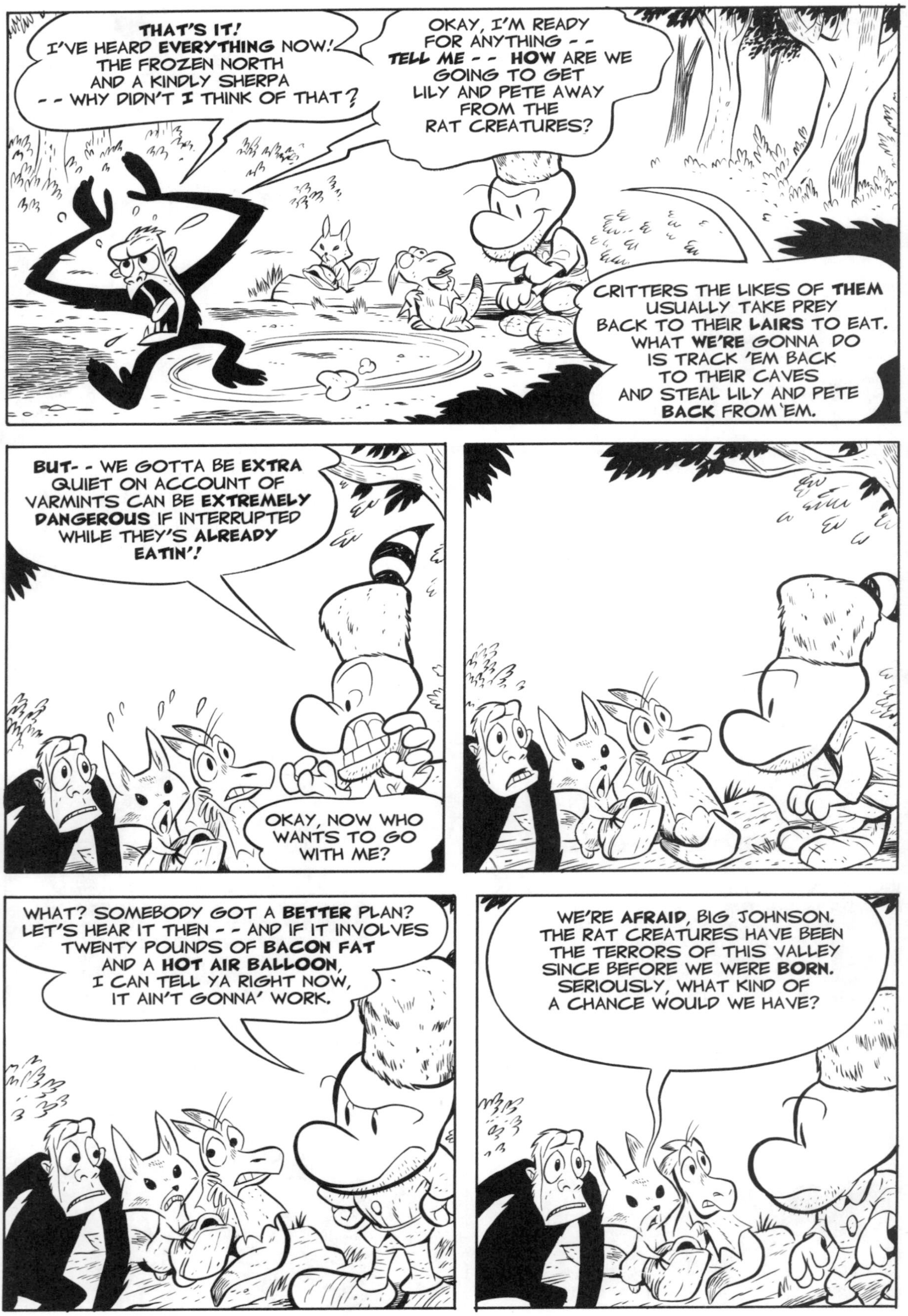
THAT'S IT! I'VE HEARD EVERYTHING NOW! THE FROZEN NORTH AND A KINDLY SHERPA - - WHY DIDN'T I THINK OF THAT?
OKAY, I'M READY FOR ANYTHING - - TELL ME - - HOW ARE WE GOING TO GET LILY AND PETE AWAY FROM THE RAT CREATURES?
CRITTERS THE LIKES OF THEM USUALLY TAKE PREY BACK TO THEIR LAIRS TO EAT. WHAT WE'RE GONNA DO IS TRACK 'EM BACK TO THEIR CAVES AND STEAL LILY AND PETE BACK FROM 'EM.
BUT- - WE GOTTA BE EXTRA QUIET ON ACCOUNT OF VARMINTS CAN BE EXTREMELY DANGEROUS IF INTERRUPTED WHILE THEY'S ALREADY EATIN'!
OKAY, NOW WHO WANTS TO GO WITH ME?
WHAT? SOMEBODY GOT A BETTER PLAN? LET'S HEAR IT THEN - - AND IF IT INVOLVES TWENTY POUNDS OF BACON FAT AND A HOT AIR BALLOON, I CAN TELL YA RIGHT NOW, IT AIN'T GONNA' WORK.
WE'RE AFRAID, BIG JOHNSON. THE RAT CREATURES HAVE BEEN THE TERRORS OF THIS VALLEY SINCE BEFORE WE WERE BORN. SERIOUSLY, WHAT KIND OF A CHANCE WOULD WE HAVE?

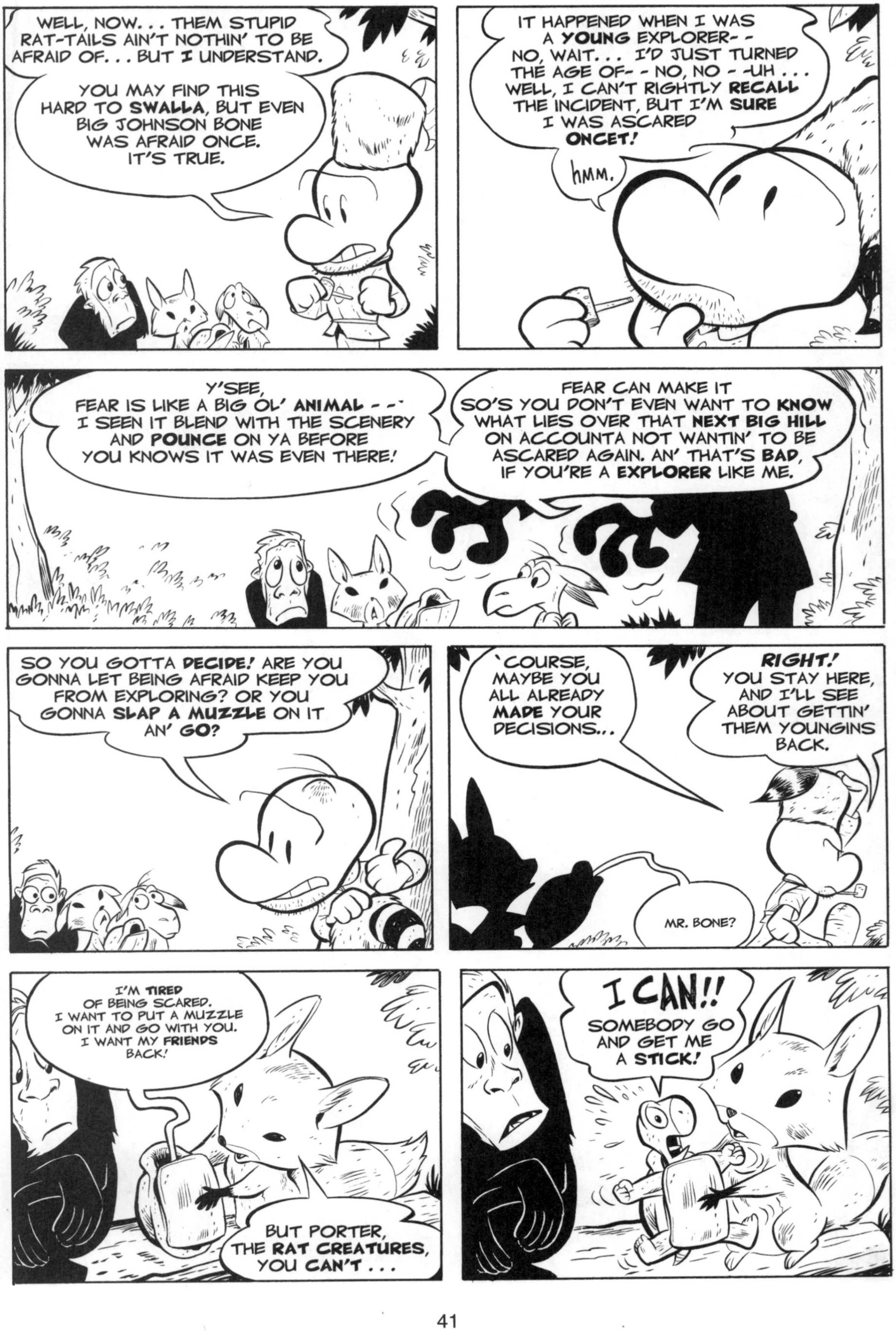
WELL, NOW... THEM STUPID RAT-TAILS AIN'T NOTHIN' TO BE AFRAID OF... BUT I UNDERSTAND.
YOU MAY FIND THIS HARD TO SWALLA, BUT EVEN BIG JOHNSON BONE WAS AFRAID ONCE. IT'S TRUE.
IT HAPPENED WHEN I WAS A YOUNG EXPLORER-- NO, WAIT... I'D JUST TURNED THE AGE OF--NO, NO--UH... WELL, I CAN'T RIGHTLY RECALL THE INCIDENT, BUT I'M SURE I WAS ASCARED ONCET!
hMM.
Y'SEE, FEAR IS LIKE A BIG OL' ANIMAL--- I SEEN IT BLEND WITH THE SCENERY AND POUNCE ON YA BEFORE YOU KNOWS IT WAS EVEN THERE!
FEAR CAN MAKE IT SO'S YOU DON'T EVEN WANT TO KNOW WHAT LIES OVER THAT NEXT BIG HILL ON ACCOUNTA NOT WANTIN' TO BE ASCARED AGAIN. AN' THAT'S BAD, IF YOU'RE A EXPLORER LIKE ME.
SO YOU GOTTA DECIDE! ARE YOU GONNA LET BEING AFRAID KEEP YOU FROM EXPLORING? OR YOU GONNA SLAP A MUZZLE ON IT AN' GO?
`COURSE, MAYBE YOU ALL ALREADY MADE YOUR DECISIONS...
RIGHT! YOU STAY HERE, AND I'LL SEE ABOUT GETTIN' THEM YOUNGINS BACK.
MR. BONE?
I'M TIRED OF BEING SCARED. I WANT TO PUT A MUZZLE ON IT AND GO WITH YOU. I WANT MY FRIENDS BACK!
BUT PORTER, THE RAT CREATURES, YOU CAN'T...
I CAN!! SOMEBODY GO AND GET ME A STICK!

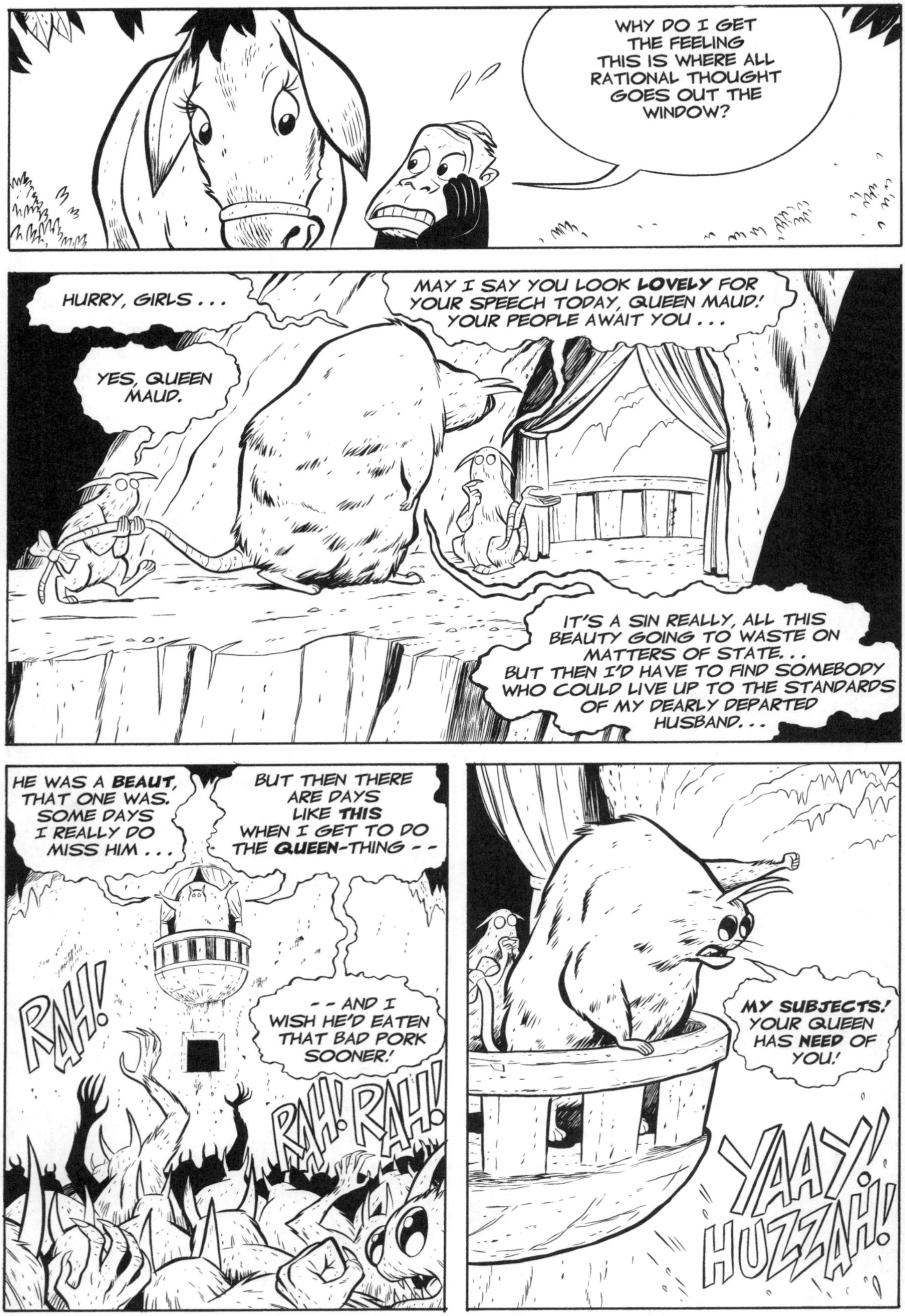
WHY DO I GET THE FEELING THIS IS WHERE ALL RATIONAL THOUGHT GOES OUT THE WINDOW?
HURRY, GIRLS . . .
MAY I SAY YOU LOOK LOVELY FOR YOUR SPEECH TODAY, QUEEN MAUD! YOUR PEOPLE AWAIT YOU . . .
YES, QUEEN MAUD.
IT'S A SIN REALLY, ALL THIS BEAUTY GOING TO WASTE ON MATTERS OF STATE. . . BUT THEN I'D HAVE TO FIND SOMEBODY WHO COULD LIVE UP TO THE STANDARDS OF MY DEARLY DEPARTED HUSBAND. . .
HE WAS A BEAUT, THAT ONE WAS. SOME DAYS I REALLY DO MISS HIM . . .
BUT THEN THERE ARE DAYS LIKE THIS WHEN I GET TO DO THE QUEEN-THING - -
RAH!
- - AND I WISH HE'D EATEN THAT BAD PORK SOONER!
RAH! RAH!
MY SUBJECTS! YOUR QUEEN HAS NEED OF YOU!
YAAY!
HUZZAH!

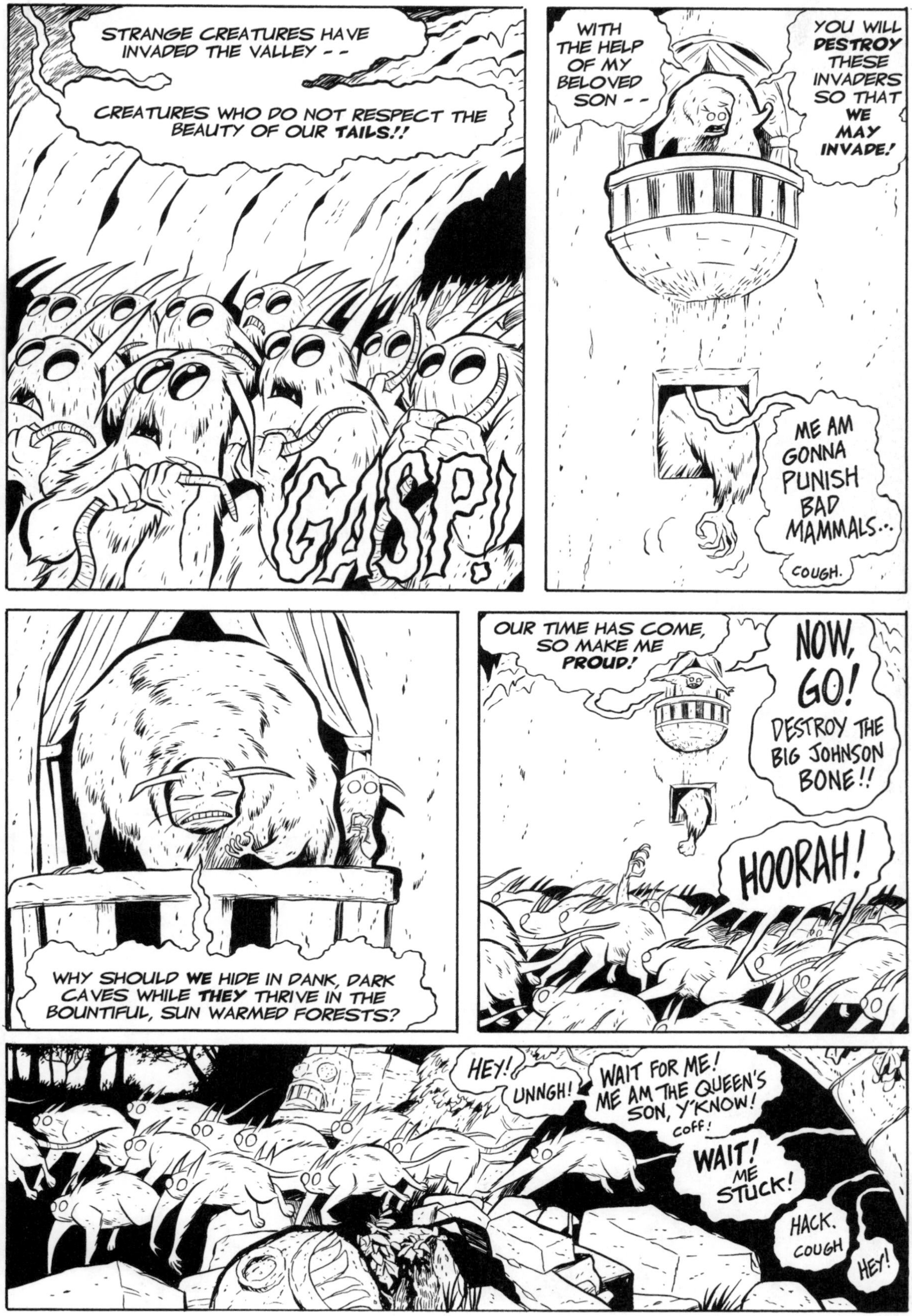
STRANGE CREATURES HAVE INVADED THE VALLEY - -
CREATURES WHO DO NOT RESPECT THE BEAUTY OF OUR TAILS!!
GASP!
WITH THE HELP OF MY BELOVED SON - -
YOU WILL DESTROY THESE INVADERS SO THAT WE MAY INVADE!
ME AM GONNA PUNISH BAD MAMMALS...
COUGH.
WHY SHOULD WE HIDE IN DANK, DARK CAVES WHILE THEY THRIVE IN THE BOUNTIFUL, SUN WARMED FORESTS?
OUR TIME HAS COME, SO MAKE ME PROUD!
NOW, GO! DESTROY THE BIG JOHNSON BONE!!
HOORAH!
HEY!
UNNGH!
WAIT FOR ME! ME AM THE QUEEN'S SON, Y'KNOW!
COFF!
WAIT! ME STUCK!
HACK. COUGH
HEY!

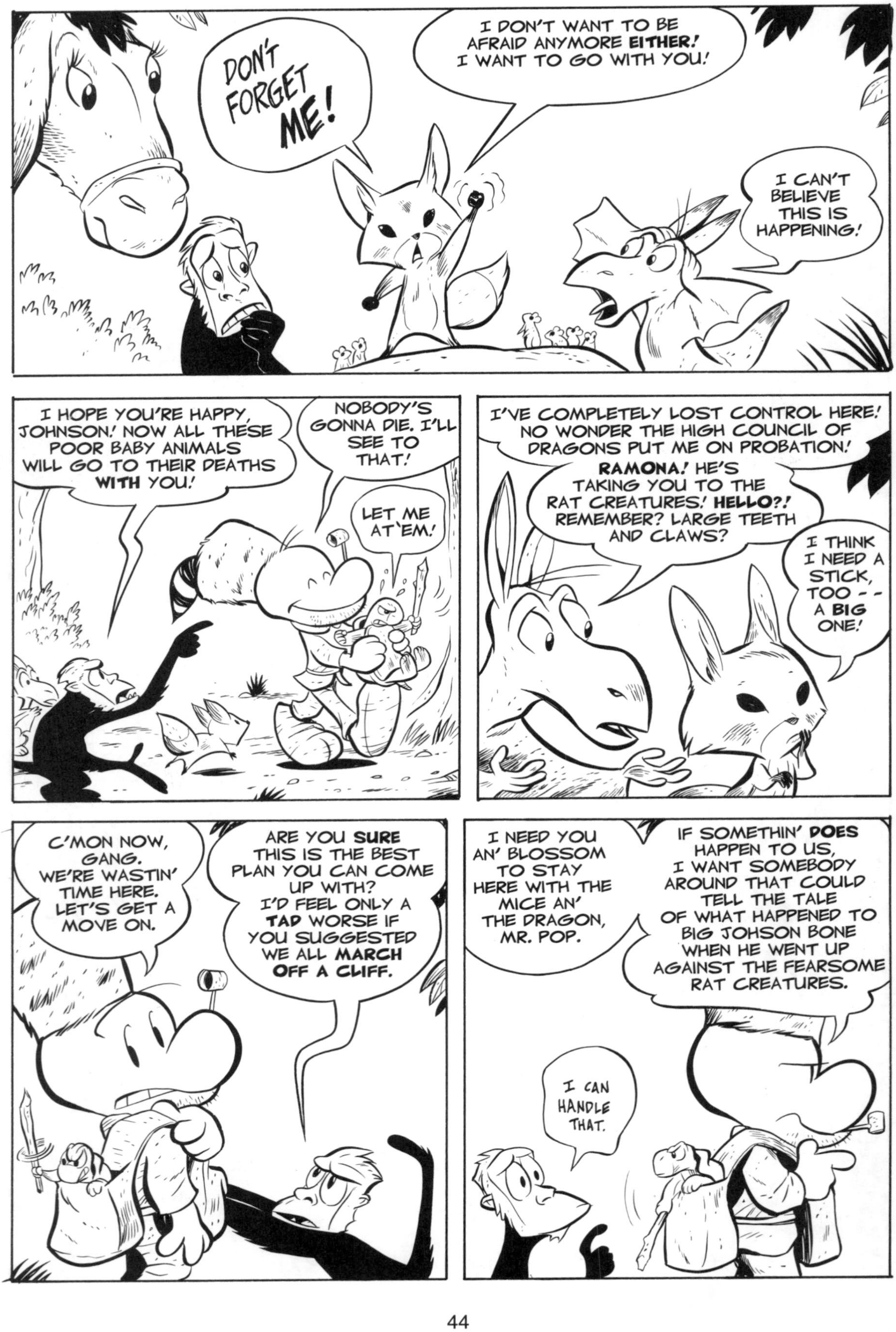
DON'T FORGET ME!
I DON'T WANT TO BE AFRAID ANYMORE EITHER! I WANT TO GO WITH YOU!
I CAN'T BELIEVE THIS IS HAPPENING!
I HOPE YOU'RE HAPPY, JOHNSON! NOW ALL THESE POOR BABY ANIMALS WILL GO TO THEIR DEATHS WITH YOU!
NOBODY'S GONNA DIE. I'LL SEE TO THAT!
LET ME AT'EM!
I'VE COMPLETELY LOST CONTROL HERE! NO WONDER THE HIGH COUNCIL OF DRAGONS PUT ME ON PROBATION!
RAMONA! HE'S TAKING YOU TO THE RAT CREATURES! HELLO?! REMEMBER? LARGE TEETH AND CLAWS?
I THINK I NEED A STICK, TOO - - A BIG ONE!
C'MON NOW, GANG. WE'RE WASTIN' TIME HERE. LET'S GET A MOVE ON.
ARE YOU SURE THIS IS THE BEST PLAN YOU CAN COME UP WITH? I'D FEEL ONLY A TAD WORSE IF YOU SUGGESTED WE ALL MARCH OFF A CLIFF.
I NEED YOU AN' BLOSSOM TO STAY HERE WITH THE MICE AN' THE DRAGON, MR. POP.
IF SOMETHIN' DOES HAPPEN TO US, I WANT SOMEBODY AROUND THAT COULD TELL THE TALE OF WHAT HAPPENED TO BIG JOHSON BONE WHEN HE WENT UP AGAINST THE FEARSOME RAT CREATURES.
I CAN HANDLE THAT.

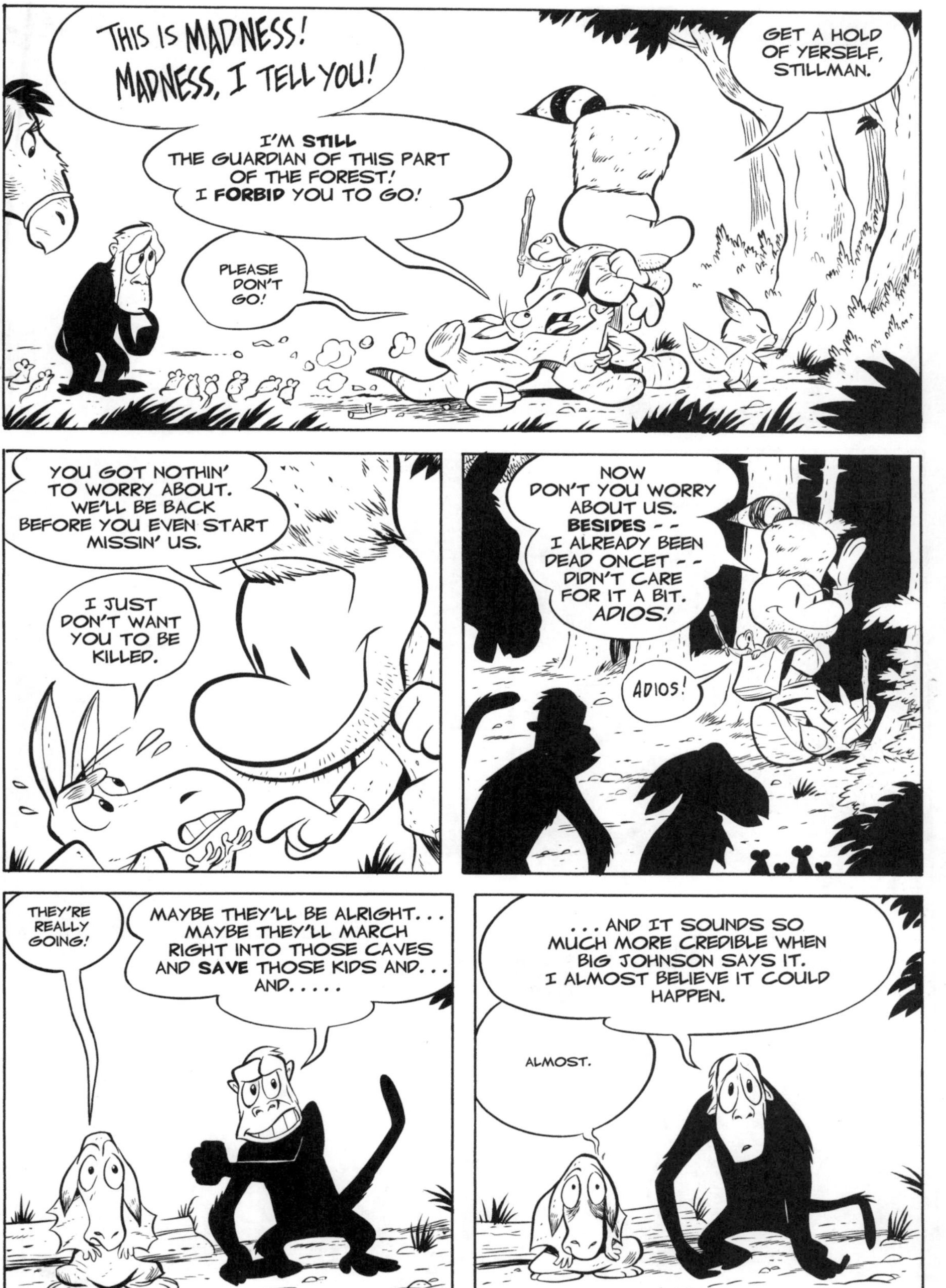
THIS IS MADNESS! MADNESS, I TELL YOU!
I'M STILL THE GUARDIAN OF THIS PART OF THE FOREST! I FORBID YOU TO GO!
GET A HOLD OF YERSELF, STILLMAN.
PLEASE DON'T GO!
YOU GOT NOTHIN' TO WORRY ABOUT. WE'LL BE BACK BEFORE YOU EVEN START MISSIN' US.
I JUST DON'T WANT YOU TO BE KILLED.
NOW DON'T YOU WORRY ABOUT US. BESIDES -- I ALREADY BEEN DEAD ONCET -- DIDN'T CARE FOR IT A BIT. ADIOS!
ADIOS!
THEY'RE REALLY GOING!
MAYBE THEY'LL BE ALRIGHT... MAYBE THEY'LL MARCH RIGHT INTO THOSE CAVES AND SAVE THOSE KIDS AND... AND.....
...AND IT SOUNDS SO MUCH MORE CREDIBLE WHEN BIG JOHNSON SAYS IT. I ALMOST BELIEVE IT COULD HAPPEN.
ALMOST.

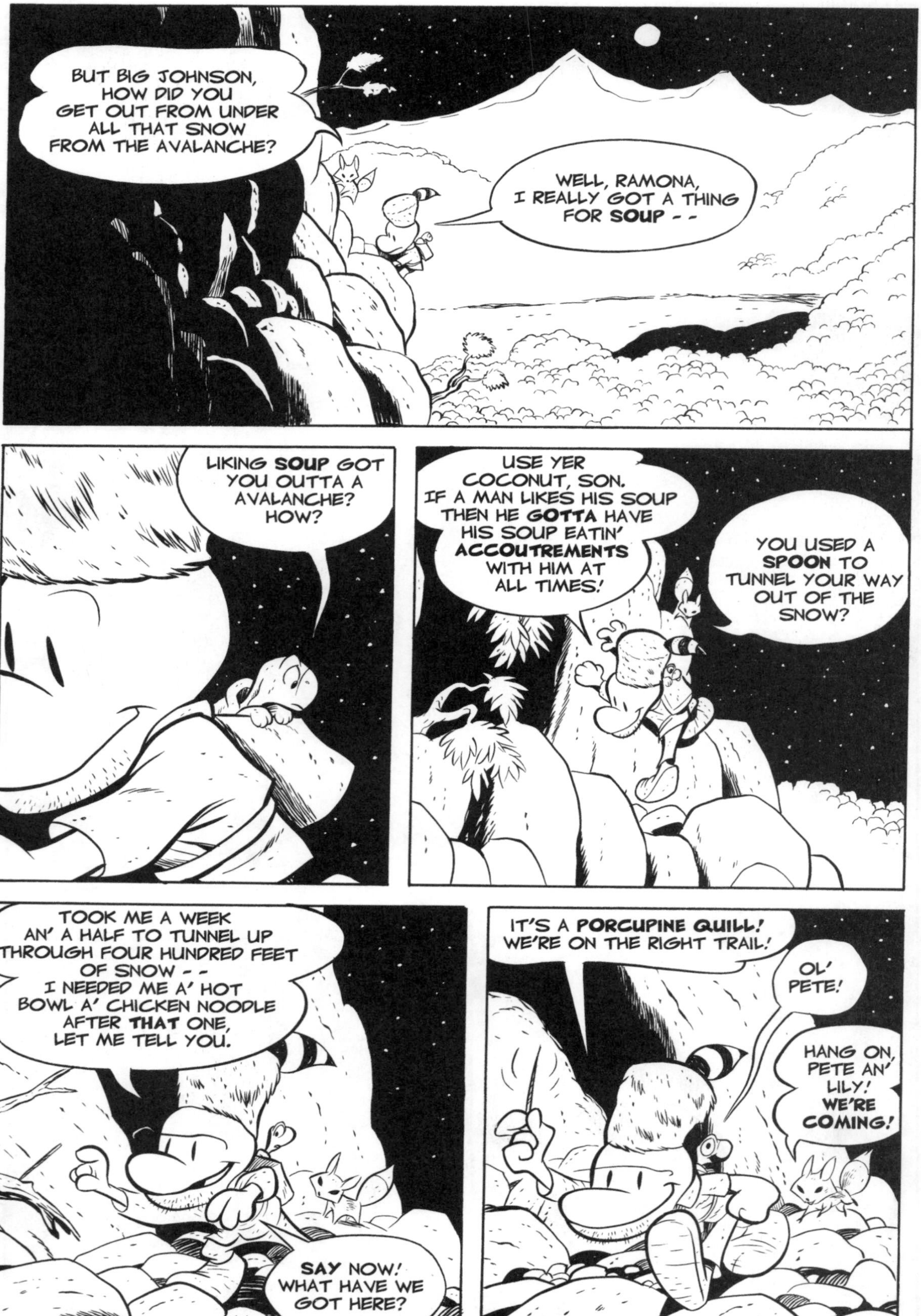
BUT BIG JOHNSON, HOW DID YOU GET OUT FROM UNDER ALL THAT SNOW FROM THE AVALANCHE?
WELL, RAMONA, I REALLY GOT A THING FOR **SOUP** - -
LIKING **SOUP** GOT YOU OUTTA A AVALANCHE? HOW?
USE YER COCONUT, SON. IF A MAN LIKES HIS SOUP THEN HE **GOTTA** HAVE HIS SOUP EATIN' **ACCOUTREMENTS** WITH HIM AT ALL TIMES!
YOU USED A **SPOON** TO TUNNEL YOUR WAY OUT OF THE SNOW?
TOOK ME A WEEK AN' A HALF TO TUNNEL UP THROUGH FOUR HUNDRED FEET OF SNOW - - I NEEDED ME A' HOT BOWL A' CHICKEN NOODLE AFTER **THAT** ONE, LET ME TELL YOU.
SAY NOW! WHAT HAVE WE GOT HERE?
IT'S A **PORCUPINE QUILL!** WE'RE ON THE RIGHT TRAIL!
OL' PETE!
HANG ON, PETE AN' LILY! **WE'RE COMING!**

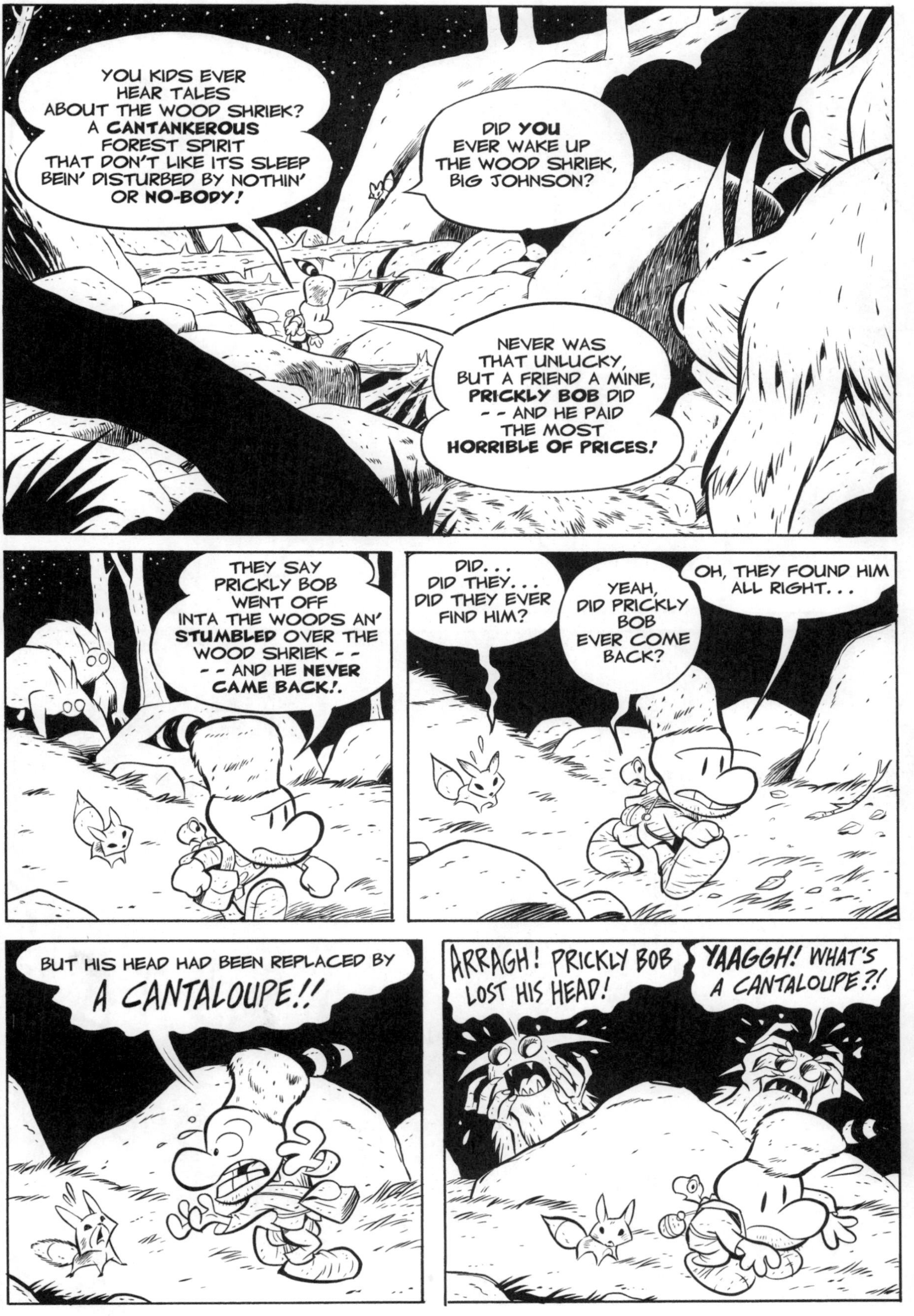
YOU KIDS EVER HEAR TALES ABOUT THE WOOD SHRIEK? A CANTANKEROUS FOREST SPIRIT THAT DON'T LIKE ITS SLEEP BEIN' DISTURBED BY NOTHIN' OR NO-BODY!
DID YOU EVER WAKE UP THE WOOD SHRIEK, BIG JOHNSON?
NEVER WAS THAT UNLUCKY, BUT A FRIEND A MINE, PRICKLY BOB DID -- AND HE PAID THE MOST HORRIBLE OF PRICES!
THEY SAY PRICKLY BOB WENT OFF INTA THE WOODS AN' STUMBLED OVER THE WOOD SHRIEK -- -- AND HE NEVER CAME BACK!.
DID... DID THEY... DID THEY EVER FIND HIM?
YEAH, DID PRICKLY BOB EVER COME BACK?
OH, THEY FOUND HIM ALL RIGHT...
BUT HIS HEAD HAD BEEN REPLACED BY A CANTALOUPE!!
ARRAGH! PRICKLY BOB LOST HIS HEAD!
YAAGGH! WHAT'S A CANTALOUPE?!

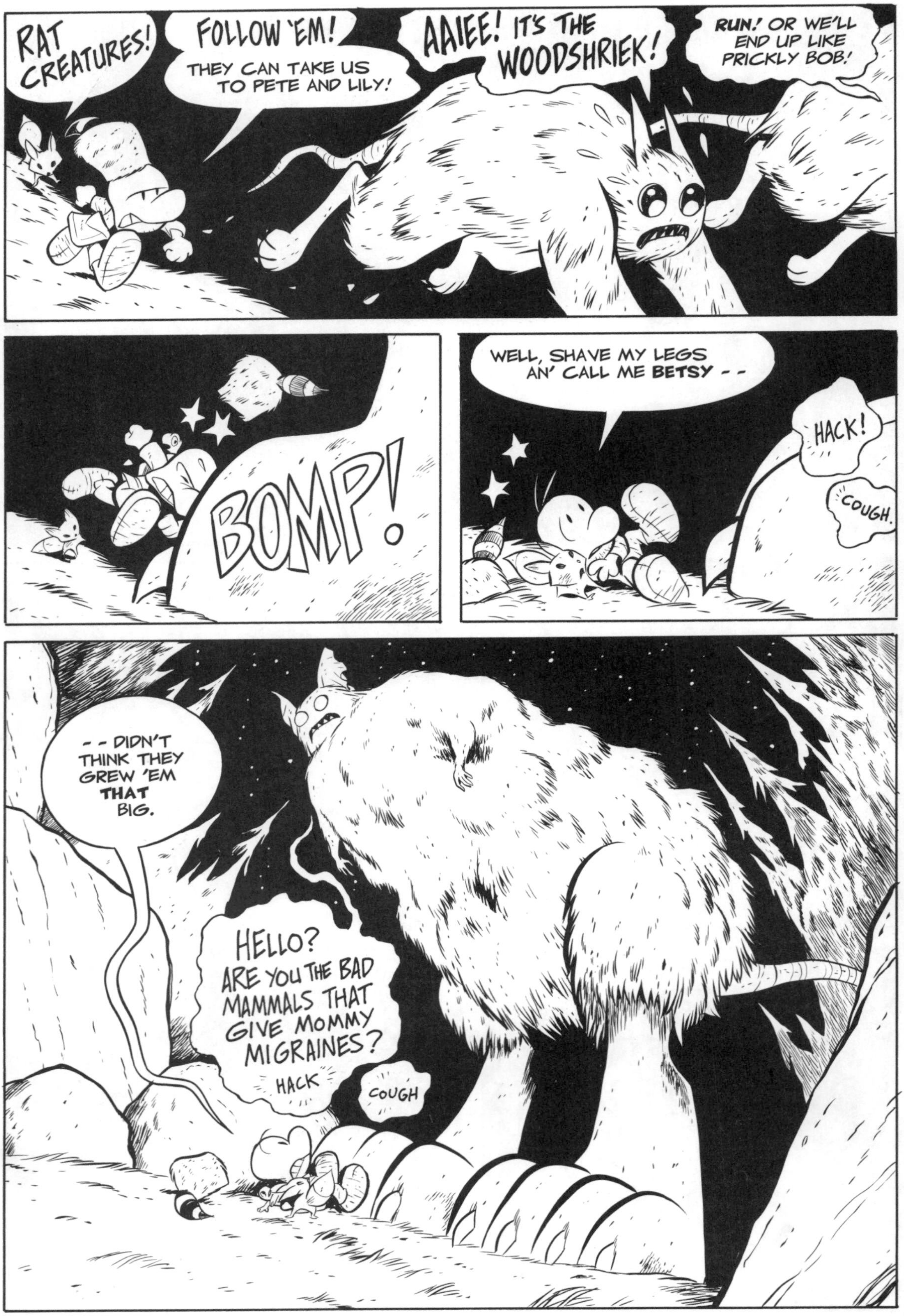

RAT CREATURES!
FOLLOW 'EM!
THEY CAN TAKE US TO PETE AND LILY!
AAIEE! IT'S THE WOODSHRIEK!
RUN! OR WE'LL END UP LIKE PRICKLY BOB!
BOMP!
WELL, SHAVE MY LEGS AN' CALL ME BETSY - -
HACK!
COUGH.
- - DIDN'T THINK THEY GREW 'EM THAT BIG.
HELLO? ARE YOU THE BAD MAMMALS THAT GIVE MOMMY MIGRAINES?
HACK
COUGH

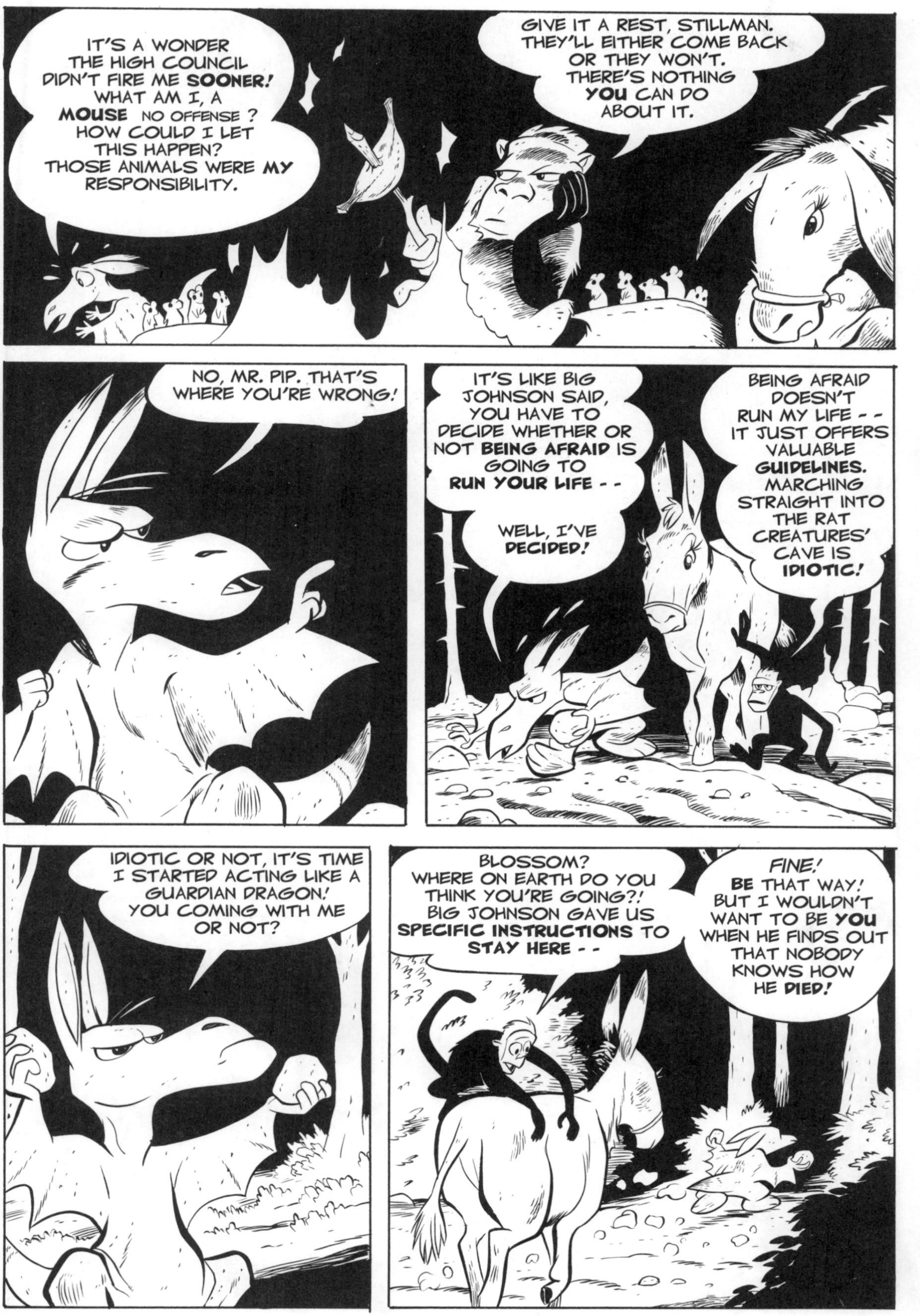
IT'S A WONDER THE HIGH COUNCIL DIDN'T FIRE ME **SOONER!** WHAT AM I, A **MOUSE** NO OFFENSE ? HOW COULD I LET THIS HAPPEN? THOSE ANIMALS WERE **MY** RESPONSIBILITY.
GIVE IT A REST, STILLMAN. THEY'LL EITHER COME BACK OR THEY WON'T. THERE'S NOTHING **YOU** CAN DO ABOUT IT.
NO, MR. PIP. THAT'S WHERE YOU'RE WRONG!
IT'S LIKE BIG JOHNSON SAID, YOU HAVE TO DECIDE WHETHER OR NOT **BEING AFRAID** IS GOING TO **RUN YOUR LIFE** - -
WELL, I'VE **DECIDED!**
BEING AFRAID DOESN'T RUN MY LIFE - - IT JUST OFFERS VALUABLE **GUIDELINES.** MARCHING STRAIGHT INTO THE RAT CREATURES' CAVE IS **IDIOTIC!**
IDIOTIC OR NOT, IT'S TIME I STARTED ACTING LIKE A GUARDIAN DRAGON! YOU COMING WITH ME OR NOT?
BLOSSOM? WHERE ON EARTH DO YOU THINK YOU'RE GOING?! BIG JOHNSON GAVE US **SPECIFIC INSTRUCTIONS** TO **STAY HERE** - -
FINE! **BE** THAT WAY! BUT I WOULDN'T WANT TO BE **YOU** WHEN HE FINDS OUT THAT NOBODY KNOWS HOW HE **DIED!**

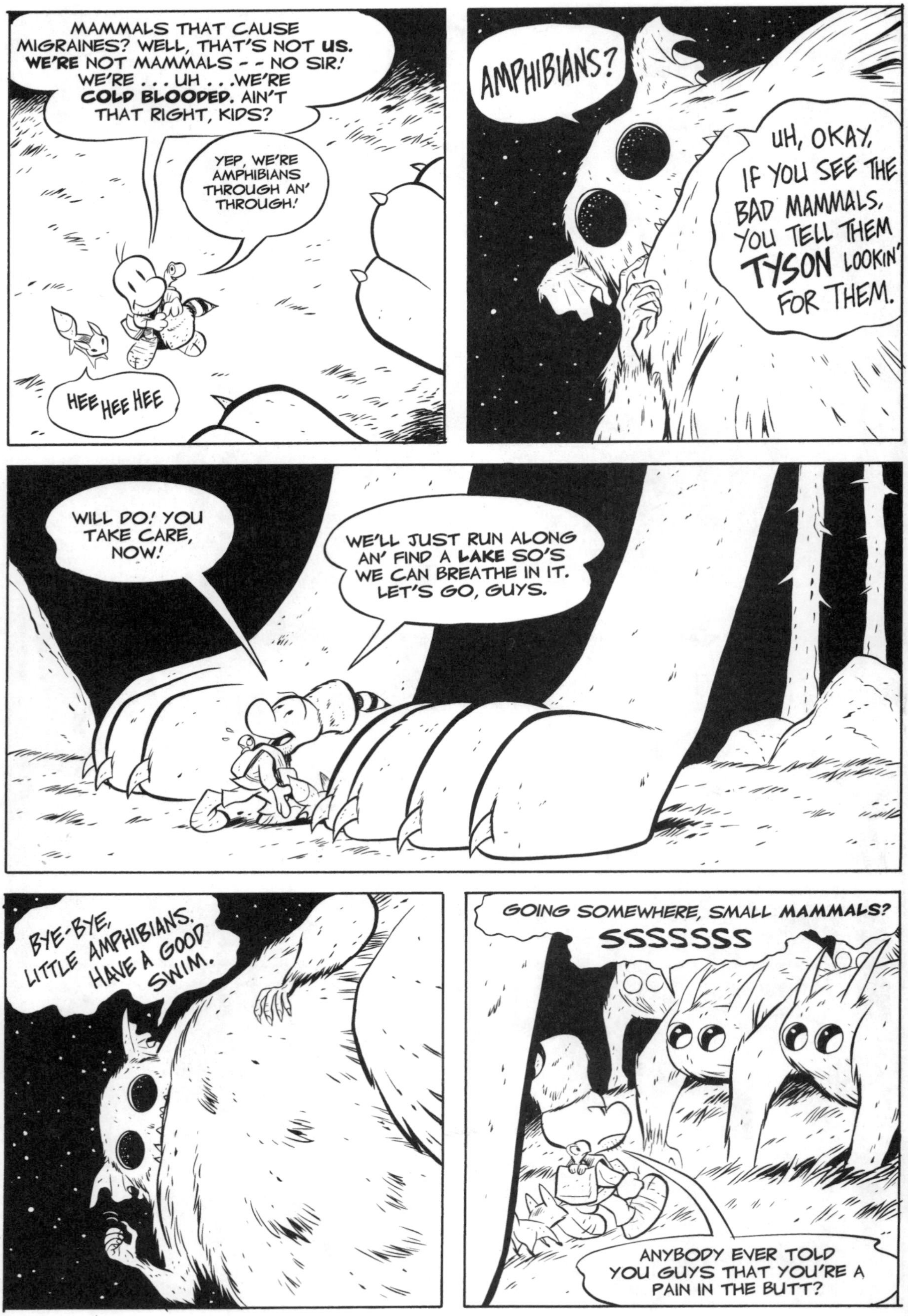
MAMMALS THAT CAUSE MIGRAINES? WELL, THAT'S NOT US. WE'RE NOT MAMMALS - - NO SIR! WE'RE . . . UH . . . WE'RE COLD BLOODED. AIN'T THAT RIGHT, KIDS?
YEP, WE'RE AMPHIBIANS THROUGH AN' THROUGH!
HEE HEE HEE
AMPHIBIANS?
UH, OKAY, IF YOU SEE THE BAD MAMMALS, YOU TELL THEM TYSON LOOKIN' FOR THEM.
WILL DO! YOU TAKE CARE, NOW!
WE'LL JUST RUN ALONG AN' FIND A LAKE SO'S WE CAN BREATHE IN IT. LET'S GO, GUYS.
BYE-BYE, LITTLE AMPHIBIANS. HAVE A GOOD SWIM.
GOING SOMEWHERE, SMALL MAMMALS?
SSSSSSS
ANYBODY EVER TOLD YOU GUYS THAT YOU'RE A PAIN IN THE BUTT?

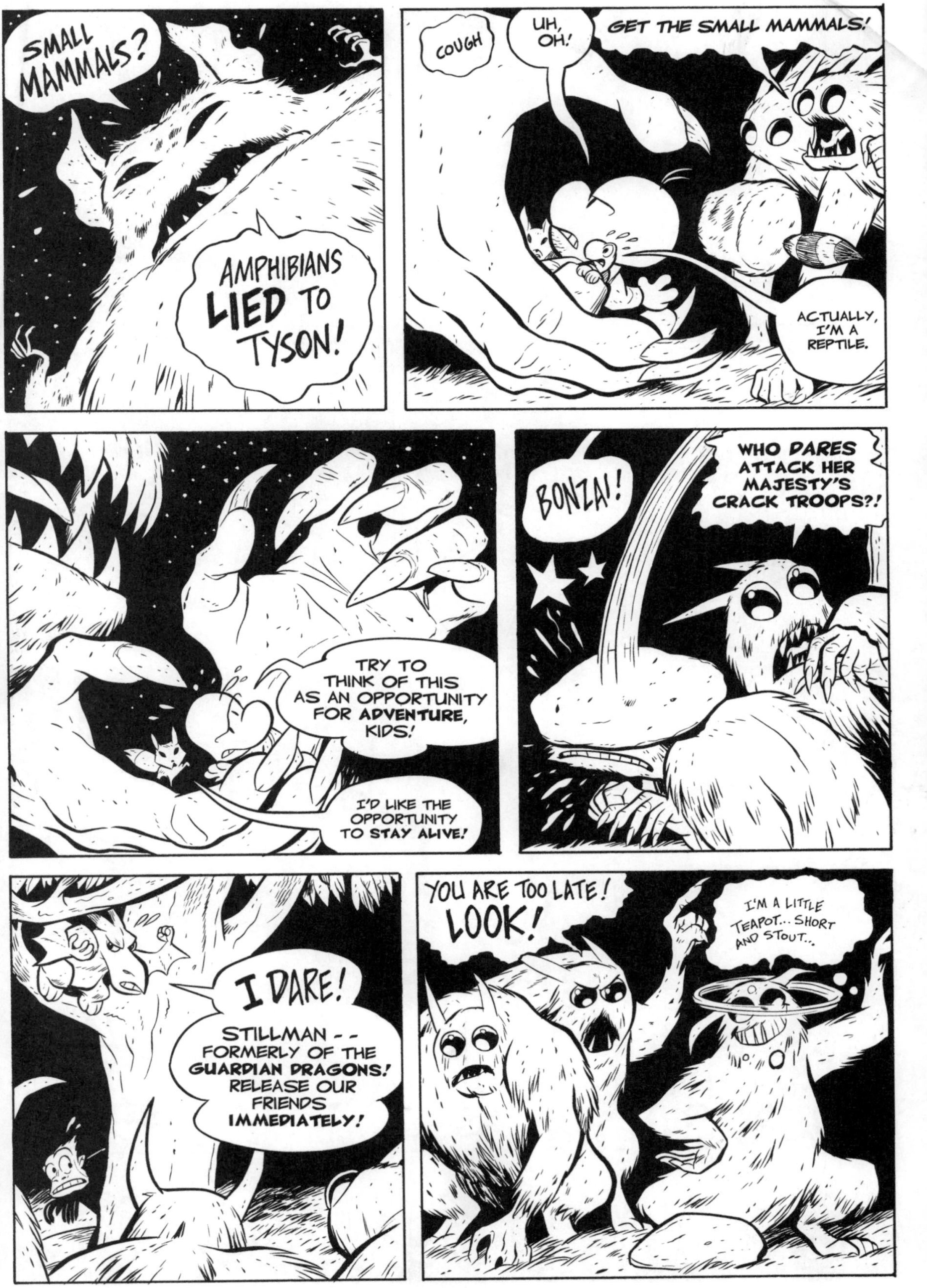
SMALL MAMMALS?
AMPHIBIANS LIED TO TYSON!
COUGH
UH, OH!
GET THE SMALL MAMMALS!
ACTUALLY, I'M A REPTILE.
TRY TO THINK OF THIS AS AN OPPORTUNITY FOR ADVENTURE, KIDS!
I'D LIKE THE OPPORTUNITY TO STAY ALIVE!
BONZAI!
WHO DARES ATTACK HER MAJESTY'S CRACK TROOPS?!
I DARE!
STILLMAN -- FORMERLY OF THE GUARDIAN DRAGONS! RELEASE OUR FRIENDS IMMEDIATELY!
YOU ARE TOO LATE! LOOK!
I'M A LITTLE TEAPOT... SHORT AND STOUT...

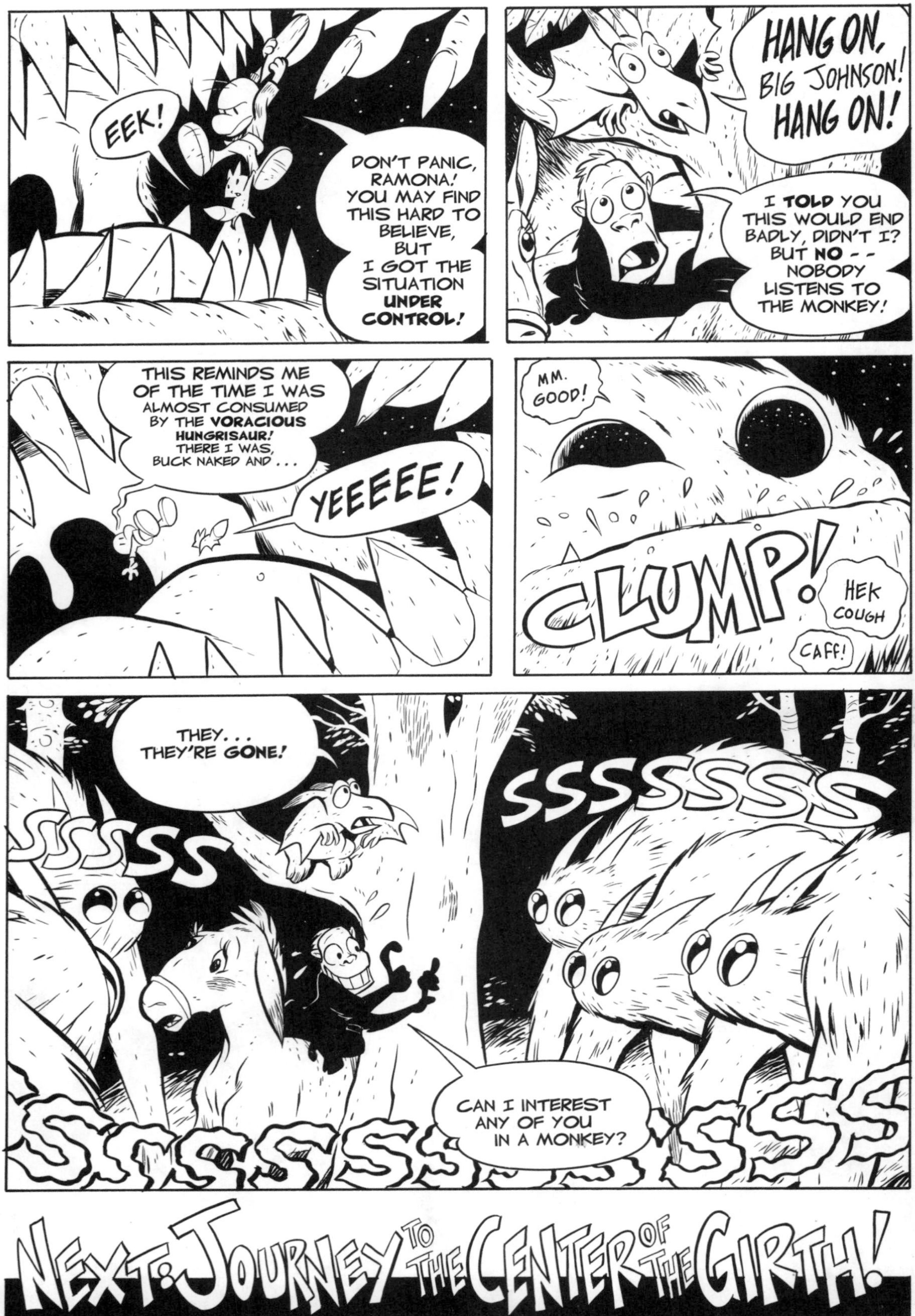
EEK!
DON'T PANIC, RAMONA! YOU MAY FIND THIS HARD TO BELIEVE, BUT I GOT THE SITUATION UNDER CONTROL!
HANG ON, BIG JOHNSON! HANG ON!
I TOLD YOU THIS WOULD END BADLY, DIDN'T I? BUT NO - - NOBODY LISTENS TO THE MONKEY!
THIS REMINDS ME OF THE TIME I WAS ALMOST CONSUMED BY THE VORACIOUS HUNGRISAUR! THERE I WAS, BUCK NAKED AND . . .
YEEEEE!
MM. GOOD!
CLUMP!
HEK COUGH
CAFF!
THEY. . . THEY'RE GONE!
SSSSSSS
SSSSS
CAN I INTEREST ANY OF YOU IN A MONKEY?
SSSSSSSSSSS
NEXT: JOURNEY TO THE CENTER OF THE GIRTH!

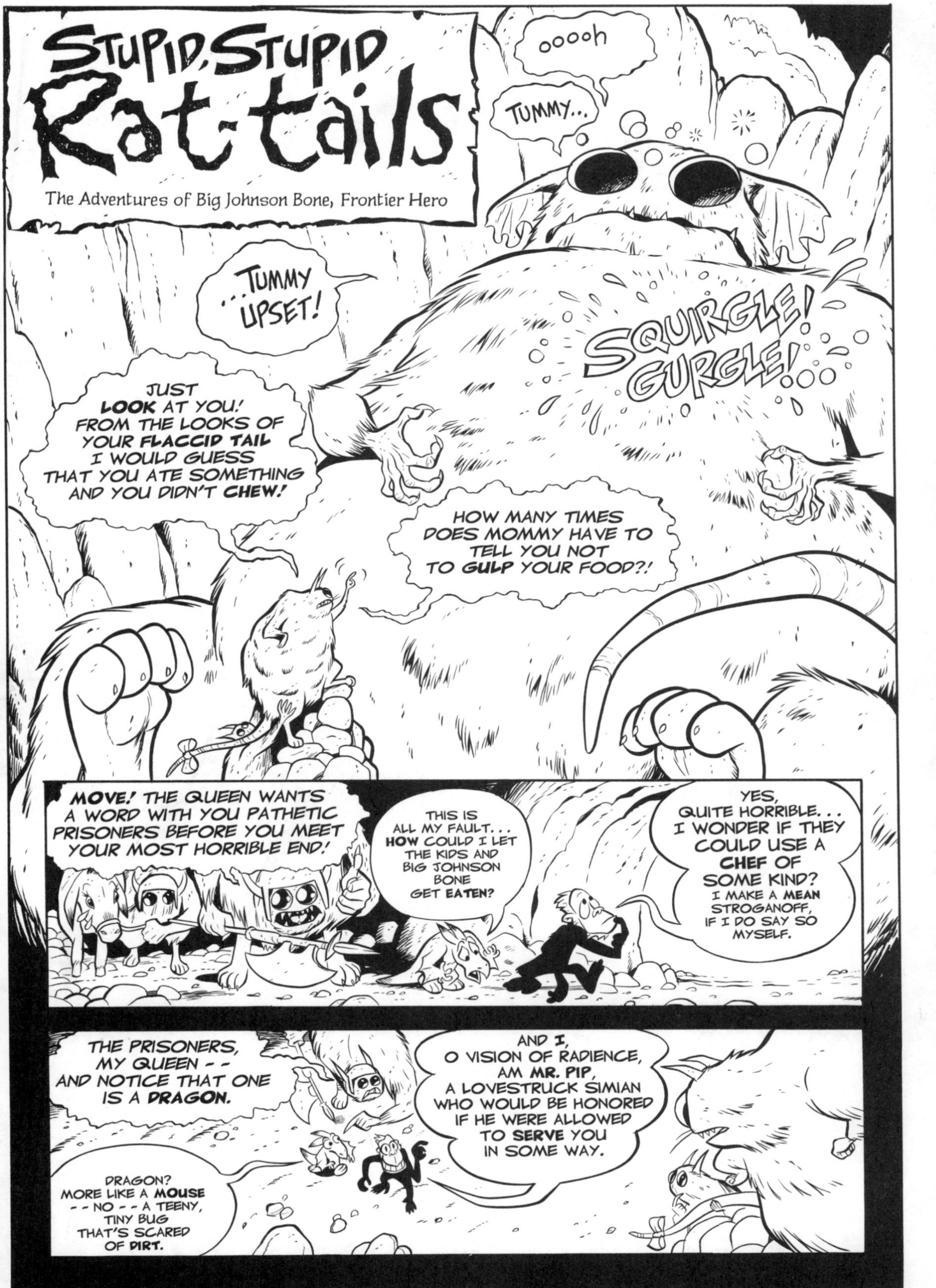

STUPID, STUPID RAT-TAILS
The Adventures of Big Johnson Bone, Frontier Hero
oooh
TUMMY...
...TUMMY UPSET!
SQUIRGLE! GURGLE!
JUST LOOK AT YOU! FROM THE LOOKS OF YOUR FLACCID TAIL I WOULD GUESS THAT YOU ATE SOMETHING AND YOU DIDN'T CHEW!
HOW MANY TIMES DOES MOMMY HAVE TO TELL YOU NOT TO GULP YOUR FOOD?!
MOVE! THE QUEEN WANTS A WORD WITH YOU PATHETIC PRISONERS BEFORE YOU MEET YOUR MOST HORRIBLE END!
THIS IS ALL MY FAULT... HOW COULD I LET THE KIDS AND BIG JOHNSON BONE GET EATEN?
YES, QUITE HORRIBLE... I WONDER IF THEY COULD USE A CHEF OF SOME KIND? I MAKE A MEAN STROGANOFF, IF I DO SAY SO MYSELF.
THE PRISONERS, MY QUEEN -- AND NOTICE THAT ONE IS A DRAGON.
DRAGON? MORE LIKE A MOUSE -- NO -- A TEENY, TINY BUG THAT'S SCARED OF DIRT.
AND I, O VISION OF RADIENCE, AM MR. PIP, A LOVESTRUCK SIMIAN WHO WOULD BE HONORED IF HE WERE ALLOWED TO SERVE YOU IN SOME WAY.

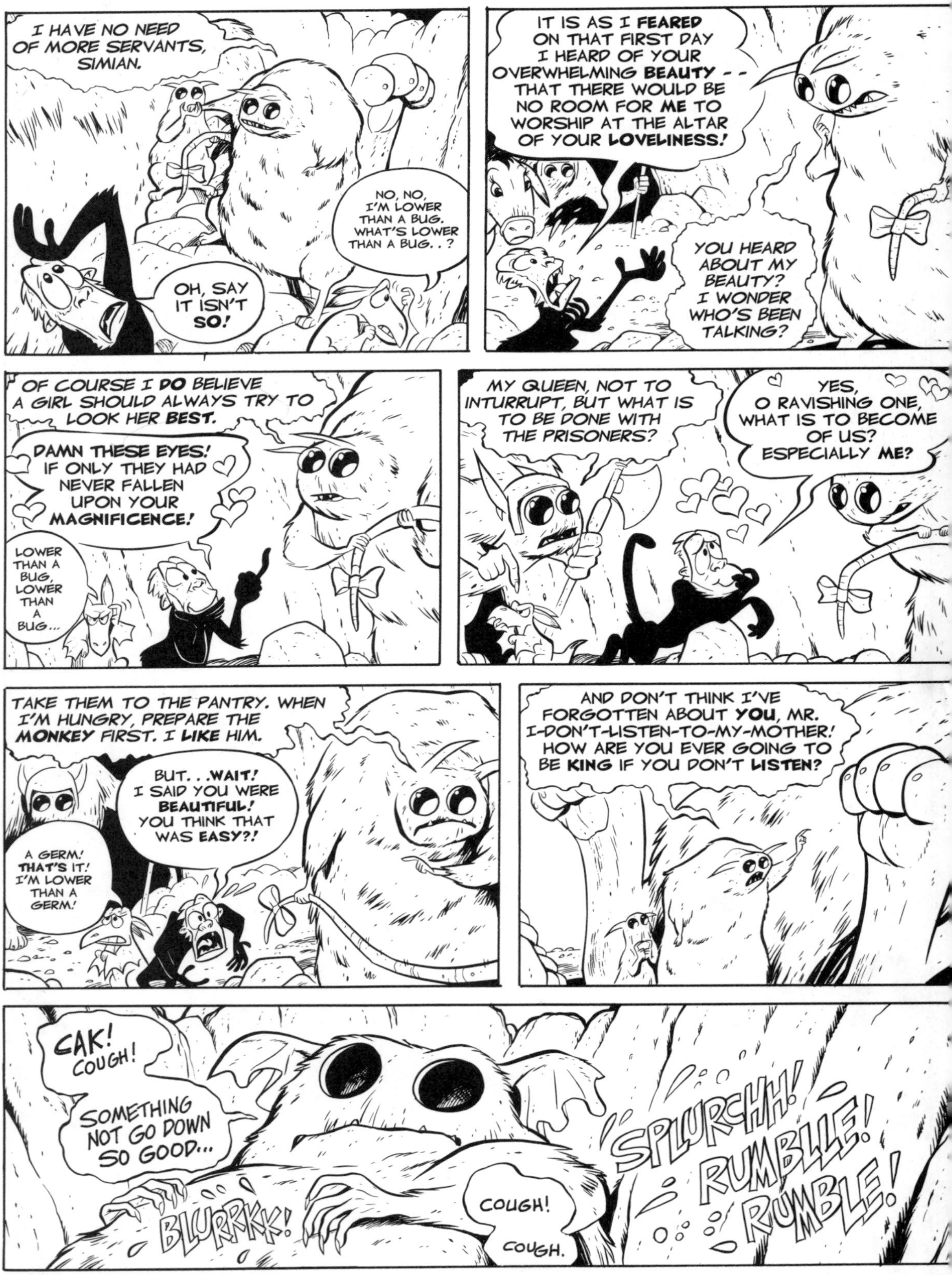
I HAVE NO NEED OF MORE SERVANTS, SIMIAN.
NO, NO, I'M LOWER THAN A BUG. WHAT'S LOWER THAN A BUG. . ?
OH, SAY IT ISN'T SO!
IT IS AS I FEARED ON THAT FIRST DAY I HEARD OF YOUR OVERWHELMING BEAUTY - - THAT THERE WOULD BE NO ROOM FOR ME TO WORSHIP AT THE ALTAR OF YOUR LOVELINESS!
YOU HEARD ABOUT MY BEAUTY? I WONDER WHO'S BEEN TALKING?
OF COURSE I DO BELIEVE A GIRL SHOULD ALWAYS TRY TO LOOK HER BEST.
DAMN THESE EYES! IF ONLY THEY HAD NEVER FALLEN UPON YOUR MAGNIFICENCE!
LOWER THAN A BUG, LOWER THAN A BUG...
MY QUEEN, NOT TO INTURRUPT, BUT WHAT IS TO BE DONE WITH THE PRISONERS?
YES, O RAVISHING ONE, WHAT IS TO BECOME OF US? ESPECIALLY ME?
TAKE THEM TO THE PANTRY. WHEN I'M HUNGRY, PREPARE THE MONKEY FIRST. I LIKE HIM.
BUT. . .WAIT! I SAID YOU WERE BEAUTIFUL! YOU THINK THAT WAS EASY?!
A GERM! THAT'S IT! I'M LOWER THAN A GERM!
AND DON'T THINK I'VE FORGOTTEN ABOUT YOU, MR. I-DON'T-LISTEN-TO-MY-MOTHER! HOW ARE YOU EVER GOING TO BE KING IF YOU DON'T LISTEN?
CAK! COUGH!
SOMETHING NOT GO DOWN SO GOOD...
BLURRKK!
COUGH! COUGH.
SPLURCHH! RUMBLLE! RUMBLE!

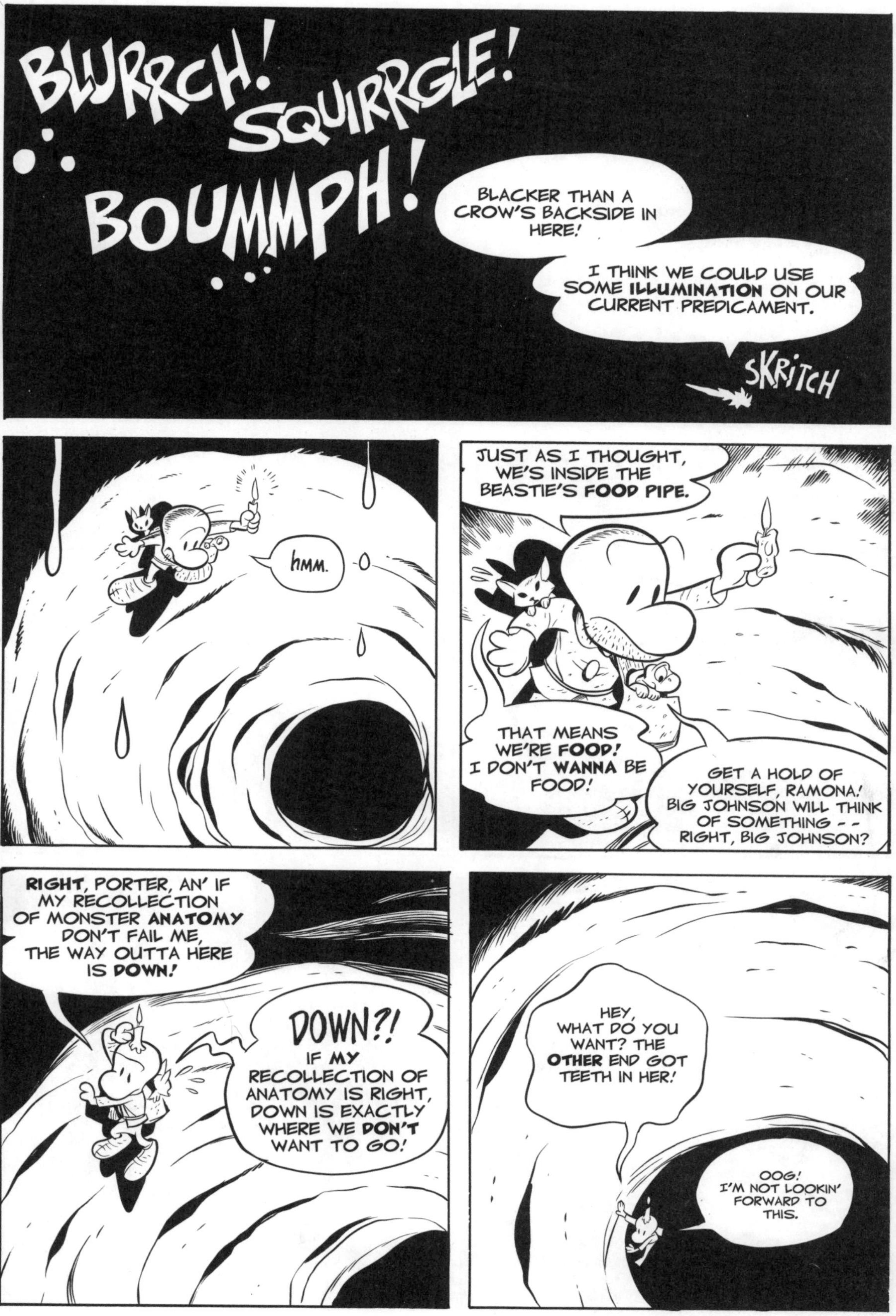
BLURRCH! SQUIRRGLE! BOUMMPH!
BLACKER THAN A CROW'S BACKSIDE IN HERE!
I THINK WE COULD USE SOME ILLUMINATION ON OUR CURRENT PREDICAMENT.
SKRITCH
hmm.
JUST AS I THOUGHT, WE'S INSIDE THE BEASTIE'S FOOD PIPE.
THAT MEANS WE'RE FOOD! I DON'T WANNA BE FOOD!
GET A HOLD OF YOURSELF, RAMONA! BIG JOHNSON WILL THINK OF SOMETHING -- RIGHT, BIG JOHNSON?
RIGHT, PORTER, AN' IF MY RECOLLECTION OF MONSTER ANATOMY DON'T FAIL ME, THE WAY OUTTA HERE IS DOWN!
DOWN?! IF MY RECOLLECTION OF ANATOMY IS RIGHT, DOWN IS EXACTLY WHERE WE DON'T WANT TO GO!
HEY, WHAT DO YOU WANT? THE OTHER END GOT TEETH IN HER!
OOG! I'M NOT LOOKIN' FORWARD TO THIS.

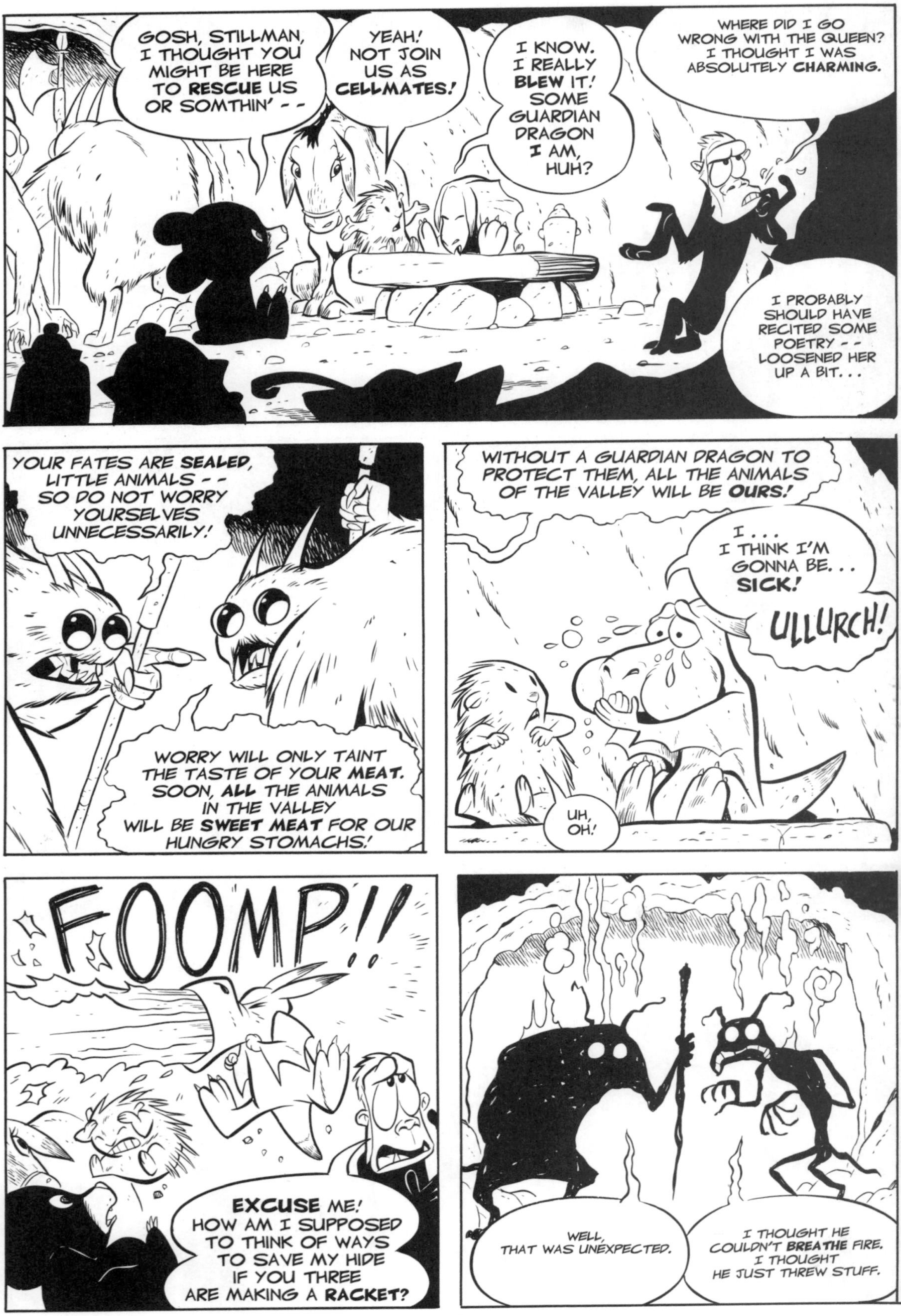
GOSH, STILLMAN, I THOUGHT YOU MIGHT BE HERE TO RESCUE US OR SOMTHIN' - -
YEAH! NOT JOIN US AS CELLMATES!
I KNOW. I REALLY BLEW IT! SOME GUARDIAN DRAGON I AM, HUH?
WHERE DID I GO WRONG WITH THE QUEEN? I THOUGHT I WAS ABSOLUTELY CHARMING.
I PROBABLY SHOULD HAVE RECITED SOME POETRY - - LOOSENED HER UP A BIT...
YOUR FATES ARE SEALED, LITTLE ANIMALS - - SO DO NOT WORRY YOURSELVES UNNECESSARILY!
WORRY WILL ONLY TAINT THE TASTE OF YOUR MEAT. SOON, ALL THE ANIMALS IN THE VALLEY WILL BE SWEET MEAT FOR OUR HUNGRY STOMACHS!
WITHOUT A GUARDIAN DRAGON TO PROTECT THEM, ALL THE ANIMALS OF THE VALLEY WILL BE OURS!
I... I THINK I'M GONNA BE... SICK!
ULLURCH!
UH, OH!
FOOMP!!
EXCUSE ME! HOW AM I SUPPOSED TO THINK OF WAYS TO SAVE MY HIDE IF YOU THREE ARE MAKING A RACKET?
WELL, THAT WAS UNEXPECTED.
I THOUGHT HE COULDN'T BREATHE FIRE. I THOUGHT HE JUST THREW STUFF.

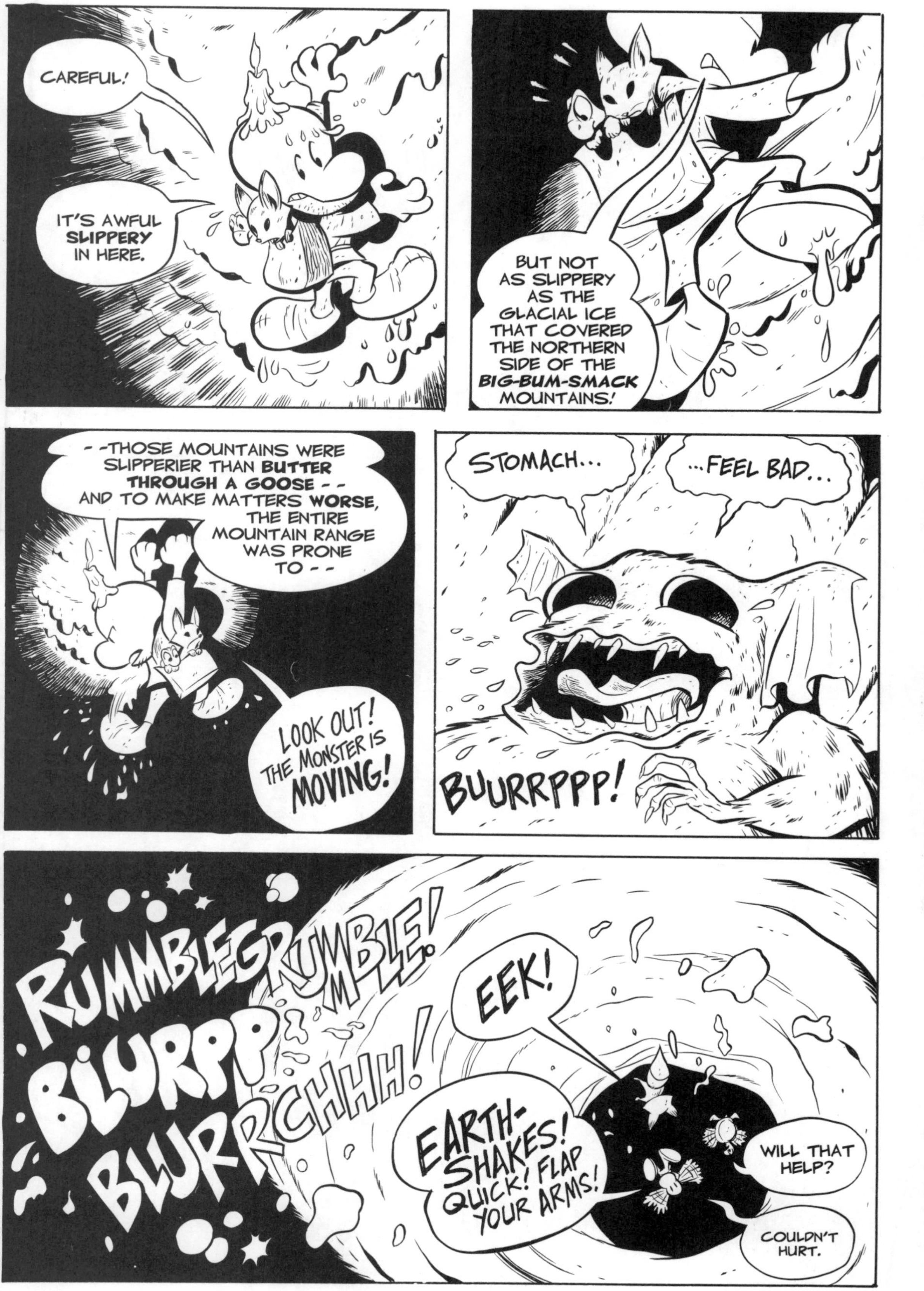
CAREFUL!
IT'S AWFUL SLIPPERY IN HERE.
BUT NOT AS SLIPPERY AS THE GLACIAL ICE THAT COVERED THE NORTHERN SIDE OF THE BIG-BUM-SMACK MOUNTAINS!
--THOSE MOUNTAINS WERE SLIPPERIER THAN BUTTER THROUGH A GOOSE -- AND TO MAKE MATTERS WORSE, THE ENTIRE MOUNTAIN RANGE WAS PRONE TO --
LOOK OUT! THE MONSTER IS MOVING!
STOMACH...
...FEEL BAD...
BUURRPPP!
RUMMBLEGRUMBLE!
BLURPP!
BLURRCHHH!
EEK!
EARTH-SHAKES! QUICK! FLAP YOUR ARMS!
WILL THAT HELP?
COULDN'T HURT.

TYSON'S BELLY SICK!

DOCTOR, YOU HAVE TO HELP MY BABY BOY!

WHOA! WOTTA REEK.

NEVER FEAR, MY QUEEN, DOC GUAM IS HERE! I WILL DETERMINE THE CAUSE OF YOUR SON'S DISCOMFORT.

BURRAPP!

YES, YES. GED ON WIT IT!

BAMMPH!

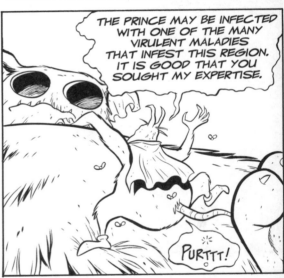

THE PRINCE MAY BE INFECTED WITH ONE OF THE MANY VIRULENT MALADIES THAT INFEST THIS REGION. IT IS GOOD THAT YOU SOUGHT MY EXPERTISE.

PURTTT!

GRRGLLE!

YES, I SEE. THE PRINCE'S AILMENT COULD BE AS SIMPLE AS AN INFLAMED BLUGOSSWICK -- OR AS DEADLY AS A WOOD ELF INFESTATION.

WURRGLLE! BLOOPURCHH!

KNEW A GUY THAT HAD WOOD ELVES -- DIDN'T LAST A MONTH.

PLEASE DOCTOR, MAKE MY BOY WELL AGAIN!

58

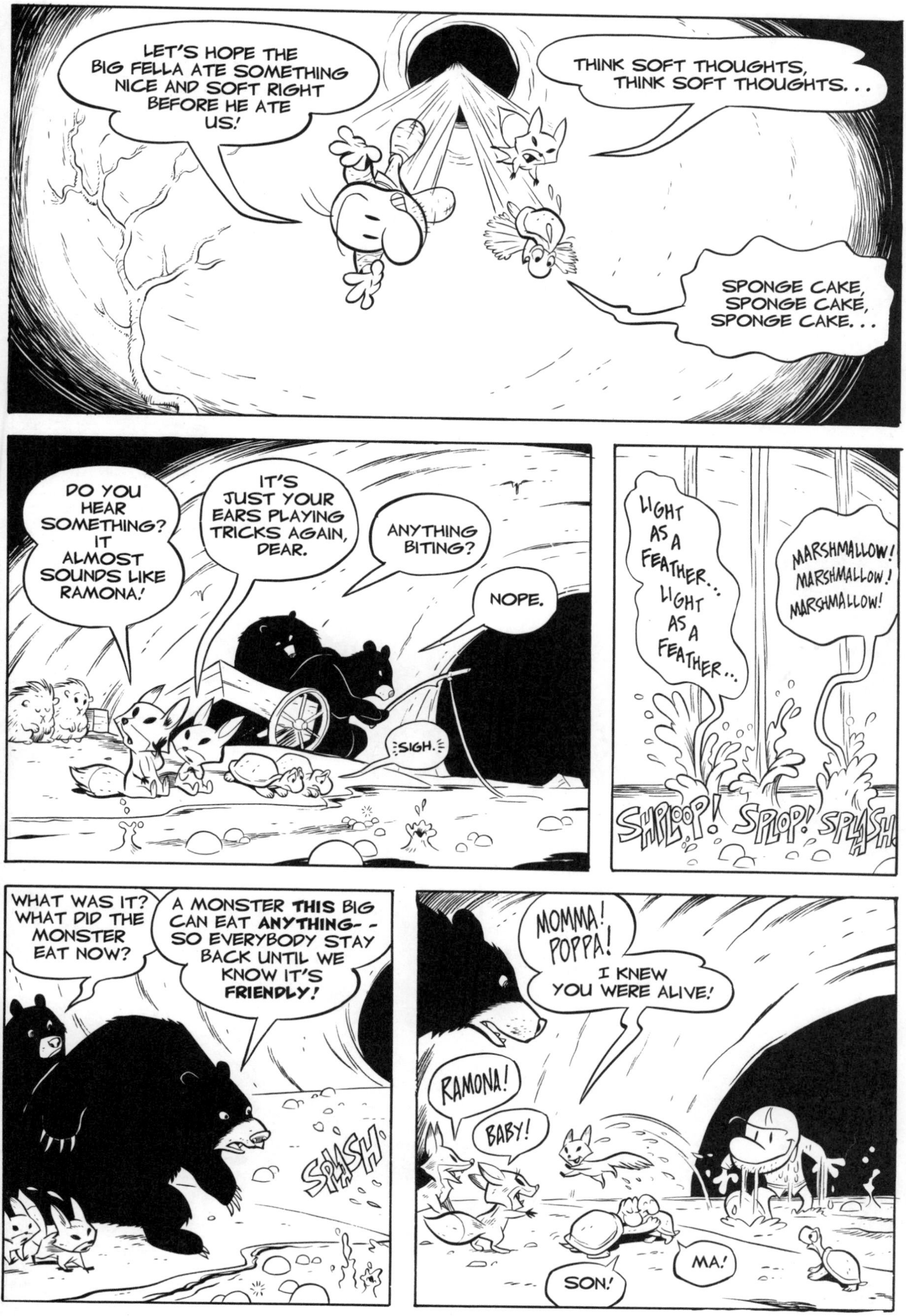
LET'S HOPE THE BIG FELLA ATE SOMETHING NICE AND SOFT RIGHT BEFORE HE ATE US!
THINK SOFT THOUGHTS, THINK SOFT THOUGHTS...
SPONGE CAKE, SPONGE CAKE, SPONGE CAKE...
DO YOU HEAR SOMETHING? IT ALMOST SOUNDS LIKE RAMONA!
IT'S JUST YOUR EARS PLAYING TRICKS AGAIN, DEAR.
ANYTHING BITING?
NOPE.
SIGH.
LIGHT AS A FEATHER... LIGHT AS A FEATHER...
MARSHMALLOW! MARSHMALLOW! MARSHMALLOW!
SHPLOOP! SPLOP! SPLASH!
WHAT WAS IT? WHAT DID THE MONSTER EAT NOW?
A MONSTER **THIS** BIG CAN EAT **ANYTHING**- - SO EVERYBODY STAY BACK UNTIL WE KNOW IT'S **FRIENDLY**!
SPLASH
MOMMA! POPPA! I KNEW YOU WERE ALIVE!
RAMONA!
BABY!
MA!
SON!

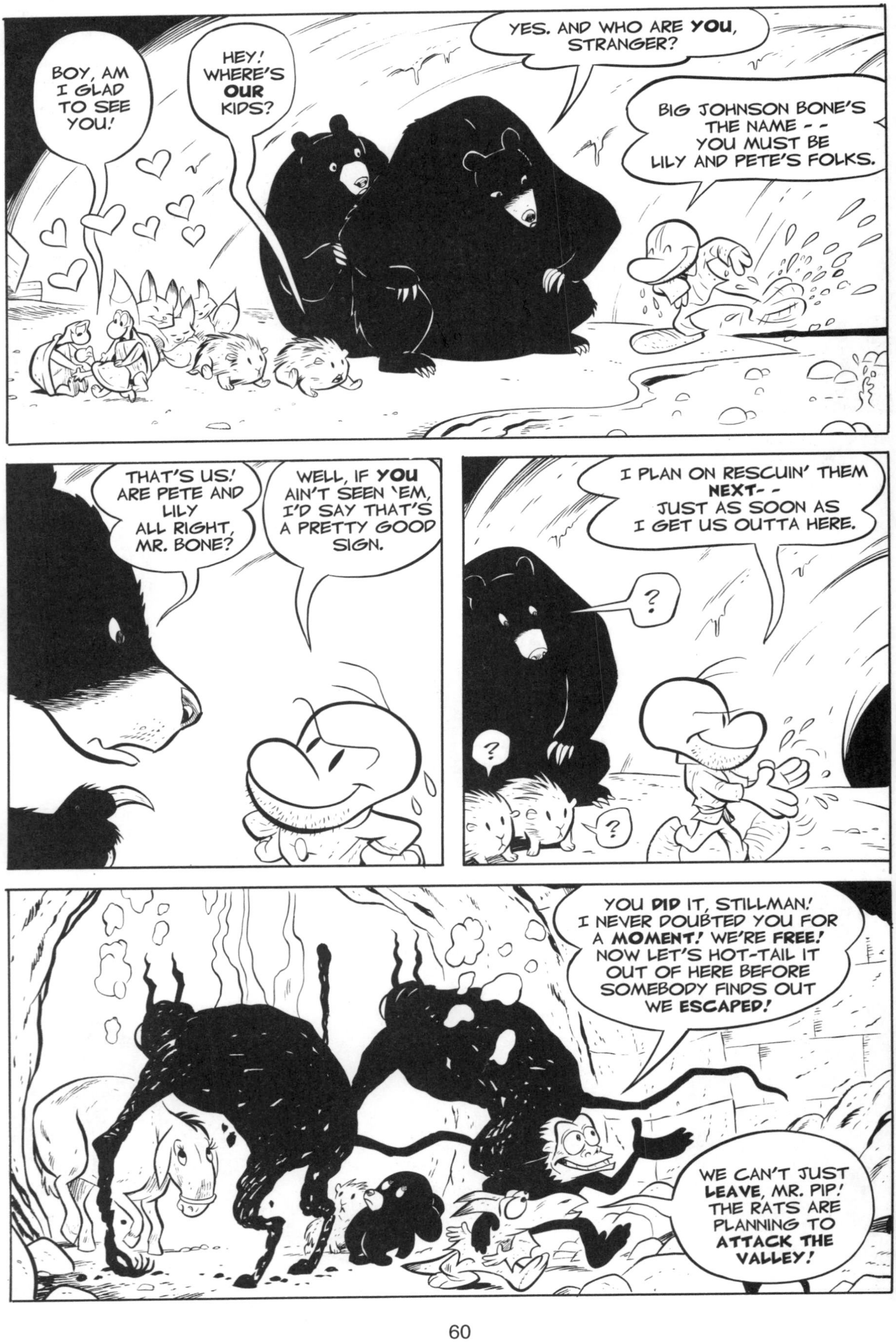

BOY, AM I GLAD TO SEE YOU!
HEY! WHERE'S **OUR** KIDS?
YES. AND WHO ARE **YOU**, STRANGER?
BIG JOHNSON BONE'S THE NAME - - YOU MUST BE LILY AND PETE'S FOLKS.
THAT'S US! ARE PETE AND LILY ALL RIGHT, MR. BONE?
WELL, IF **YOU** AIN'T SEEN 'EM, I'D SAY THAT'S A PRETTY GOOD SIGN.
I PLAN ON RESCUIN' THEM **NEXT**- - JUST AS SOON AS I GET US OUTTA HERE.
?
?
?
YOU **DID** IT, STILLMAN! I NEVER DOUBTED YOU FOR A **MOMENT**! WE'RE **FREE**! NOW LET'S HOT-TAIL IT OUT OF HERE BEFORE SOMEBODY FINDS OUT WE **ESCAPED**!
WE CAN'T JUST **LEAVE**, MR. PIP! THE RATS ARE PLANNING TO **ATTACK THE VALLEY**!

YOU CAN LEAVE IF YOU WANT, BUT **I'VE GOT** RESPONSIBILITIES. I'M GOING BACK TO DEAL WITH THE **QUEEN!**

WAIT! I'VE GOT A **BETTER** IDEA! WE COULD RUN AND HIDE IN THE WOODS! WOULDN'T **THAT** MAKE THE QUEEN ANGRY-- **HIDING** AND ALL? **ARE YOU LISTENING TO ME!?**

SHOULDN'T WE GO AFTER THEM?

I'M AFRAID IF I MOVE -- I'LL CRUMBLE TO DUST.

I DIDN'T EVEN THINK OF THAT.

DOCTOR?

CAN YOU GIVE ME ANY WORDS OF ENCOURAGEMENT?

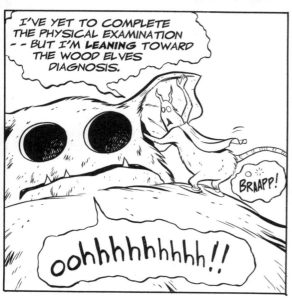

I'VE YET TO COMPLETE THE PHYSICAL EXAMINATION -- BUT I'M **LEANING** TOWARD THE WOOD ELVES DIAGNOSIS.

BRAAPP!

ooohhhhhhhhhh!!

☀ **YEEEEEE**

BEGGING **THE QUEEN'S PARDON!**

OW! OW! OOTCH! **OW!!**

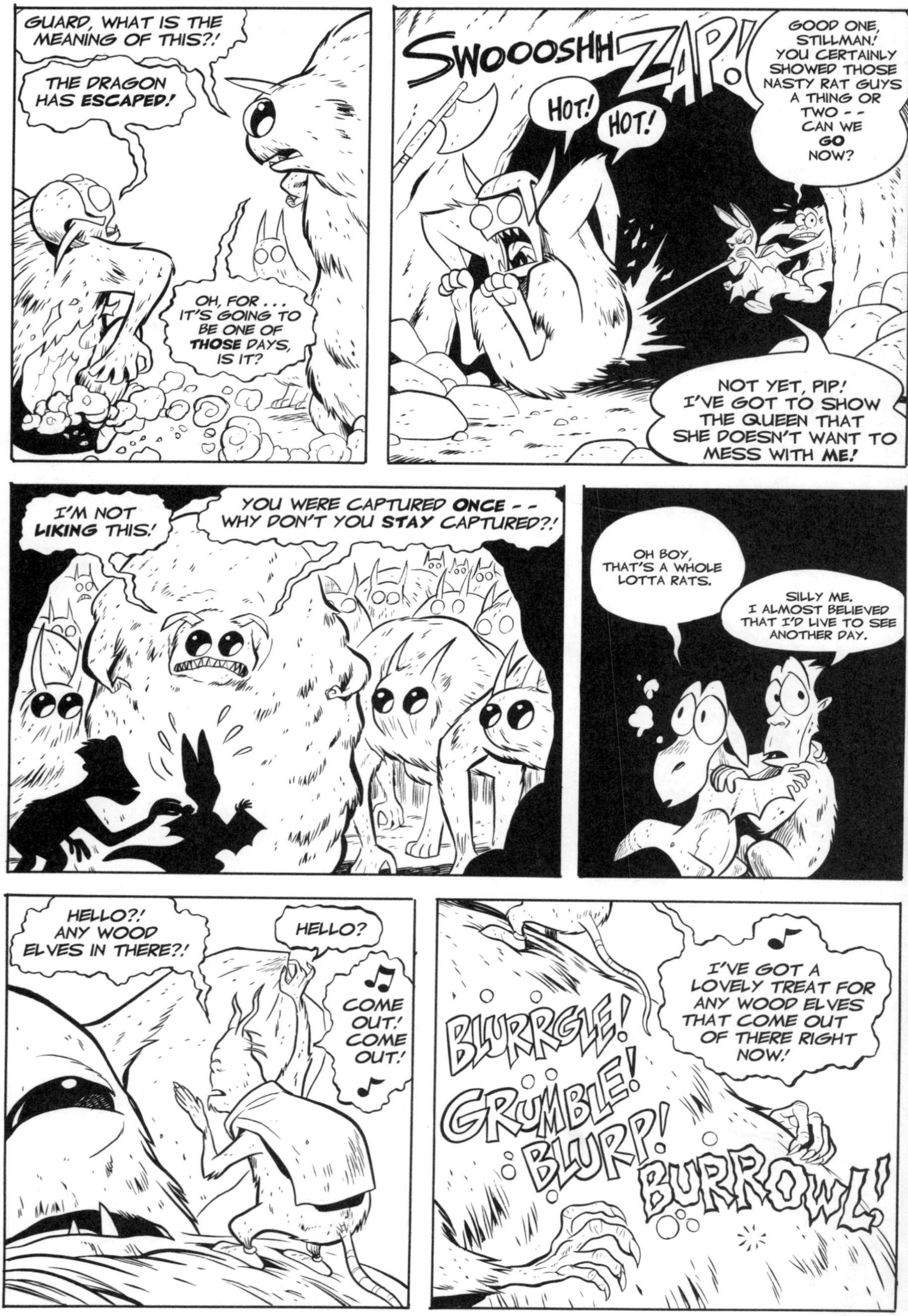
GUARD, WHAT IS THE MEANING OF THIS?!
THE DRAGON HAS ESCAPED!
OH, FOR . . . IT'S GOING TO BE ONE OF THOSE DAYS, IS IT?
SWOOOSHH
ZAP!
HOT!
HOT!
GOOD ONE, STILLMAN! YOU CERTAINLY SHOWED THOSE NASTY RAT GUYS A THING OR TWO - - CAN WE GO NOW?
NOT YET, PIP! I'VE GOT TO SHOW THE QUEEN THAT SHE DOESN'T WANT TO MESS WITH ME!
I'M NOT LIKING THIS!
YOU WERE CAPTURED ONCE - - WHY DON'T YOU STAY CAPTURED?!
OH BOY, THAT'S A WHOLE LOTTA RATS.
SILLY ME. I ALMOST BELIEVED THAT I'D LIVE TO SEE ANOTHER DAY.
HELLO?! ANY WOOD ELVES IN THERE?!
HELLO?
COME OUT! COME OUT!
I'VE GOT A LOVELY TREAT FOR ANY WOOD ELVES THAT COME OUT OF THERE RIGHT NOW!
BLURRGLE!
GRUMBLE!
BLURP!
BURROWL!

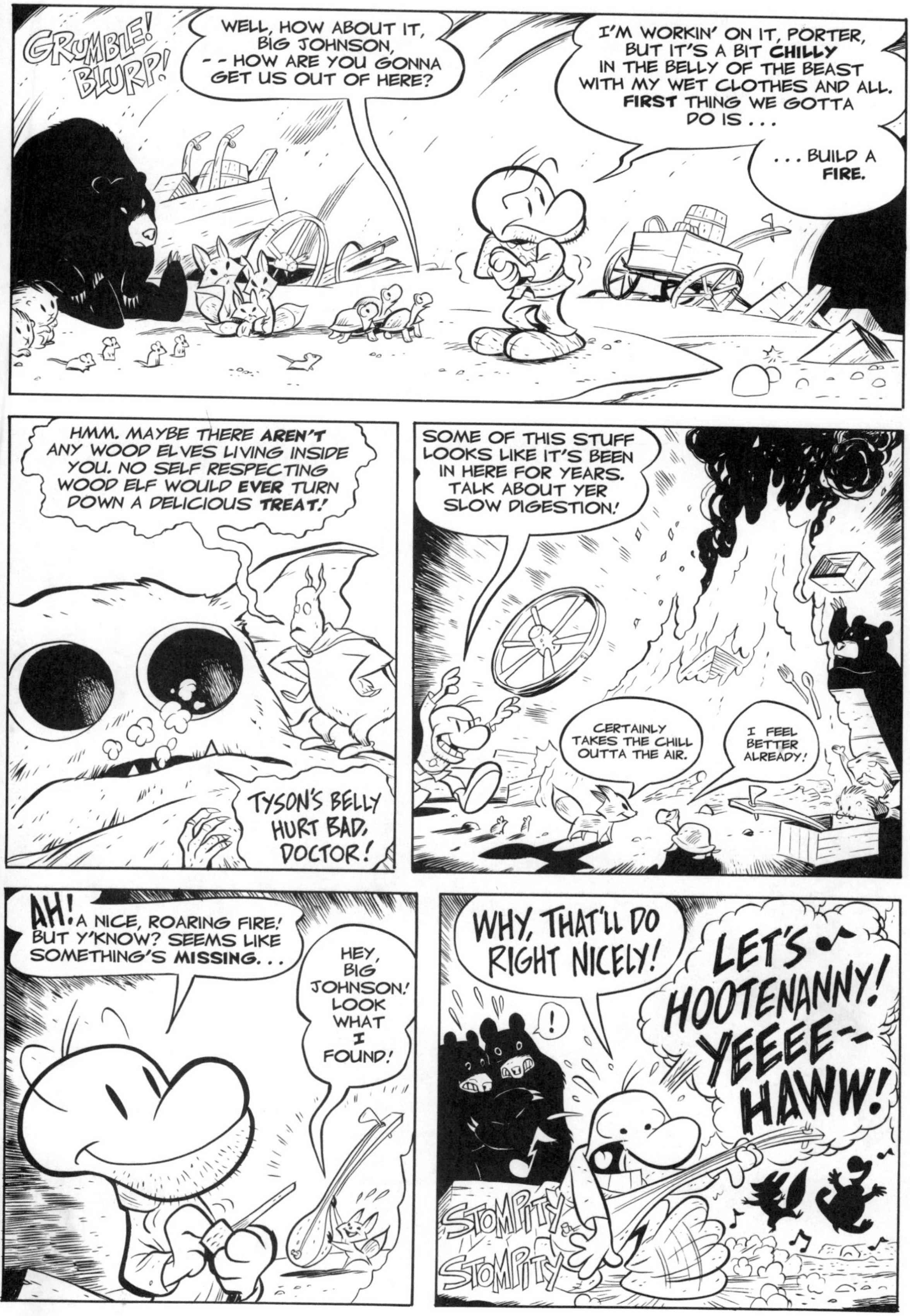
GRUMBLE! BLURP!
WELL, HOW ABOUT IT, BIG JOHNSON, - - HOW ARE YOU GONNA GET US OUT OF HERE?
I'M WORKIN' ON IT, PORTER, BUT IT'S A BIT CHILLY IN THE BELLY OF THE BEAST WITH MY WET CLOTHES AND ALL. FIRST THING WE GOTTA DO IS . . .
. . . BUILD A FIRE.
HMM. MAYBE THERE AREN'T ANY WOOD ELVES LIVING INSIDE YOU. NO SELF RESPECTING WOOD ELF WOULD EVER TURN DOWN A DELICIOUS TREAT!
TYSON'S BELLY HURT BAD, DOCTOR!
SOME OF THIS STUFF LOOKS LIKE IT'S BEEN IN HERE FOR YEARS. TALK ABOUT YER SLOW DIGESTION!
CERTAINLY TAKES THE CHILL OUTTA THE AIR.
I FEEL BETTER ALREADY!
AH! A NICE, ROARING FIRE! BUT Y'KNOW? SEEMS LIKE SOMETHING'S MISSING. . .
HEY, BIG JOHNSON! LOOK WHAT I FOUND!
WHY, THAT'LL DO RIGHT NICELY!
!
LET'S HOOTENANNY! YEEEE-HAWW!
STOMPITY STOMPITY

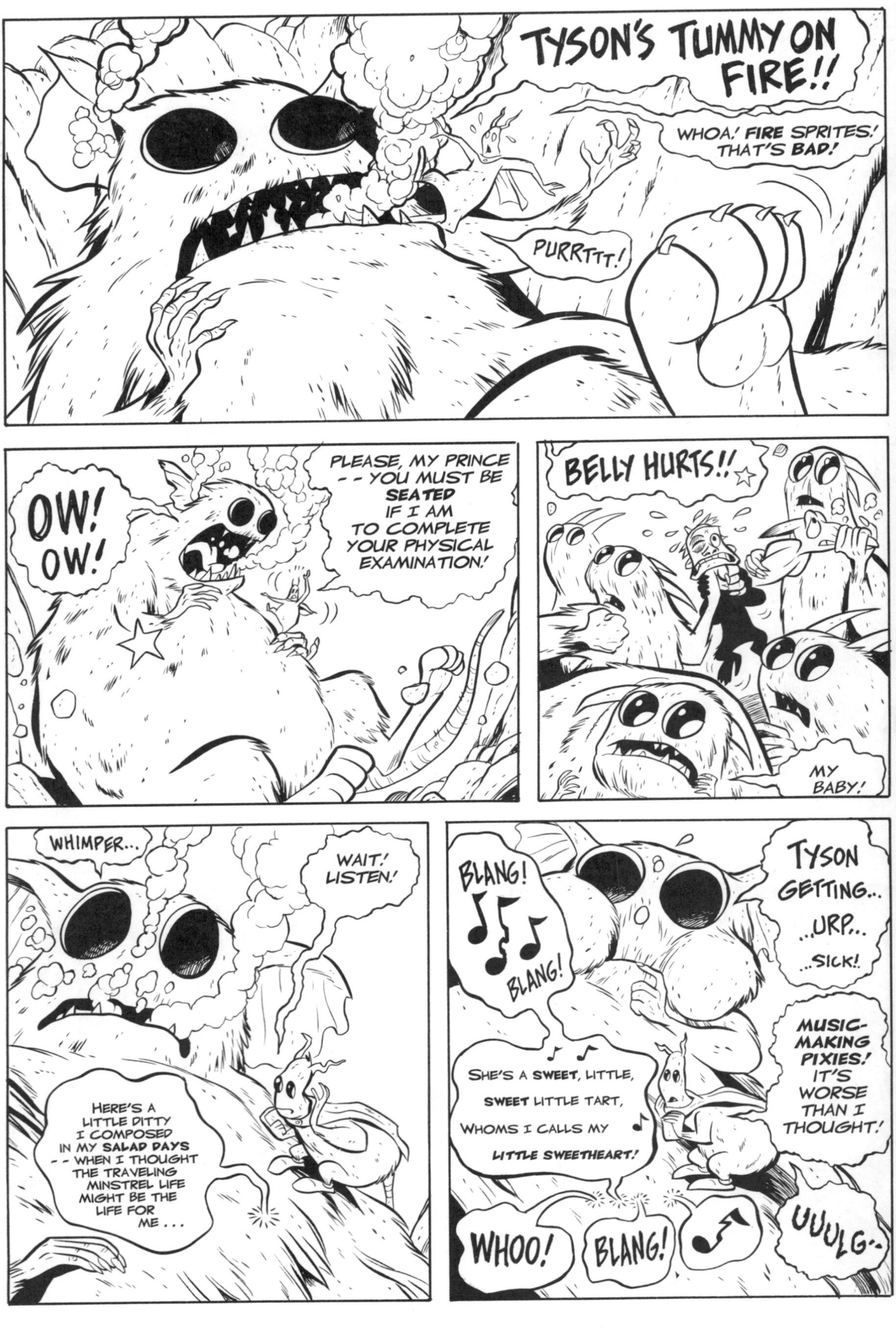
TYSON'S TUMMY ON FIRE!!
WHOA! FIRE SPRITES! THAT'S BAD!
PURRTTT!
OW! OW!
PLEASE, MY PRINCE - - YOU MUST BE SEATED IF I AM TO COMPLETE YOUR PHYSICAL EXAMINATION!
BELLY HURTS!!
MY BABY!
WHIMPER...
WAIT! LISTEN!
HERE'S A LITTLE DITTY I COMPOSED IN MY SALAD DAYS - - WHEN I THOUGHT THE TRAVELING MINSTREL LIFE MIGHT BE THE LIFE FOR ME . . .
BLANG!
BLANG!
TYSON GETTING... ...URP... ...SICK!
SHE'S A SWEET, LITTLE, SWEET LITTLE TART, WHOMS I CALLS MY LITTLE SWEETHEART!
MUSIC-MAKING PIXIES! IT'S WORSE THAN I THOUGHT!
WHOO!
BLANG!
UUULG..

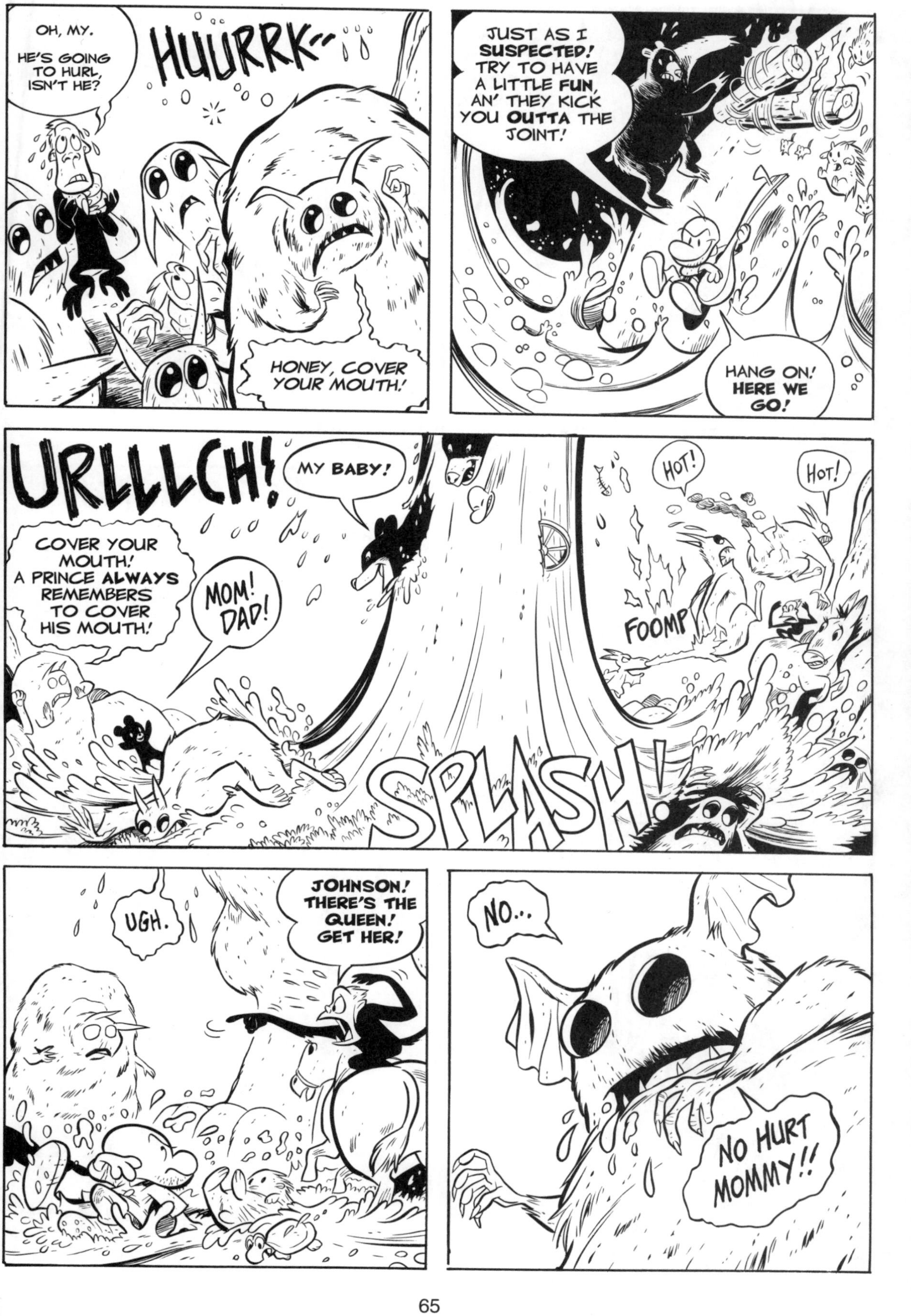
OH, MY.
HE'S GOING TO HURL, ISN'T HE?
HUURRK
HONEY, COVER YOUR MOUTH!
JUST AS I SUSPECTED! TRY TO HAVE A LITTLE FUN, AN' THEY KICK YOU OUTTA THE JOINT!
HANG ON! HERE WE GO!
URLLLCH!
MY BABY!
COVER YOUR MOUTH! A PRINCE ALWAYS REMEMBERS TO COVER HIS MOUTH!
MOM! DAD!
HOT!
HOT!
FOOMP
SPLASH!
UGH.
JOHNSON! THERE'S THE QUEEN! GET HER!
NO...
NO HURT MOMMY!!

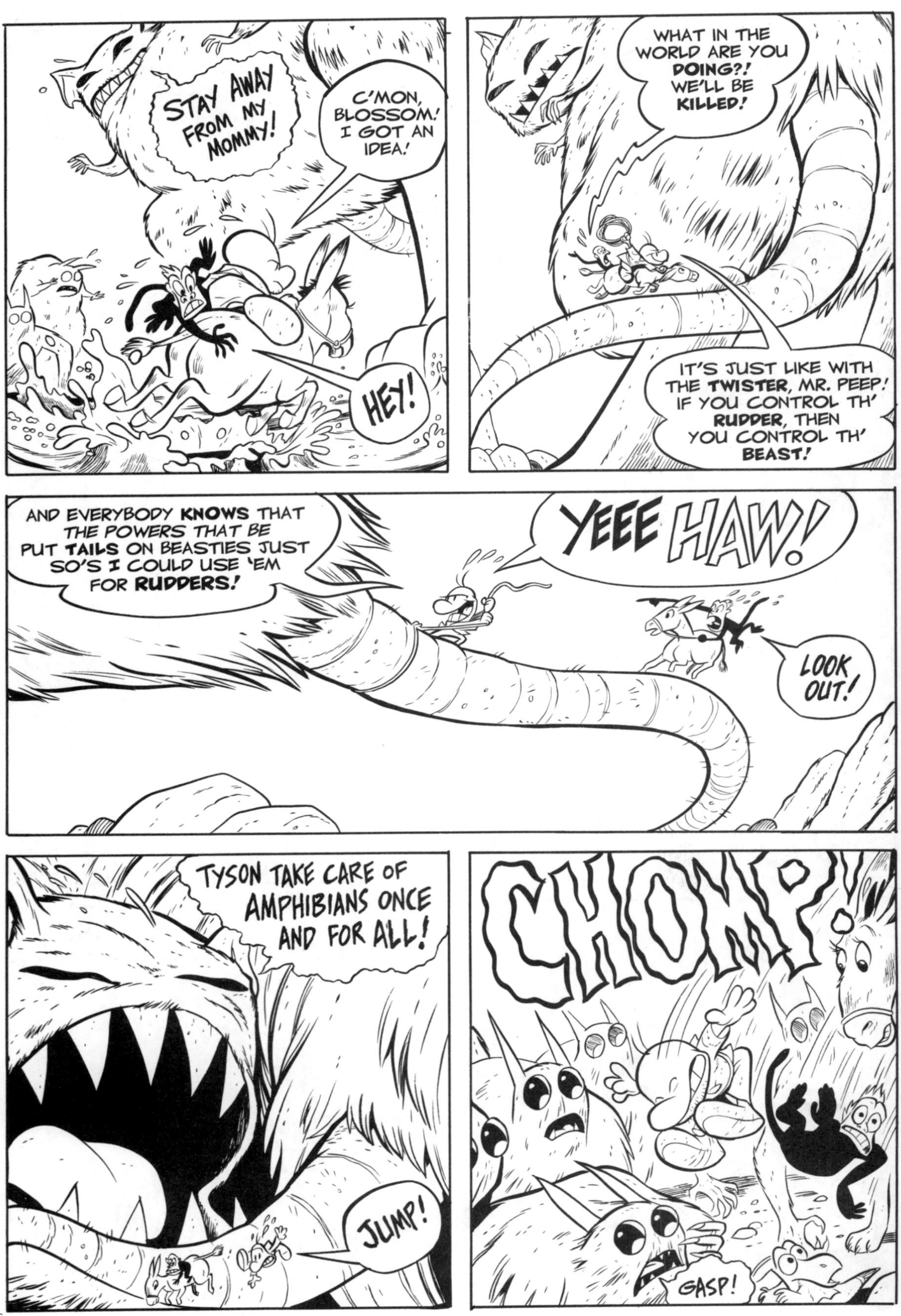
STAY AWAY FROM MY MOMMY!
C'MON, BLOSSOM! I GOT AN IDEA!
HEY!
WHAT IN THE WORLD ARE YOU DOING?! WE'LL BE KILLED!
IT'S JUST LIKE WITH THE TWISTER, MR. PEEP! IF YOU CONTROL TH' RUDDER, THEN YOU CONTROL TH' BEAST!
AND EVERYBODY KNOWS THAT THE POWERS THAT BE PUT TAILS ON BEASTIES JUST SO'S I COULD USE 'EM FOR RUDDERS!
YEEE HAW!
LOOK OUT!
TYSON TAKE CARE OF AMPHIBIANS ONCE AND FOR ALL!
JUMP!
CHOMP!
GASP!

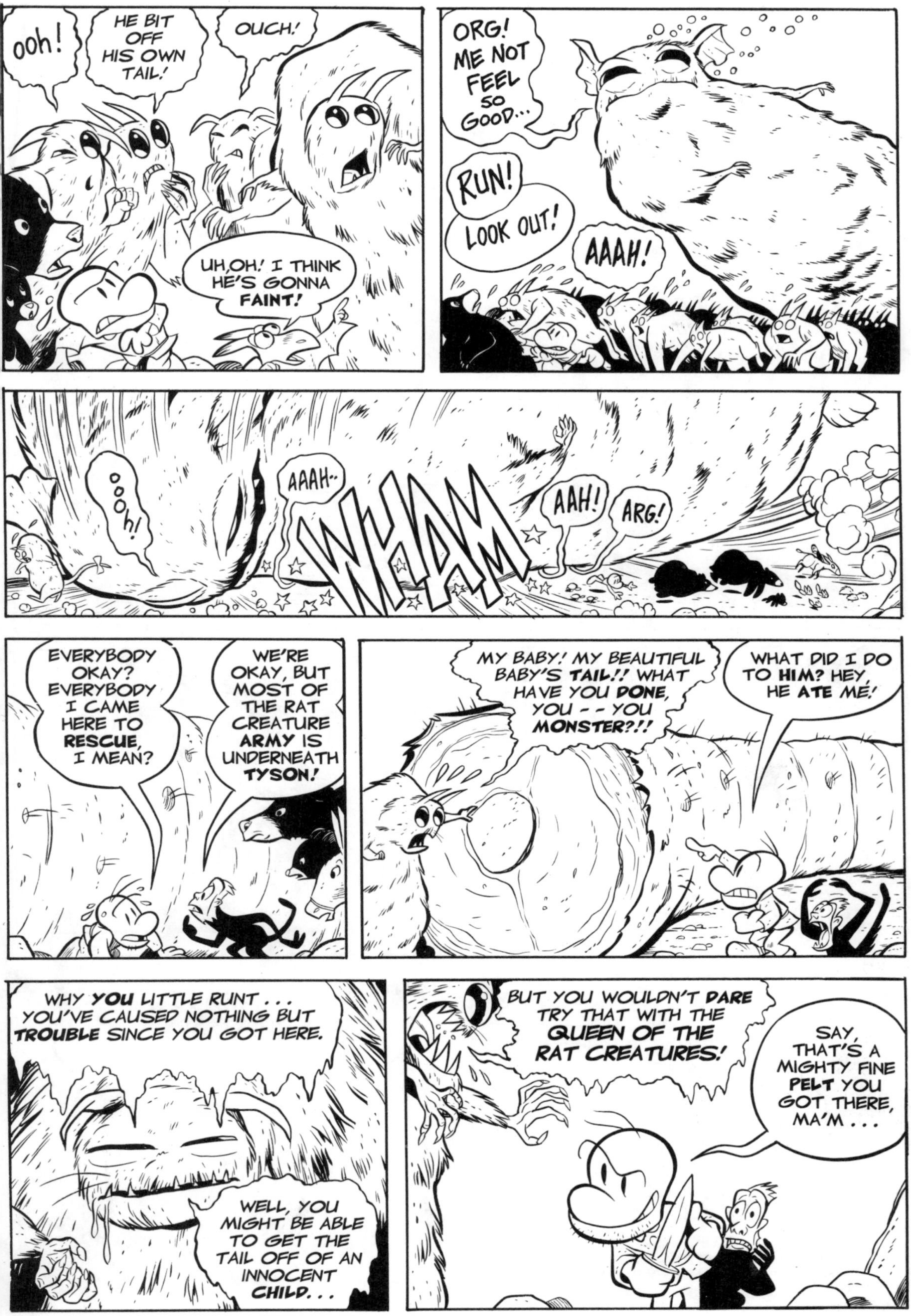

ooh!
HE BIT OFF HIS OWN TAIL!
OUCH!
UH, OH! I THINK HE'S GONNA FAINT!
ORG! ME NOT FEEL SO GOOD...
RUN!
LOOK OUT!
AAAH!
OOOh!
AAAH..
WHAM
AAH!
ARG!
EVERYBODY OKAY? EVERYBODY I CAME HERE TO RESCUE, I MEAN?
WE'RE OKAY, BUT MOST OF THE RAT CREATURE ARMY IS UNDERNEATH TYSON!
MY BABY! MY BEAUTIFUL BABY'S TAIL!! WHAT HAVE YOU DONE, YOU - - YOU MONSTER?!!
WHAT DID I DO TO HIM? HEY, HE ATE ME!
WHY YOU LITTLE RUNT . . . YOU'VE CAUSED NOTHING BUT TROUBLE SINCE YOU GOT HERE.
WELL, YOU MIGHT BE ABLE TO GET THE TAIL OFF OF AN INNOCENT CHILD . . .
BUT YOU WOULDN'T DARE TRY THAT WITH THE QUEEN OF THE RAT CREATURES!
SAY, THAT'S A MIGHTY FINE PELT YOU GOT THERE, MA'M . . .

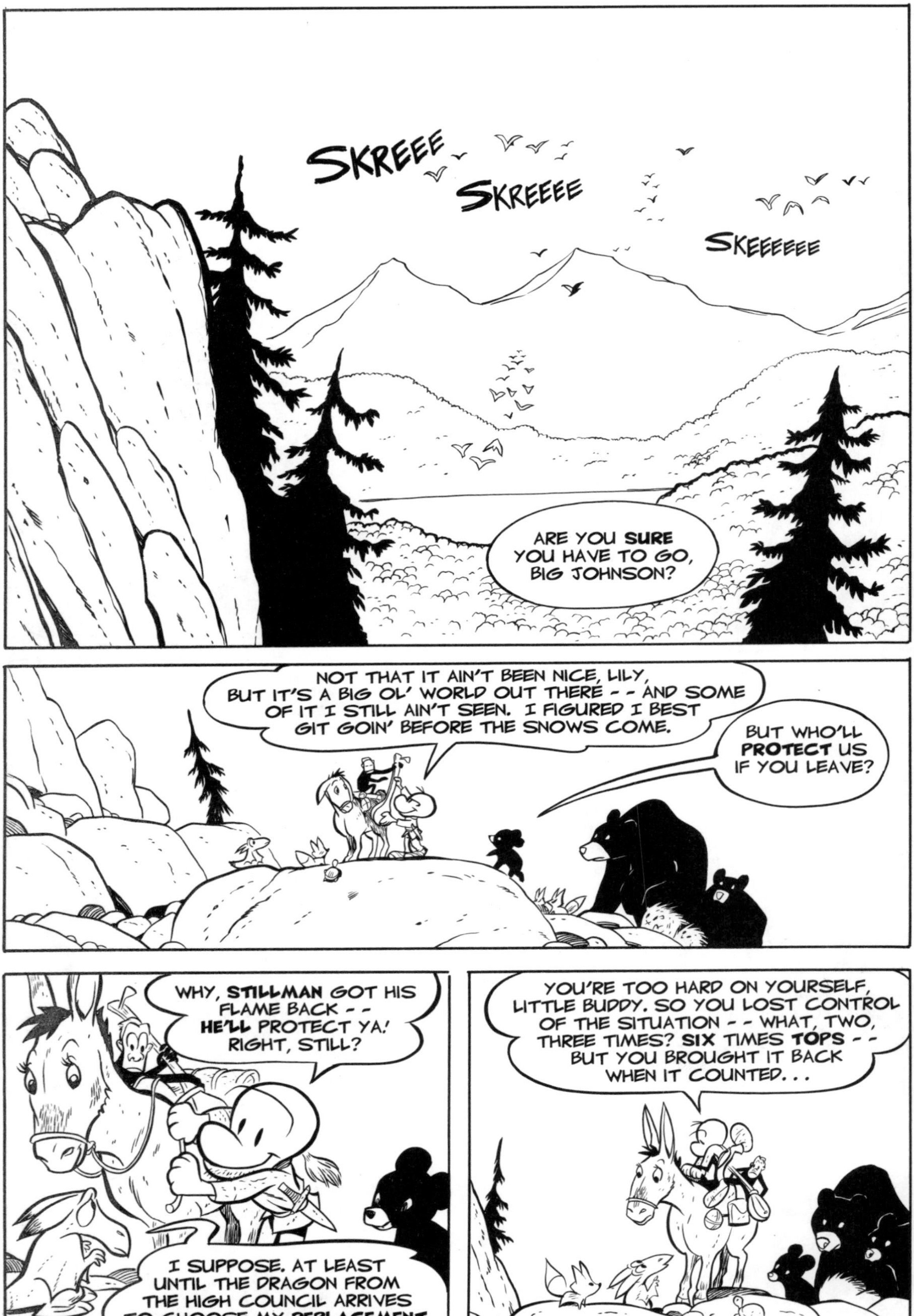
SKREEE
SKREEEE
SKEEEEEE
ARE YOU **SURE** YOU HAVE TO GO, BIG JOHNSON?
NOT THAT IT AIN'T BEEN NICE, LILY, BUT IT'S A BIG OL' WORLD OUT THERE -- AND SOME OF IT I STILL AIN'T SEEN. I FIGURED I BEST GIT GOIN' BEFORE THE SNOWS COME.
BUT WHO'LL **PROTECT** US IF YOU LEAVE?
WHY, **STILLMAN** GOT HIS FLAME BACK -- **HE'LL** PROTECT YA! RIGHT, STILL?
I SUPPOSE. AT LEAST UNTIL THE DRAGON FROM THE HIGH COUNCIL ARRIVES TO CHOOSE MY **REPLACEMENT**.
YOU'RE TOO HARD ON YOURSELF, LITTLE BUDDY. SO YOU LOST CONTROL OF THE SITUATION -- WHAT, TWO, THREE TIMES? **SIX** TIMES **TOPS** -- BUT YOU BROUGHT IT BACK WHEN IT COUNTED...

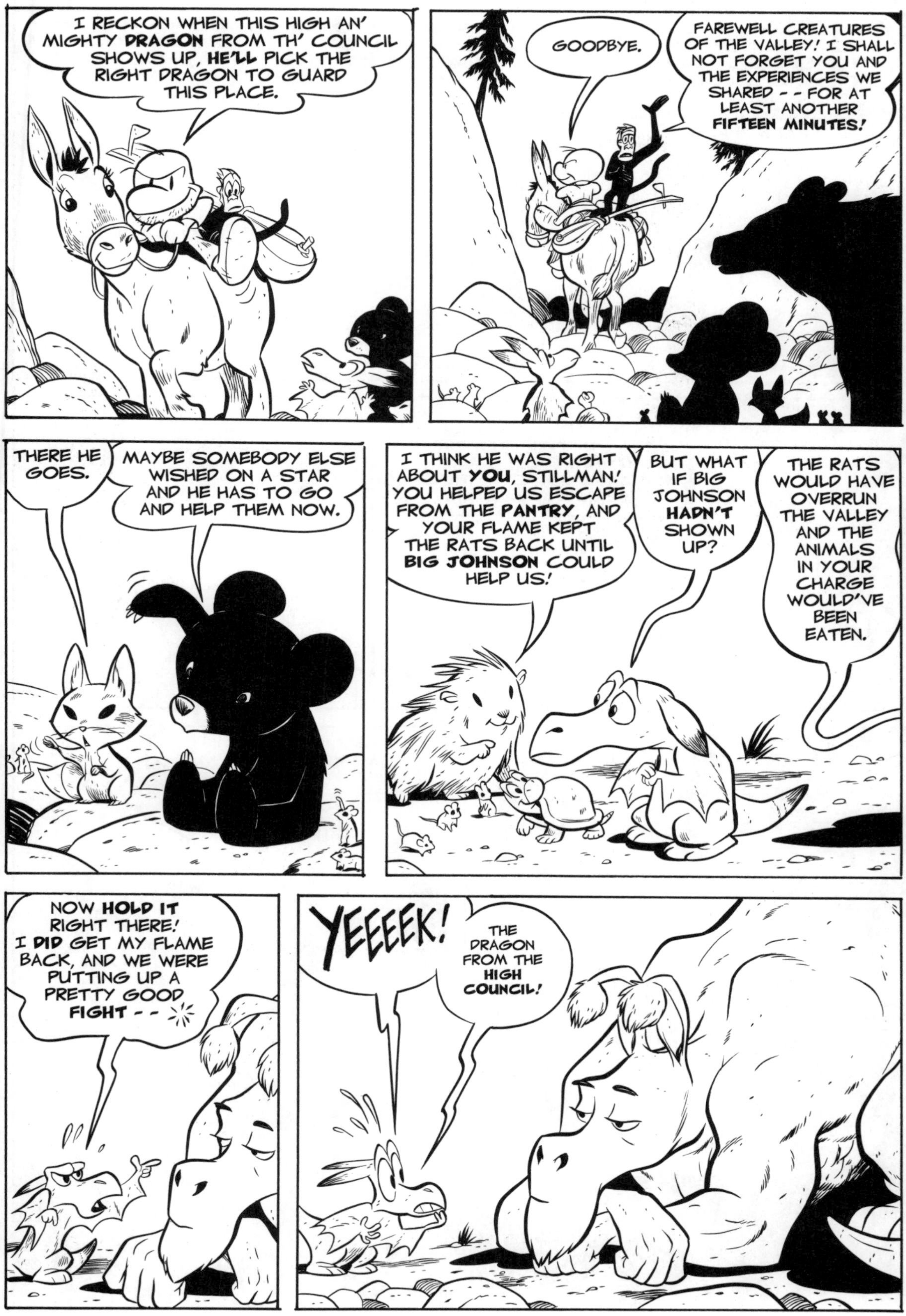
I RECKON WHEN THIS HIGH AN' MIGHTY **DRAGON** FROM TH' COUNCIL SHOWS UP, **HE'LL** PICK THE RIGHT DRAGON TO GUARD THIS PLACE.
GOODBYE.
FAREWELL CREATURES OF THE VALLEY! I SHALL NOT FORGET YOU AND THE EXPERIENCES WE SHARED -- FOR AT LEAST ANOTHER **FIFTEEN MINUTES!**
THERE HE GOES.
MAYBE SOMEBODY ELSE WISHED ON A STAR AND HE HAS TO GO AND HELP THEM NOW.
I THINK HE WAS RIGHT ABOUT **YOU**, STILLMAN! YOU HELPED US ESCAPE FROM THE **PANTRY**, AND YOUR FLAME KEPT THE RATS BACK UNTIL **BIG JOHNSON** COULD HELP US!
BUT WHAT IF BIG JOHNSON **HADN'T** SHOWN UP?
THE RATS WOULD HAVE OVERRUN THE VALLEY AND THE ANIMALS IN YOUR CHARGE WOULD'VE BEEN EATEN.
NOW **HOLD IT** RIGHT THERE! I **DID** GET MY FLAME BACK, AND WE WERE PUTTING UP A PRETTY GOOD **FIGHT** --
YEEEEK!
THE DRAGON FROM THE **HIGH COUNCIL!**

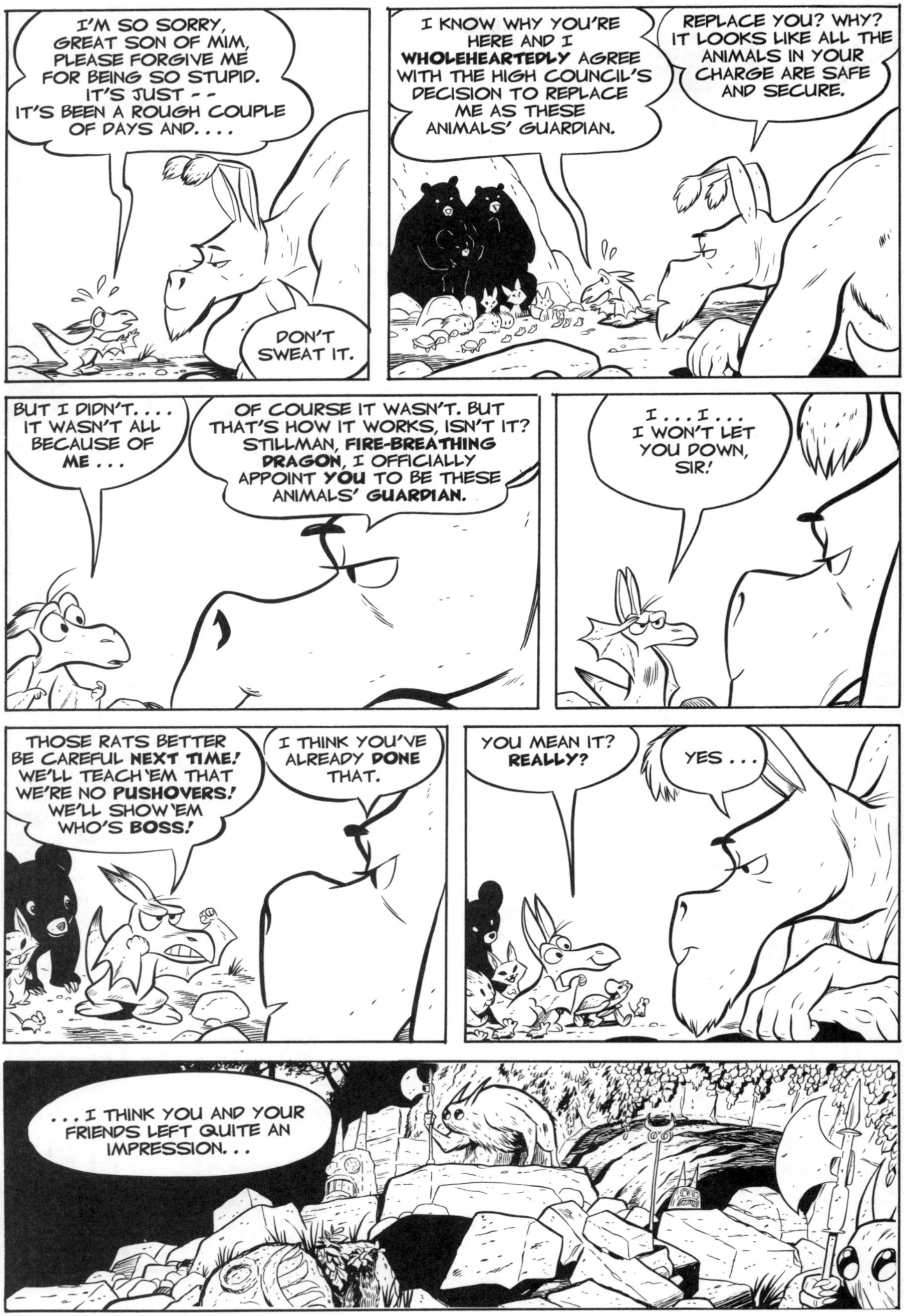
I'M SO SORRY, GREAT SON OF MIM, PLEASE FORGIVE ME FOR BEING SO STUPID. IT'S JUST - - IT'S BEEN A ROUGH COUPLE OF DAYS AND. . . .
DON'T SWEAT IT.
I KNOW WHY YOU'RE HERE AND I **WHOLEHEARTEDLY** AGREE WITH THE HIGH COUNCIL'S DECISION TO REPLACE ME AS THESE ANIMALS' GUARDIAN.
REPLACE YOU? WHY? IT LOOKS LIKE ALL THE ANIMALS IN YOUR CHARGE ARE SAFE AND SECURE.
BUT I DIDN'T. . . . IT WASN'T ALL BECAUSE OF **ME** . . .
OF COURSE IT WASN'T. BUT THAT'S HOW IT WORKS, ISN'T IT? STILLMAN, **FIRE-BREATHING DRAGON**, I OFFICIALLY APPOINT **YOU** TO BE THESE ANIMALS' **GUARDIAN.**
I . . . I . . . I WON'T LET YOU DOWN, SIR!
THOSE RATS BETTER BE CAREFUL **NEXT TIME!** WE'LL TEACH 'EM THAT WE'RE NO **PUSHOVERS!** WE'LL SHOW 'EM WHO'S **BOSS!**
I THINK YOU'VE ALREADY **DONE** THAT.
YOU MEAN IT? **REALLY?**
YES . . .
. . . I THINK YOU AND YOUR FRIENDS LEFT QUITE AN IMPRESSION. . .

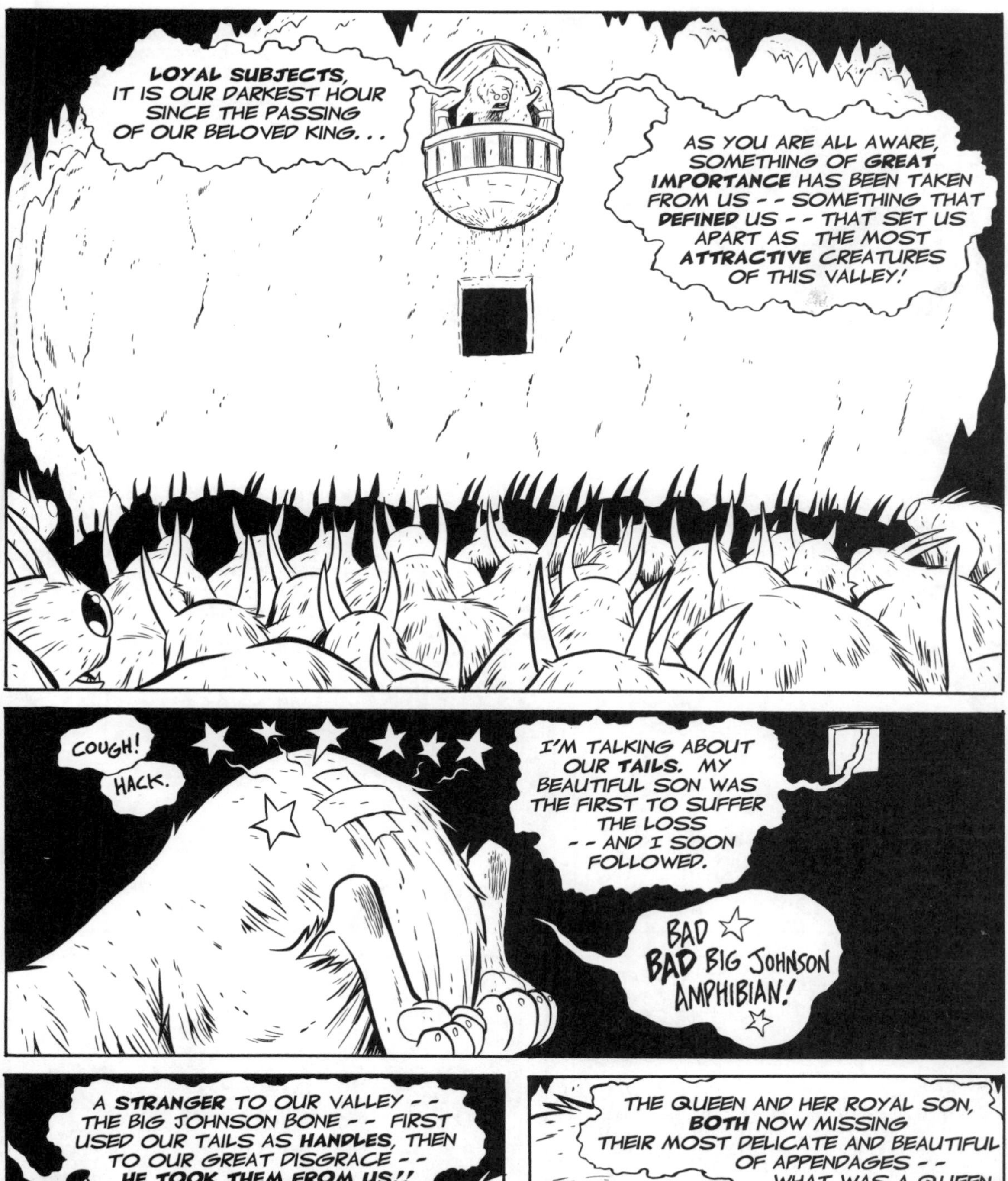

LOYAL SUBJECTS, IT IS OUR DARKEST HOUR SINCE THE PASSING OF OUR BELOVED KING. . .
AS YOU ARE ALL AWARE, SOMETHING OF GREAT IMPORTANCE HAS BEEN TAKEN FROM US - - SOMETHING THAT DEFINED US - - THAT SET US APART AS THE MOST ATTRACTIVE CREATURES OF THIS VALLEY!
COUGH!
HACK.
I'M TALKING ABOUT OUR TAILS. MY BEAUTIFUL SON WAS THE FIRST TO SUFFER THE LOSS - - AND I SOON FOLLOWED.
BAD BAD BIG JOHNSON AMPHIBIAN!
A STRANGER TO OUR VALLEY - - THE BIG JOHNSON BONE - - FIRST USED OUR TAILS AS HANDLES, THEN TO OUR GREAT DISGRACE - - HE TOOK THEM FROM US!!
THE QUEEN AND HER ROYAL SON, BOTH NOW MISSING THEIR MOST DELICATE AND BEAUTIFUL OF APPENDAGES - - WHAT WAS A QUEEN TO DO?

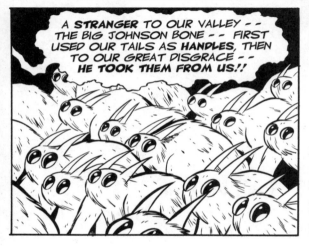

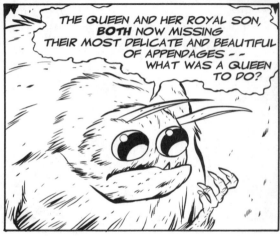

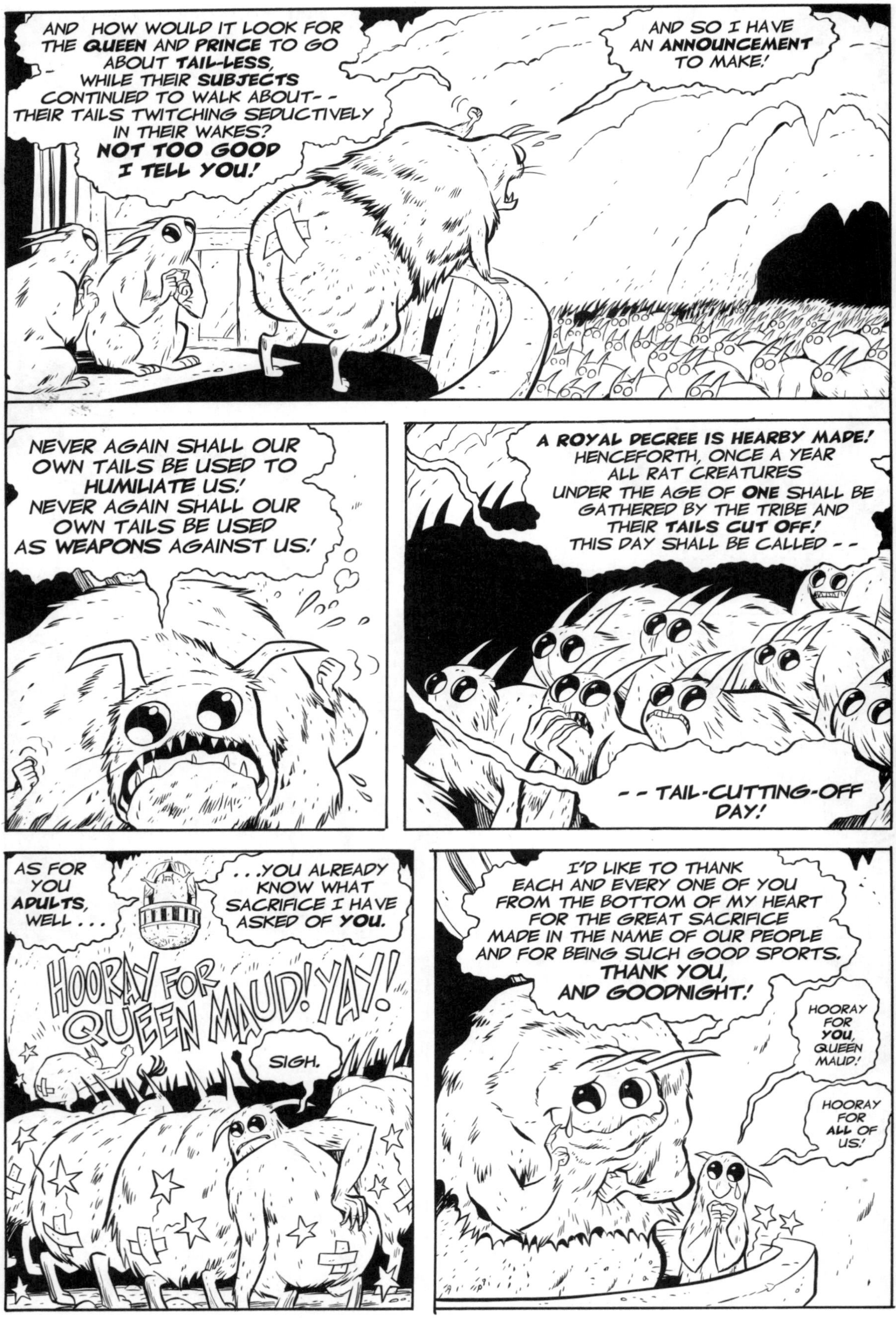
AND HOW WOULD IT LOOK FOR THE QUEEN AND PRINCE TO GO ABOUT TAIL-LESS, WHILE THEIR SUBJECTS CONTINUED TO WALK ABOUT- - THEIR TAILS TWITCHING SEDUCTIVELY IN THEIR WAKES? NOT TOO GOOD I TELL YOU!
AND SO I HAVE AN ANNOUNCEMENT TO MAKE!
NEVER AGAIN SHALL OUR OWN TAILS BE USED TO HUMILIATE US! NEVER AGAIN SHALL OUR OWN TAILS BE USED AS WEAPONS AGAINST US!
A ROYAL DECREE IS HEARBY MADE! HENCEFORTH, ONCE A YEAR ALL RAT CREATURES UNDER THE AGE OF ONE SHALL BE GATHERED BY THE TRIBE AND THEIR TAILS CUT OFF! THIS DAY SHALL BE CALLED - -
- - TAIL-CUTTING-OFF DAY!
AS FOR YOU ADULTS, WELL . . .
. . .YOU ALREADY KNOW WHAT SACRIFICE I HAVE ASKED OF YOU.
HOORAY FOR QUEEN MAUD! YAY!
SIGH.
I'D LIKE TO THANK EACH AND EVERY ONE OF YOU FROM THE BOTTOM OF MY HEART FOR THE GREAT SACRIFICE MADE IN THE NAME OF OUR PEOPLE AND FOR BEING SUCH GOOD SPORTS. THANK YOU, AND GOODNIGHT!
HOORAY FOR YOU, QUEEN MAUD!
HOORAY FOR ALL OF US!

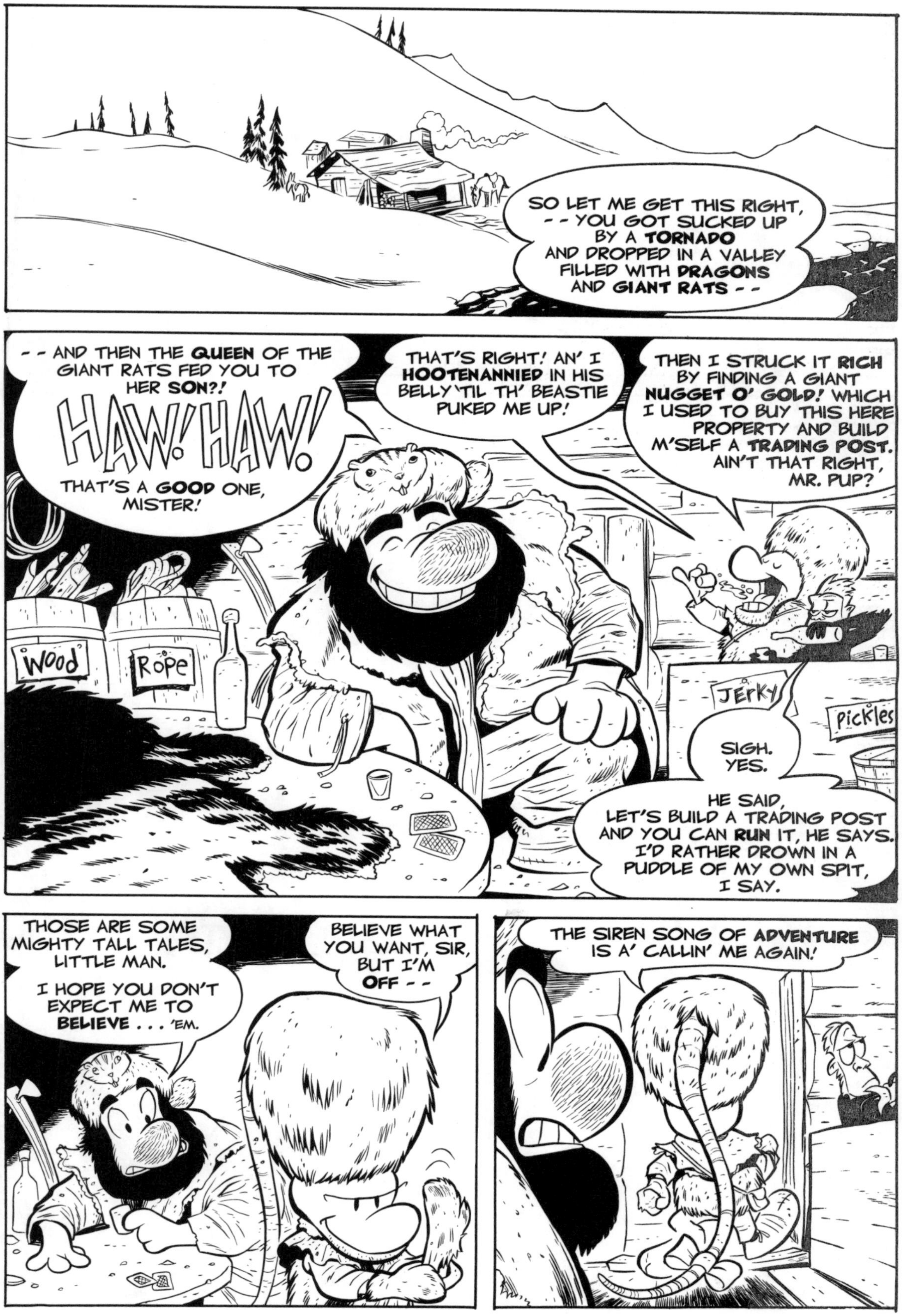
SO LET ME GET THIS RIGHT, - - YOU GOT SUCKED UP BY A **TORNADO** AND DROPPED IN A VALLEY FILLED WITH **DRAGONS** AND **GIANT RATS** - -
- - AND THEN THE **QUEEN** OF THE GIANT RATS FED YOU TO HER **SON?!**
HAW! HAW!
THAT'S A **GOOD** ONE, MISTER!
THAT'S RIGHT! AN' I **HOOTENANNIED** IN HIS BELLY 'TIL TH' BEASTIE PUKED ME UP!
THEN I STRUCK IT **RICH** BY FINDING A GIANT **NUGGET O' GOLD!** WHICH I USED TO BUY THIS HERE PROPERTY AND BUILD M'SELF A **TRADING POST.** AIN'T THAT RIGHT, MR. PUP?
Wood
Rope
Jerky
Pickles
SIGH. YES.
HE SAID, LET'S BUILD A TRADING POST AND YOU CAN **RUN** IT, HE SAYS. I'D RATHER DROWN IN A PUDDLE OF MY OWN SPIT, I SAY.
THOSE ARE SOME MIGHTY TALL TALES, LITTLE MAN.
I HOPE YOU DON'T EXPECT ME TO **BELIEVE** . . . 'EM.
BELIEVE WHAT YOU WANT, SIR, BUT I'M **OFF** - -
THE SIREN SONG OF **ADVENTURE** IS A' CALLIN' ME AGAIN!

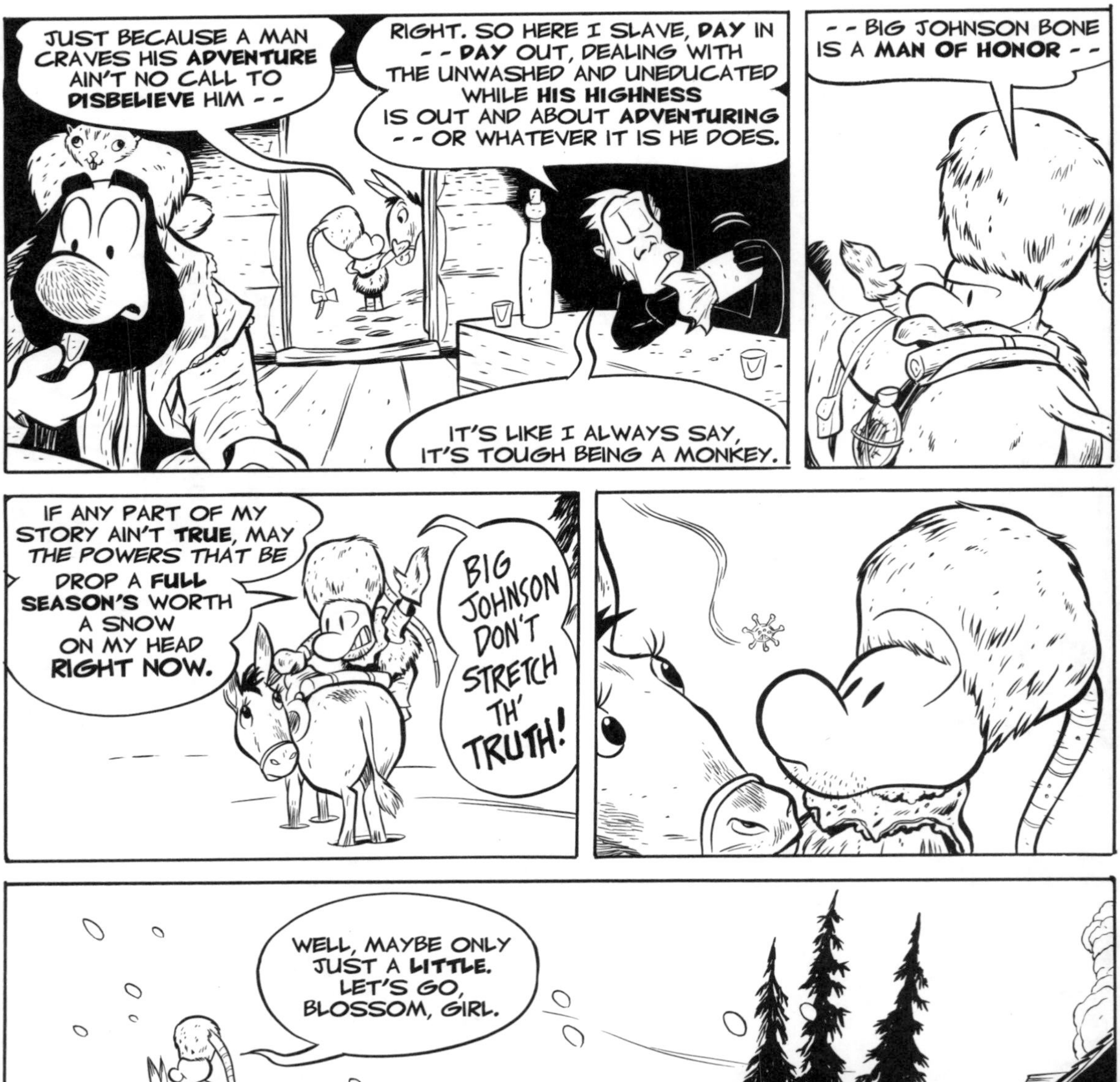

JUST BECAUSE A MAN CRAVES HIS ADVENTURE AIN'T NO CALL TO DISBELIEVE HIM - -
RIGHT. SO HERE I SLAVE, DAY IN - - DAY OUT, DEALING WITH THE UNWASHED AND UNEDUCATED WHILE HIS HIGHNESS IS OUT AND ABOUT ADVENTURING - - OR WHATEVER IT IS HE DOES.
IT'S LIKE I ALWAYS SAY, IT'S TOUGH BEING A MONKEY.
- - BIG JOHNSON BONE IS A MAN OF HONOR - -
IF ANY PART OF MY STORY AIN'T TRUE, MAY THE POWERS THAT BE DROP A FULL SEASON'S WORTH A SNOW ON MY HEAD RIGHT NOW.
BIG JOHNSON DON'T STRETCH TH' TRUTH!
WELL, MAYBE ONLY JUST A LITTLE. LET'S GO, BLOSSOM, GIRL.
THE END

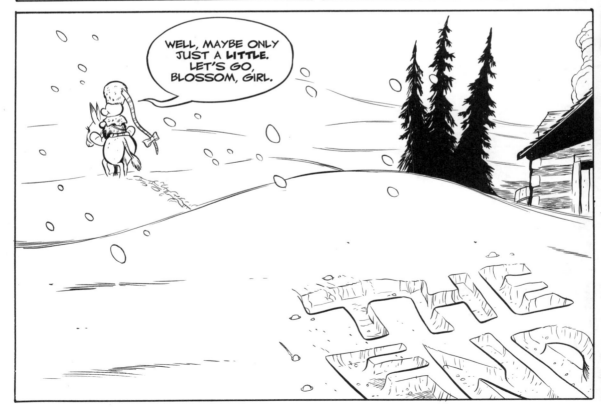

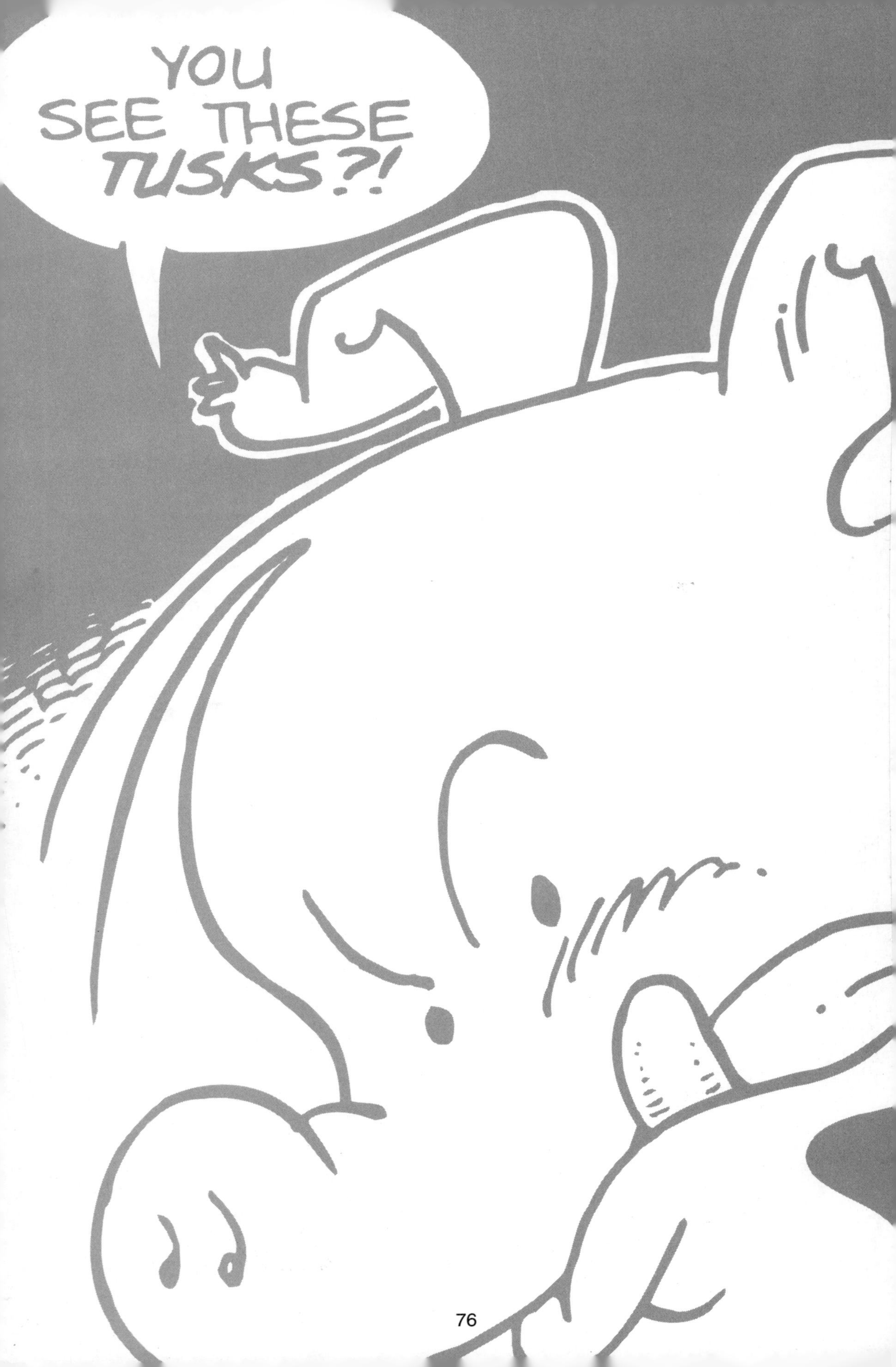
YOU SEE THESE *TUSKS*?!

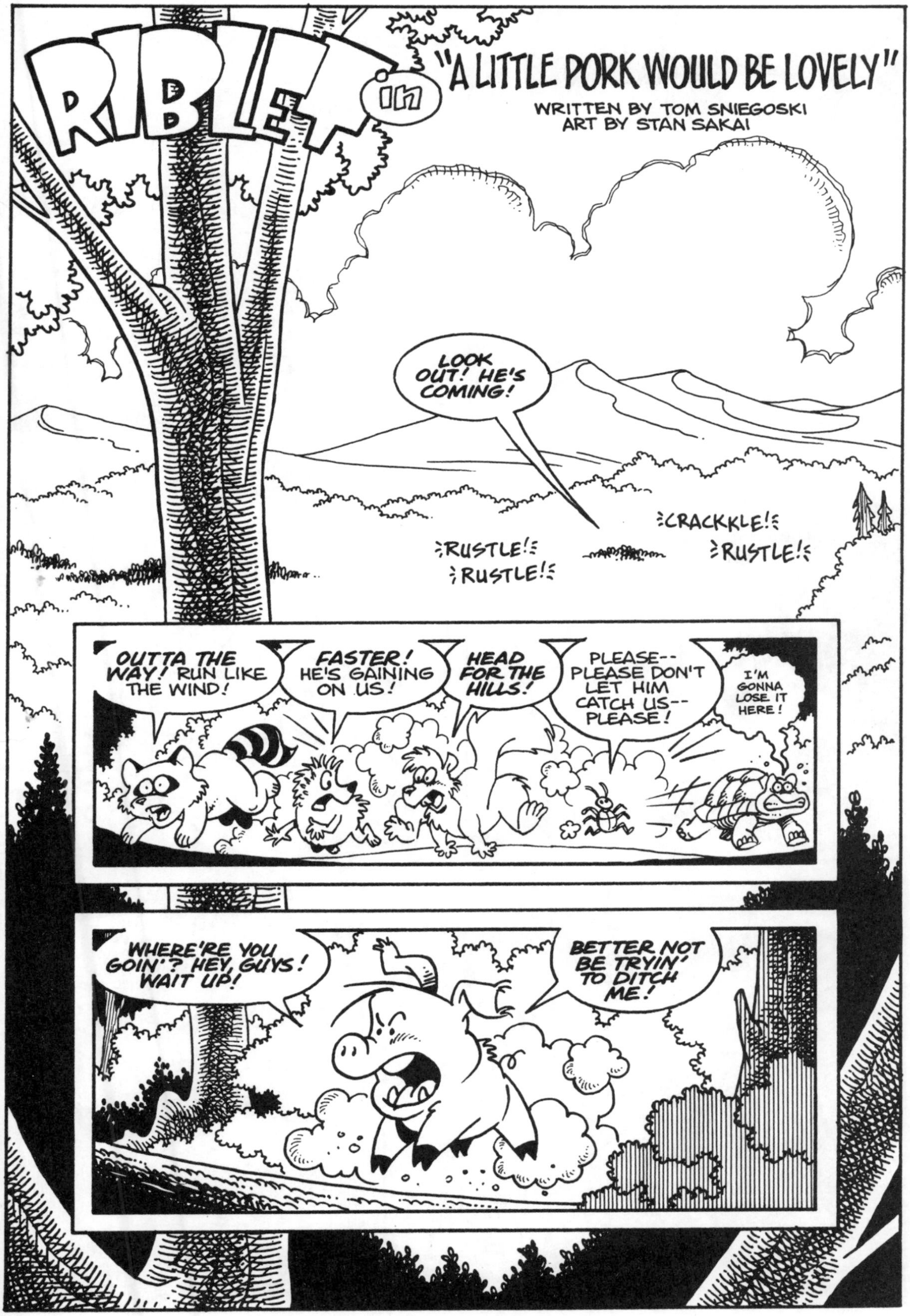
RIBLET in
"A LITTLE PORK WOULD BE LOVELY"
WRITTEN BY TOM SNIEGOSKI
ART BY STAN SAKAI
LOOK OUT! HE'S COMING!
CRACKKLE!
RUSTLE!
RUSTLE!
RUSTLE!
OUTTA THE WAY! RUN LIKE THE WIND!
FASTER! HE'S GAINING ON US!
HEAD FOR THE HILLS!
PLEASE-- PLEASE DON'T LET HIM CATCH US-- PLEASE!
I'M GONNA LOSE IT HERE!
WHERE'RE YOU GOIN'? HEY, GUYS! WAIT UP!
BETTER NOT BE TRYIN' TO DITCH ME!

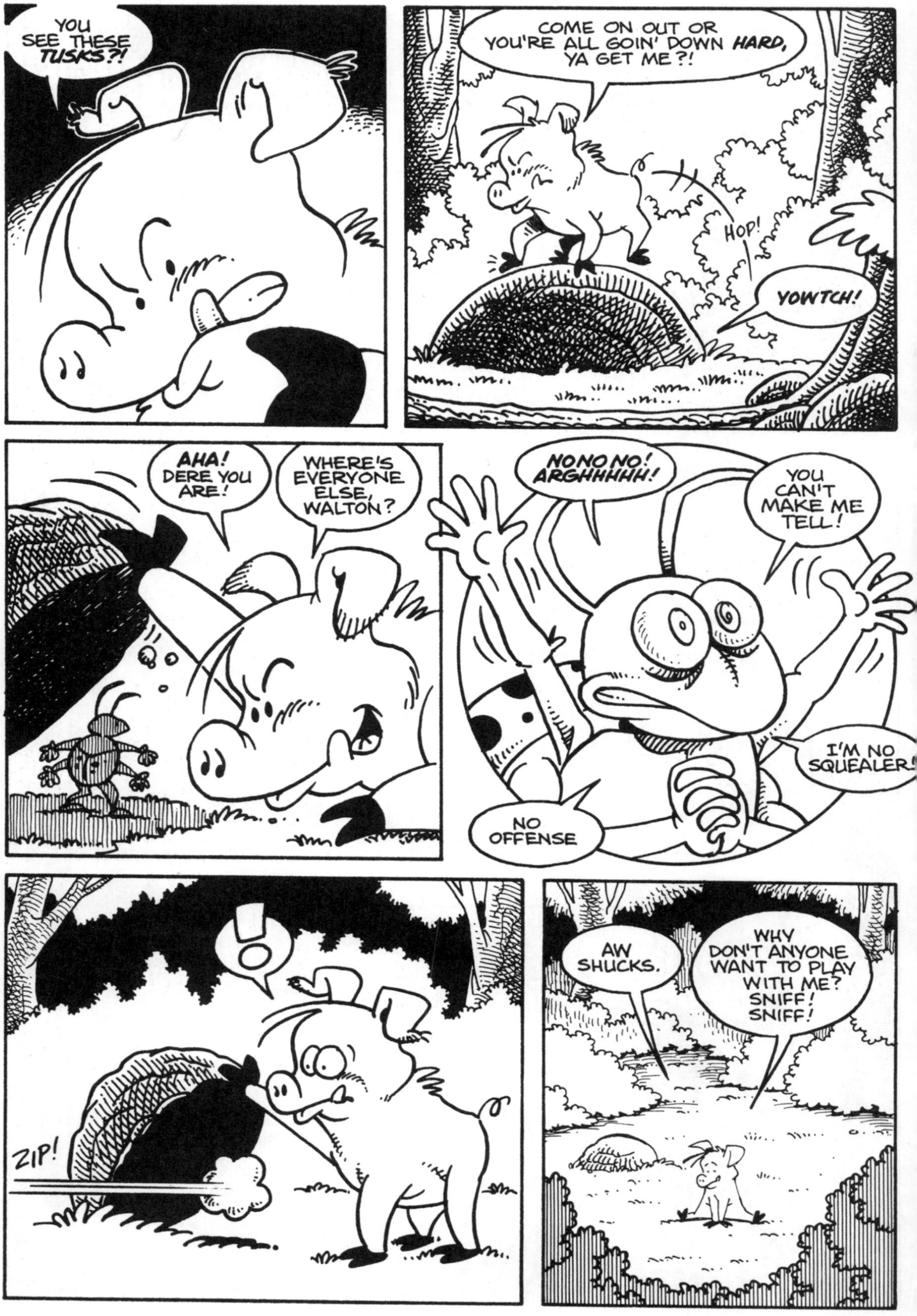
YOU SEE THESE TUSKS?!
COME ON OUT OR YOU'RE ALL GOIN' DOWN HARD, YA GET ME?!
HOP!
YOWTCH!
AHA! DERE YOU ARE!
WHERE'S EVERYONE ELSE, WALTON?
NONONO! ARGHHHHH!
YOU CAN'T MAKE ME TELL!
I'M NO SQUEALER!
NO OFFENSE
!
ZIP!
AW SHUCKS.
WHY DON'T ANYONE WANT TO PLAY WITH ME? SNIFF! SNIFF!

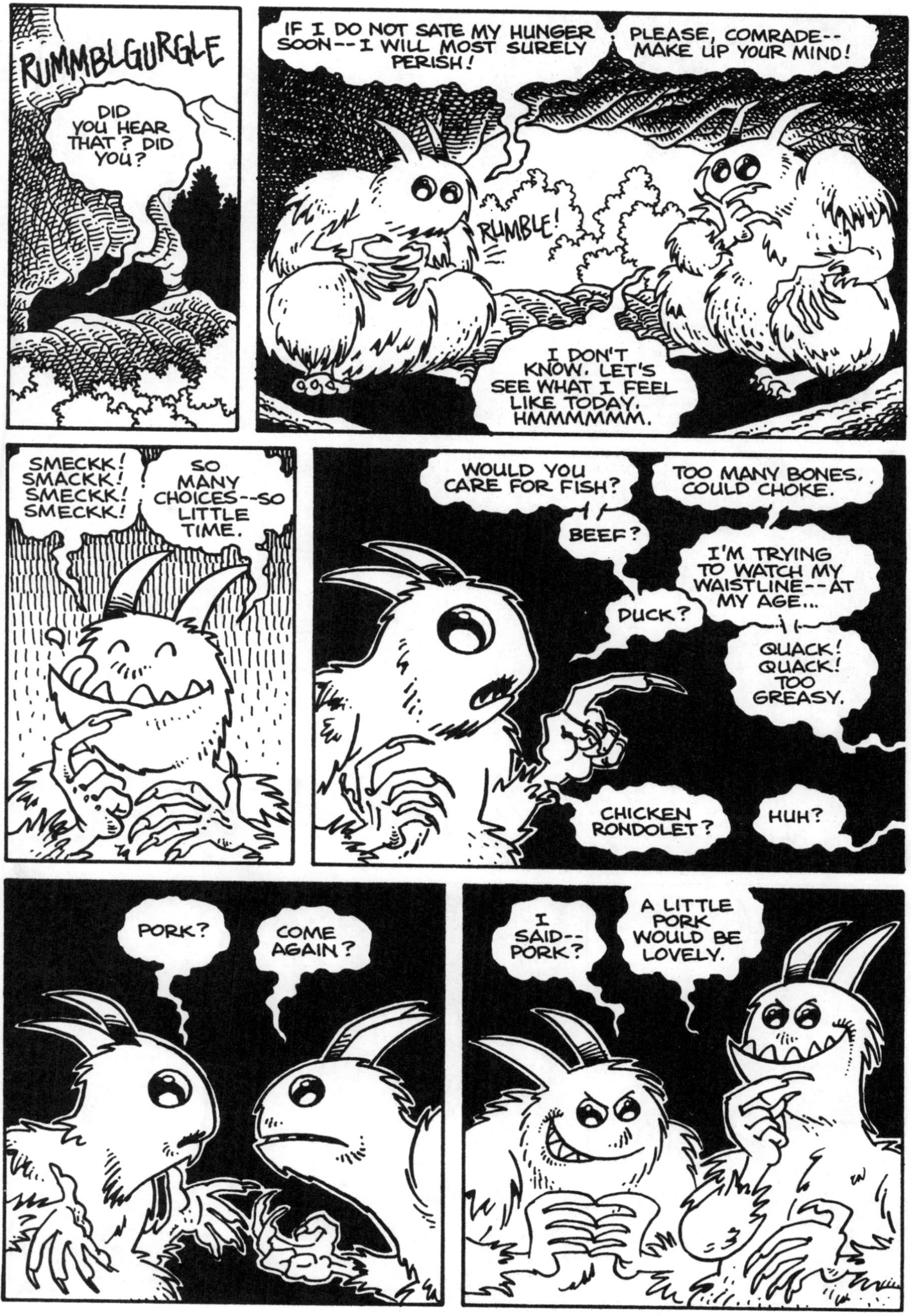
RUMMBLGURGLE
DID YOU HEAR THAT? DID YOU?
IF I DO NOT SATE MY HUNGER SOON--I WILL MOST SURELY PERISH!
PLEASE, COMRADE--MAKE UP YOUR MIND!
RUMBLE!
I DON'T KNOW. LET'S SEE WHAT I FEEL LIKE TODAY. HMMMMMM.
SMECKK! SMACKK! SMECKK! SMECKK!
SO MANY CHOICES--SO LITTLE TIME.
WOULD YOU CARE FOR FISH?
TOO MANY BONES. COULD CHOKE.
BEEF?
I'M TRYING TO WATCH MY WAISTLINE--AT MY AGE...
DUCK?
QUACK! QUACK! TOO GREASY.
CHICKEN RONDOLET?
HUH?
PORK?
COME AGAIN?
I SAID--PORK?
A LITTLE PORK WOULD BE LOVELY.

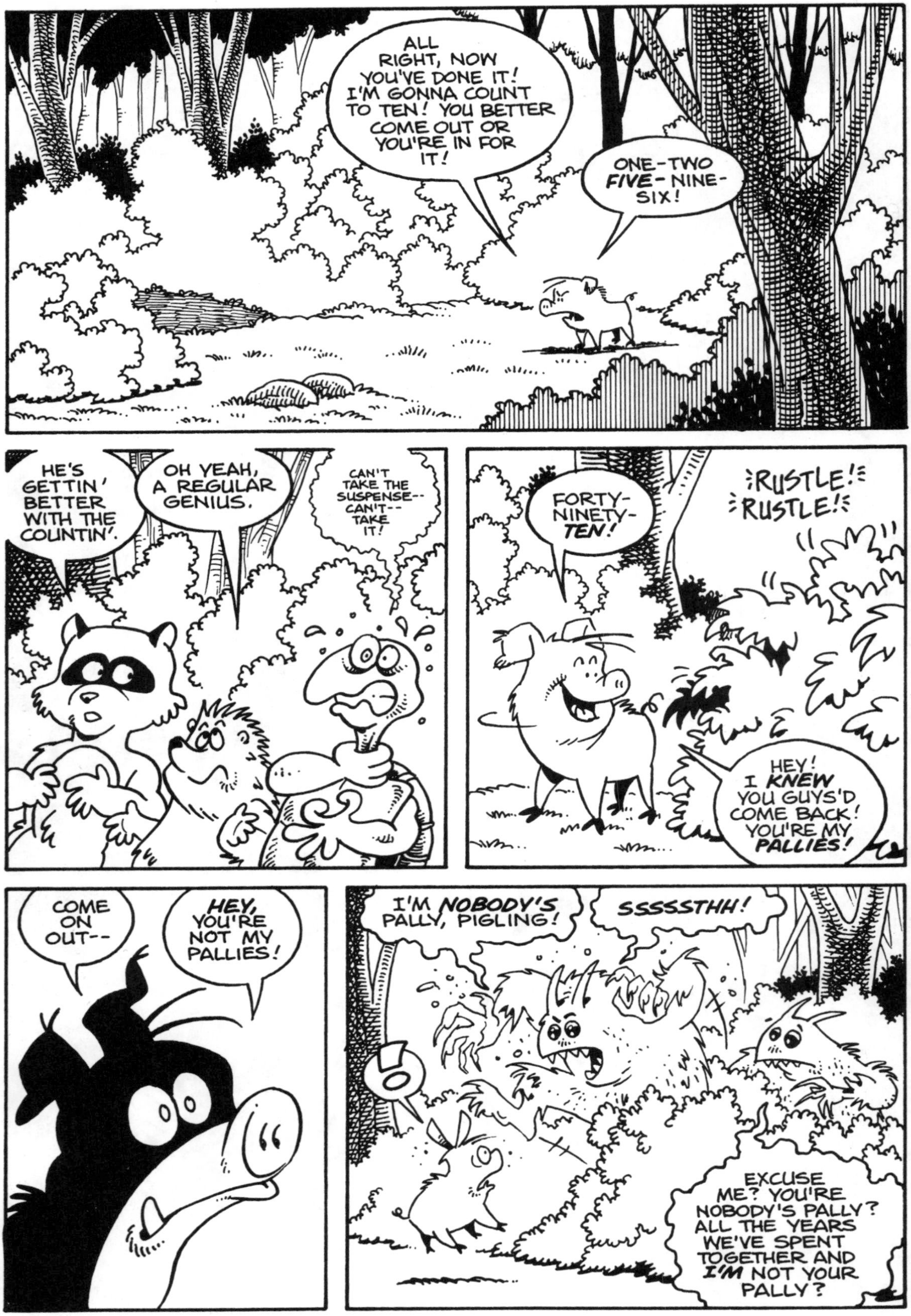

ALL RIGHT, NOW YOU'VE DONE IT! I'M GONNA COUNT TO TEN! YOU BETTER COME OUT OR YOU'RE IN FOR IT!
ONE-TWO *FIVE*-NINE-SIX!
HE'S GETTIN' BETTER WITH THE COUNTIN'.
OH YEAH, A REGULAR GENIUS.
CAN'T TAKE THE SUSPENSE-- CAN'T-- TAKE IT!
FORTY-NINETY-*TEN*!
RUSTLE! RUSTLE!
HEY! I *KNEW* YOU GUYS'D COME BACK! YOU'RE MY *PALLIES*!
COME ON OUT--
HEY, YOU'RE NOT MY PALLIES!
I'M *NOBODY'S* PALLY, PIGLING!
SSSSSTHH!
EXCUSE ME? YOU'RE NOBODY'S PALLY? ALL THE YEARS WE'VE SPENT TOGETHER AND *I'M* NOT YOUR PALLY?

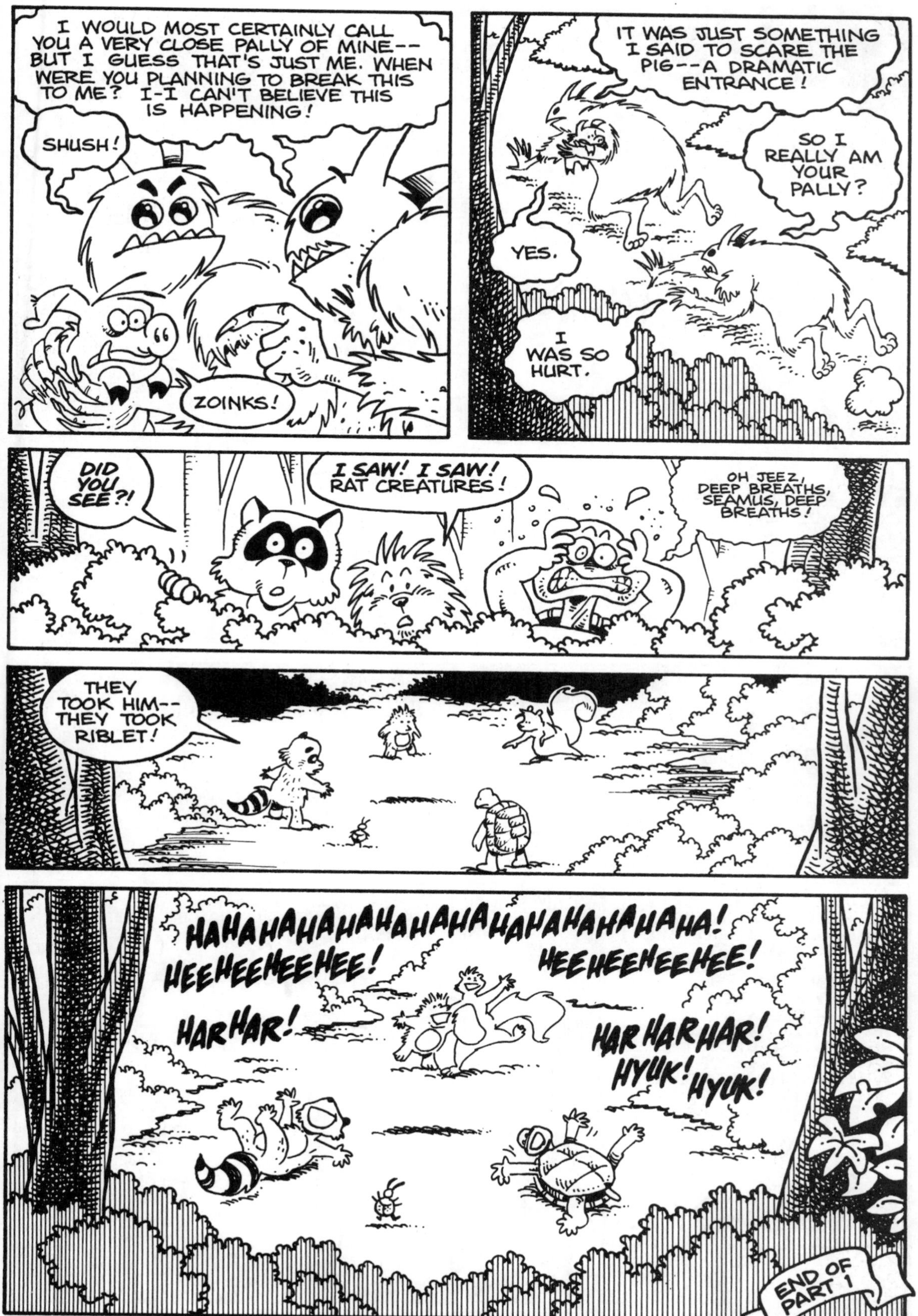
I WOULD MOST CERTAINLY CALL YOU A VERY CLOSE PALLY OF MINE-- BUT I GUESS THAT'S JUST ME. WHEN WERE YOU PLANNING TO BREAK THIS TO ME? I-I CAN'T BELIEVE THIS IS HAPPENING!
SHUSH!
ZOINKS!
IT WAS JUST SOMETHING I SAID TO SCARE THE PIG--A DRAMATIC ENTRANCE!
SO I REALLY AM YOUR PALLY?
YES.
I WAS SO HURT.
DID YOU SEE?!
I SAW! I SAW! RAT CREATURES!
OH JEEZ, DEEP BREATHS, SEAMUS, DEEP BREATHS!
THEY TOOK HIM-- THEY TOOK RIBLET!
HAHAHAHAHAHAHAHAHAHAHAHAHAHAHAHA!
HEEHEEHEEHEE!
HEEHEEHEEHEE!
HARHAR!
HAR HAR HAR!
HYUK! HYUK!
END OF PART 1

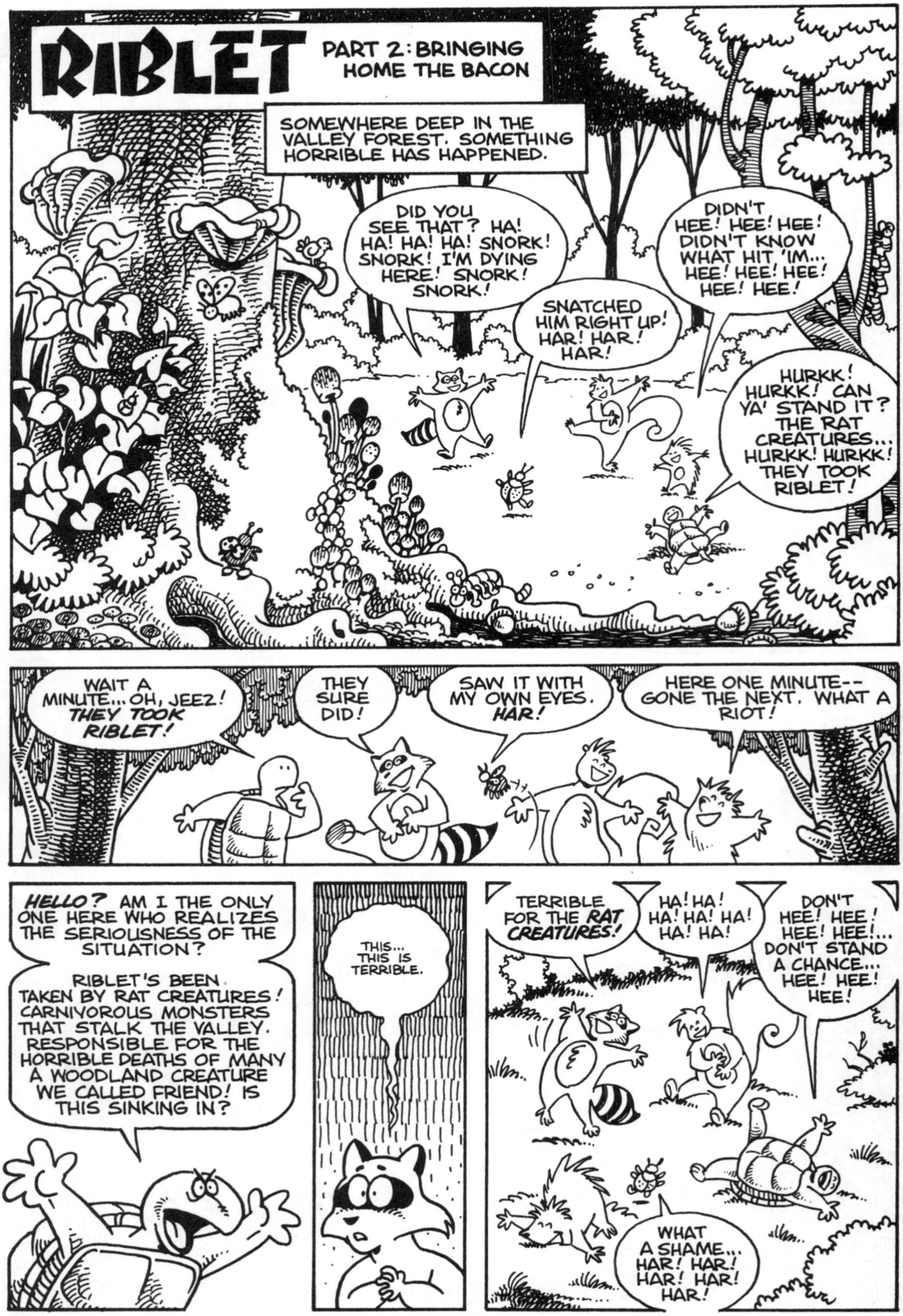
RIBLET
PART 2: BRINGING HOME THE BACON
SOMEWHERE DEEP IN THE VALLEY FOREST. SOMETHING HORRIBLE HAS HAPPENED.
DID YOU SEE THAT? HA! HA! HA! HA! SNORK! SNORK! I'M DYING HERE! SNORK! SNORK!
SNATCHED HIM RIGHT UP! HAR! HAR! HAR!
DIDN'T HEE! HEE! HEE! DIDN'T KNOW WHAT HIT 'IM... HEE! HEE! HEE! HEE! HEE!
HURKK! HURKK! CAN YA' STAND IT? THE RAT CREATURES... HURKK! HURKK! THEY TOOK RIBLET!
WAIT A MINUTE... OH, JEEZ! *THEY TOOK RIBLET!*
THEY SURE DID!
SAW IT WITH MY OWN EYES. *HAR!*
HERE ONE MINUTE-- GONE THE NEXT. WHAT A RIOT!
HELLO? AM I THE ONLY ONE HERE WHO REALIZES THE SERIOUSNESS OF THE SITUATION?
RIBLET'S BEEN TAKEN BY RAT CREATURES! CARNIVOROUS MONSTERS THAT STALK THE VALLEY. RESPONSIBLE FOR THE HORRIBLE DEATHS OF MANY A WOODLAND CREATURE WE CALLED FRIEND! IS THIS SINKING IN?
THIS... THIS IS TERRIBLE.
TERRIBLE FOR THE *RAT CREATURES!*
HA! HA! HA! HA! HA! HA! HA!
DON'T HEE! HEE! HEE! HEE!... DON'T STAND A CHANCE... HEE! HEE! HEE!
WHAT A SHAME... HAR! HAR! HAR! HAR! HAR!

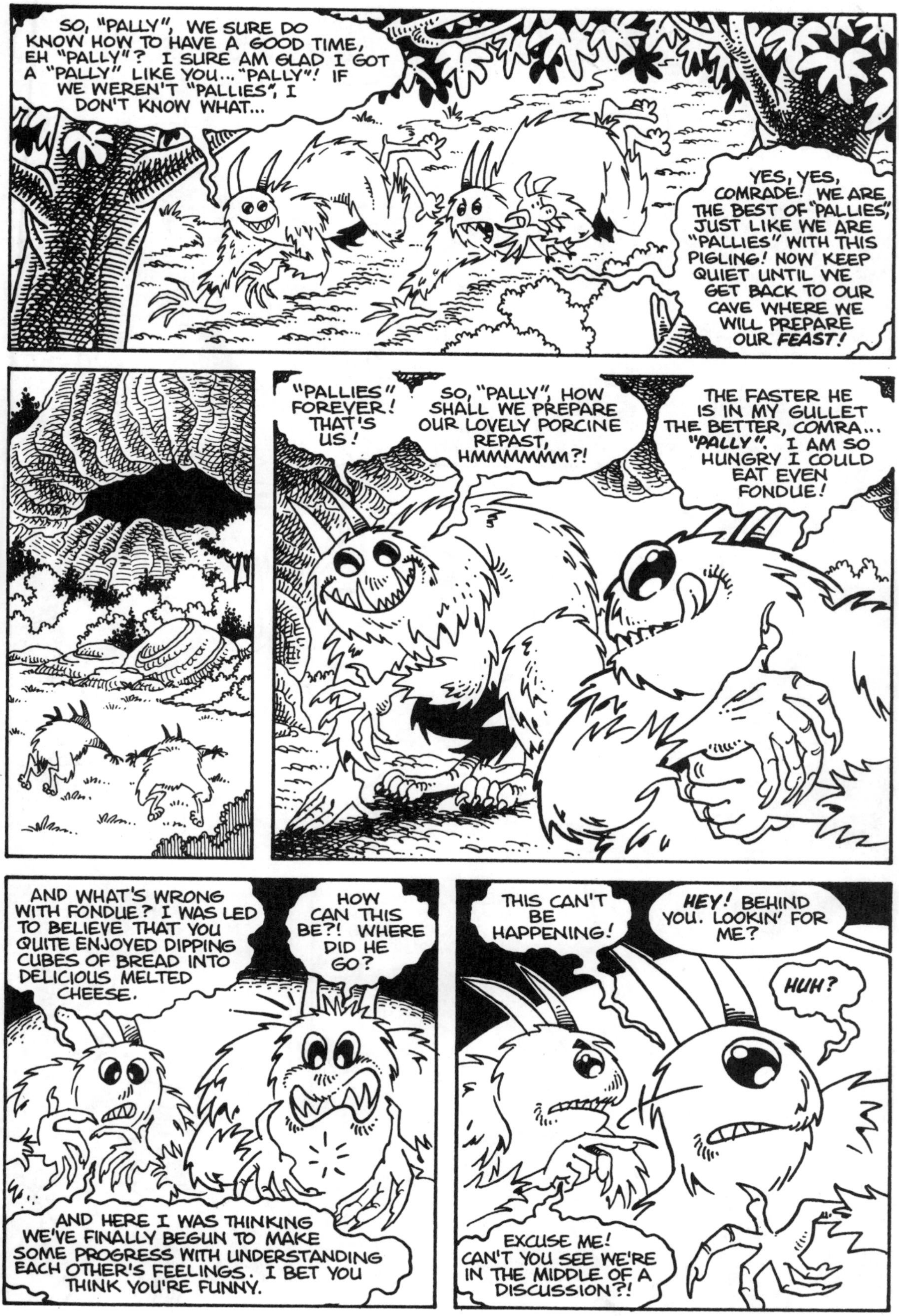

SO, "PALLY", WE SURE DO KNOW HOW TO HAVE A GOOD TIME, EH "PALLY"? I SURE AM GLAD I GOT A "PALLY" LIKE YOU... "PALLY"! IF WE WEREN'T "PALLIES", I DON'T KNOW WHAT...
YES, YES, COMRADE! WE ARE THE BEST OF "PALLIES", JUST LIKE WE ARE "PALLIES" WITH THIS PIGLING! NOW KEEP QUIET UNTIL WE GET BACK TO OUR CAVE WHERE WE WILL PREPARE OUR *FEAST*!
"PALLIES" FOREVER! THAT'S US!
SO, "PALLY", HOW SHALL WE PREPARE OUR LOVELY PORCINE REPAST, HMMMMMM?!
THE FASTER HE IS IN MY GULLET THE BETTER, COMRA... *"PALLY"*. I AM SO HUNGRY I COULD EAT EVEN FONDUE!
AND WHAT'S WRONG WITH FONDUE? I WAS LED TO BELIEVE THAT YOU QUITE ENJOYED DIPPING CUBES OF BREAD INTO DELICIOUS MELTED CHEESE.
HOW CAN THIS BE?! WHERE DID HE GO?
AND HERE I WAS THINKING WE'VE FINALLY BEGUN TO MAKE SOME PROGRESS WITH UNDERSTANDING EACH OTHER'S FEELINGS. I BET YOU THINK YOU'RE FUNNY.
THIS CAN'T BE HAPPENING!
HEY! BEHIND YOU. LOOKIN' FOR ME?
HUH?
EXCUSE ME! CAN'T YOU SEE WE'RE IN THE MIDDLE OF A DISCUSSION?!

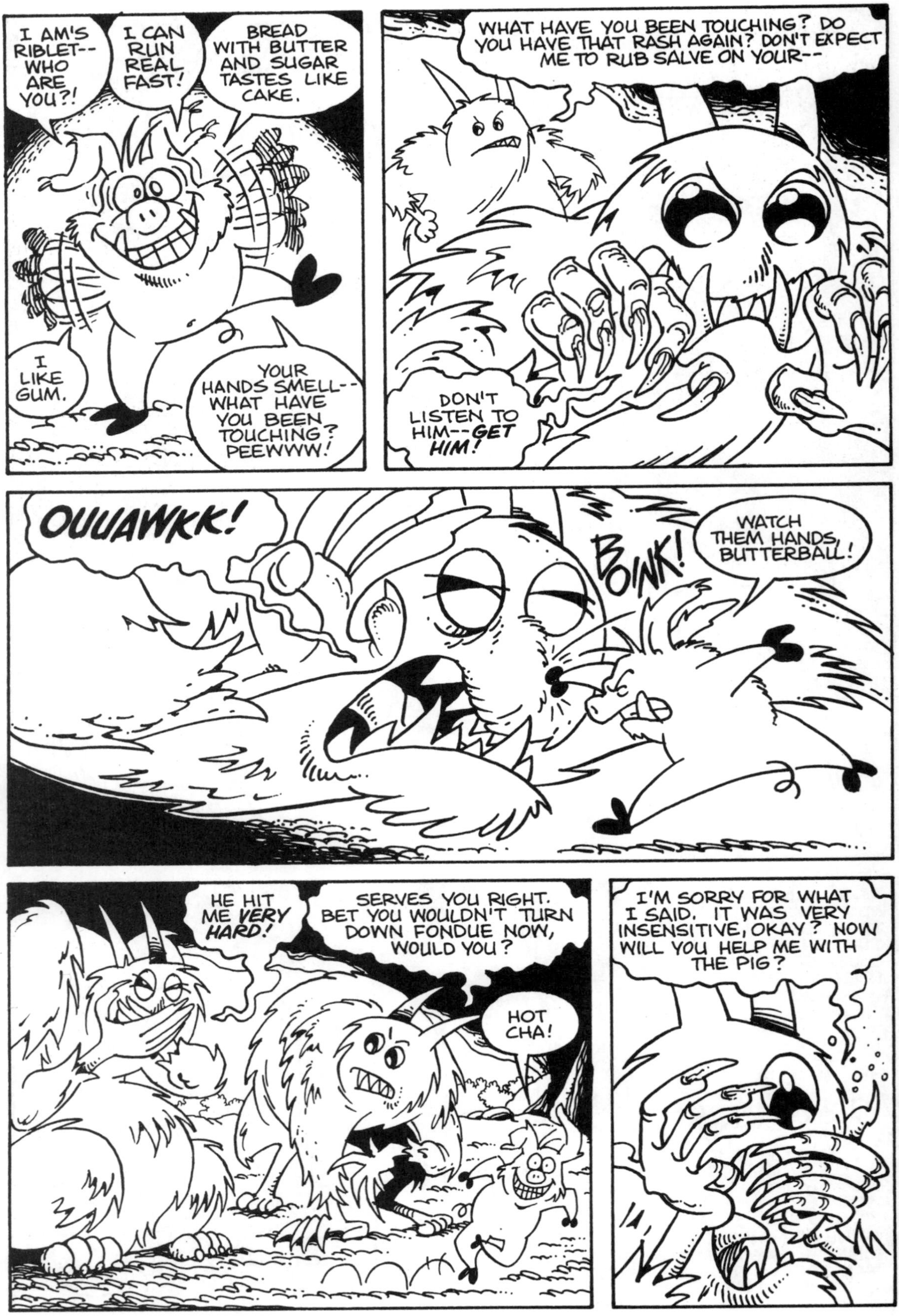
I AM'S RIBLET-- WHO ARE YOU?!
I CAN RUN REAL FAST!
BREAD WITH BUTTER AND SUGAR TASTES LIKE CAKE.
I LIKE GUM.
YOUR HANDS SMELL-- WHAT HAVE YOU BEEN TOUCHING? PEEWWW!
WHAT HAVE YOU BEEN TOUCHING? DO YOU HAVE THAT RASH AGAIN? DON'T EXPECT ME TO RUB SALVE ON YOUR--
DON'T LISTEN TO HIM--GET HIM!
OUUAWKK!
BOINK!
WATCH THEM HANDS, BUTTERBALL!
HE HIT ME VERY HARD!
SERVES YOU RIGHT. BET YOU WOULDN'T TURN DOWN FONDUE NOW, WOULD YOU?
HOT CHA!
I'M SORRY FOR WHAT I SAID. IT WAS VERY INSENSITIVE, OKAY? NOW WILL YOU HELP ME WITH THE PIG?

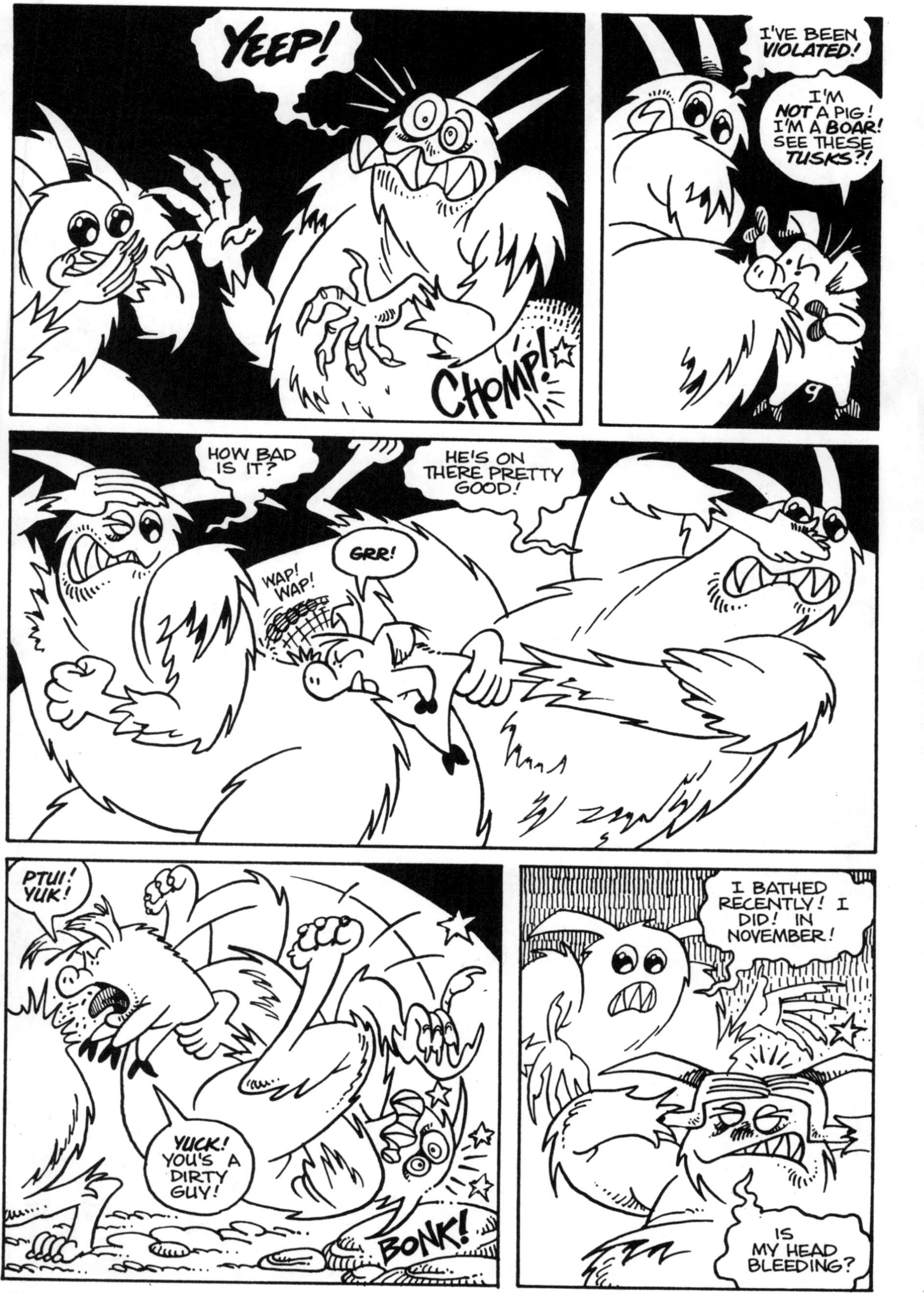
YEEP!
CHOMP!
I'VE BEEN VIOLATED!
I'M NOT A PIG! I'M A BOAR! SEE THESE TUSKS?!
HOW BAD IS IT?
HE'S ON THERE PRETTY GOOD!
GRR!
WAP! WAP!
PTUI! YUK!
YUCK! YOU'S A DIRTY GUY!
BONK!
I BATHED RECENTLY! I DID! IN NOVEMBER!
IS MY HEAD BLEEDING?

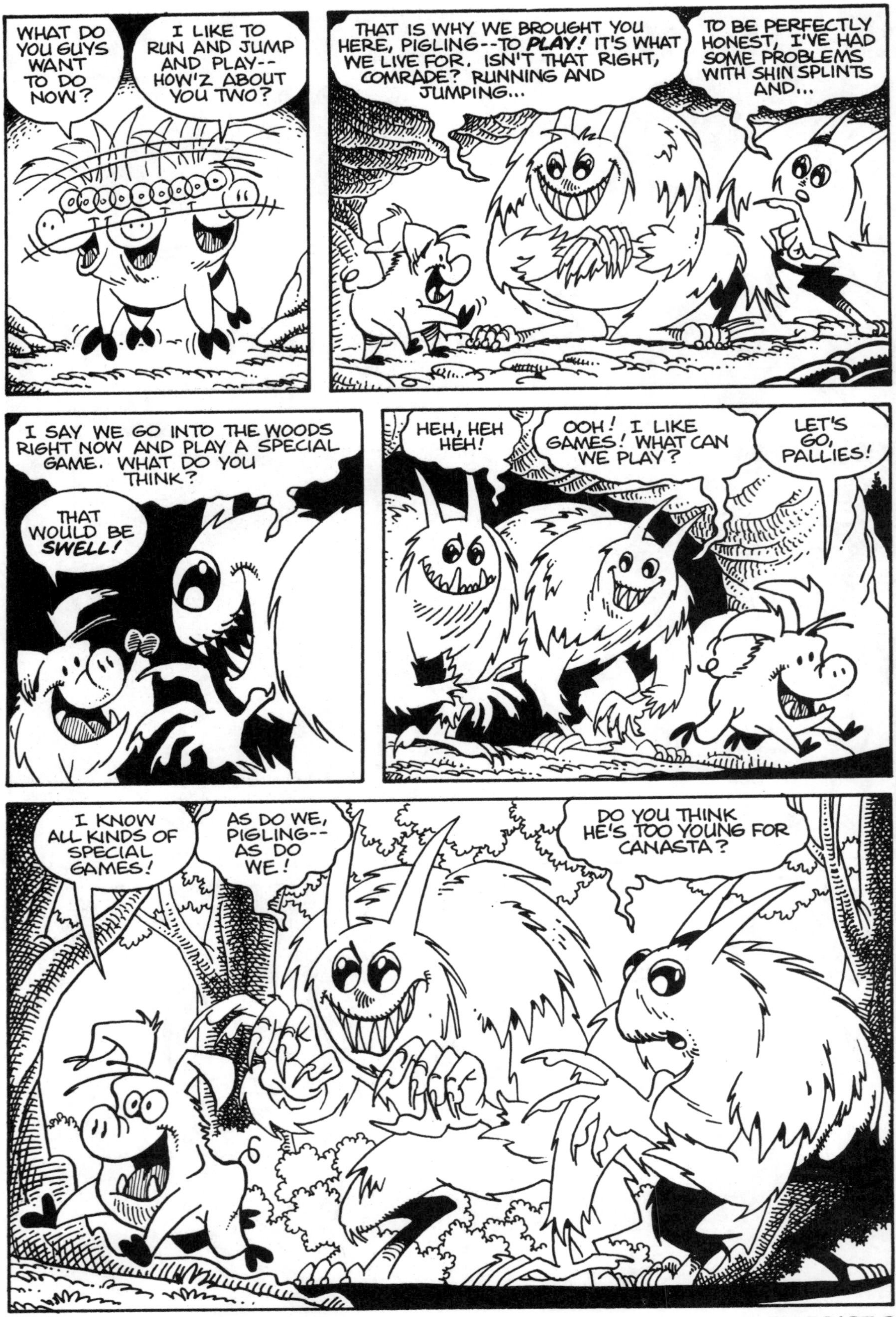
WHAT DO YOU GUYS WANT TO DO NOW?
I LIKE TO RUN AND JUMP AND PLAY-- HOW'Z ABOUT YOU TWO?
THAT IS WHY WE BROUGHT YOU HERE, PIGLING--TO **PLAY!** IT'S WHAT WE LIVE FOR. ISN'T THAT RIGHT, COMRADE? RUNNING AND JUMPING...
TO BE PERFECTLY HONEST, I'VE HAD SOME PROBLEMS WITH SHIN SPLINTS AND...
I SAY WE GO INTO THE WOODS RIGHT NOW AND PLAY A SPECIAL GAME. WHAT DO YOU THINK?
THAT WOULD BE **SWELL!**
HEH, HEH HEH!
OOH! I LIKE GAMES! WHAT CAN WE PLAY?
LET'S GO, PALLIES!
I KNOW ALL KINDS OF SPECIAL GAMES!
AS DO WE, PIGLING-- AS DO WE!
DO YOU THINK HE'S TOO YOUNG FOR CANASTA?

END OF PART 2

RIBLET PART 3 FUN & GAMES

SOMEWHERE, DEEP IN THE VALLEY FOREST--SOMETHING HORRIBLE HAS HAPPENED. A BABY BOAR, NAMED RIBLET, HAS BEEN STOLEN AWAY BY THE FEARSOME RAT CREATURES.

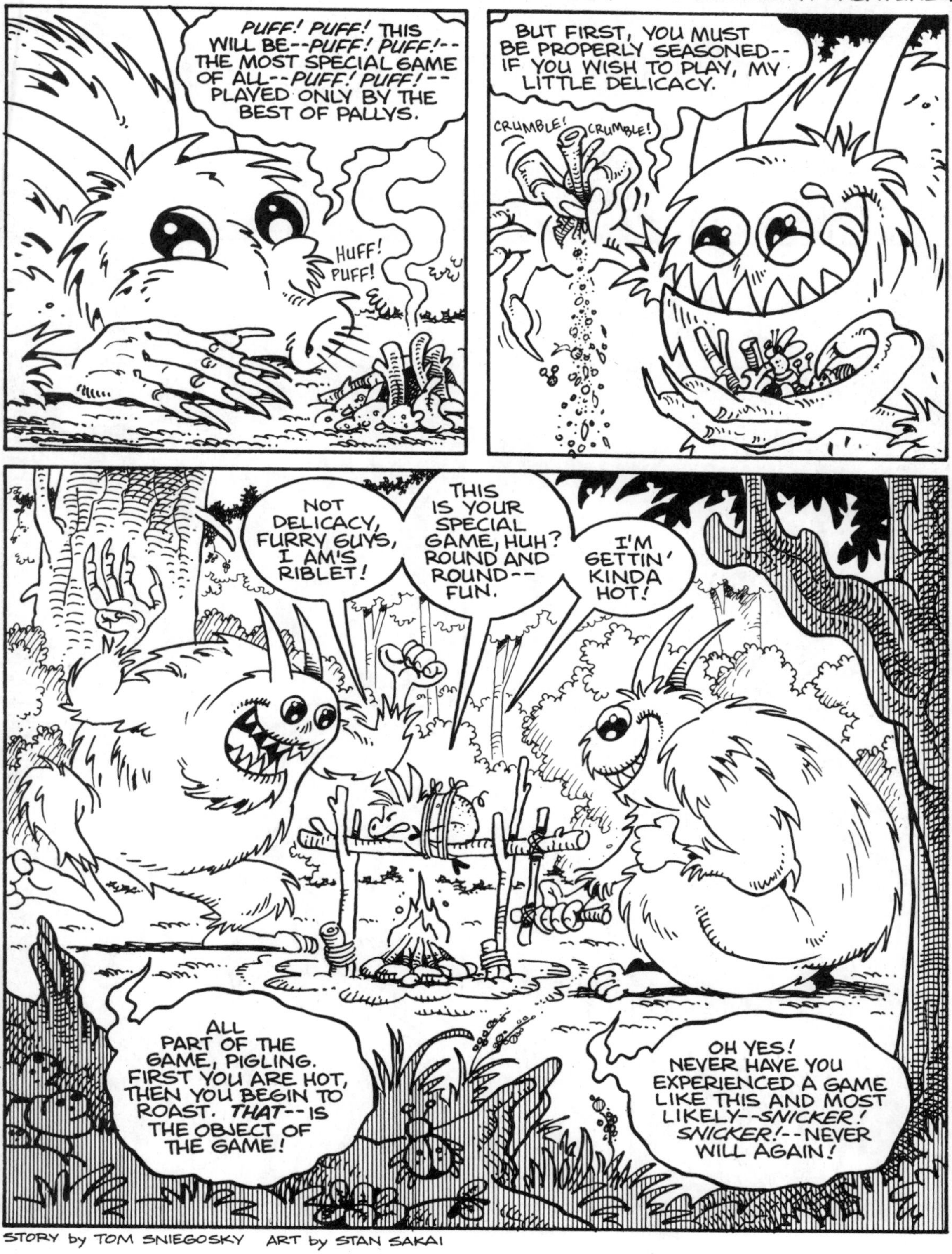
PUFF! PUFF! THIS WILL BE--PUFF! PUFF!--THE MOST SPECIAL GAME OF ALL--PUFF! PUFF!--PLAYED ONLY BY THE BEST OF PALLYS.
HUFF! PUFF!
BUT FIRST, YOU MUST BE PROPERLY SEASONED--IF YOU WISH TO PLAY, MY LITTLE DELICACY.
CRUMBLE! CRUMBLE!
NOT DELICACY, FURRY GUYS, I AM'S RIBLET!
THIS IS YOUR SPECIAL GAME, HUH? ROUND AND ROUND--FUN.
I'M GETTIN' KINDA HOT!
ALL PART OF THE GAME, PIGLING. FIRST YOU ARE HOT, THEN YOU BEGIN TO ROAST. THAT--IS THE OBJECT OF THE GAME!
OH YES! NEVER HAVE YOU EXPERIENCED A GAME LIKE THIS AND MOST LIKELY--SNICKER! SNICKER!--NEVER WILL AGAIN!

STORY by TOM SNIEGOSKY ART by STAN SAKAI

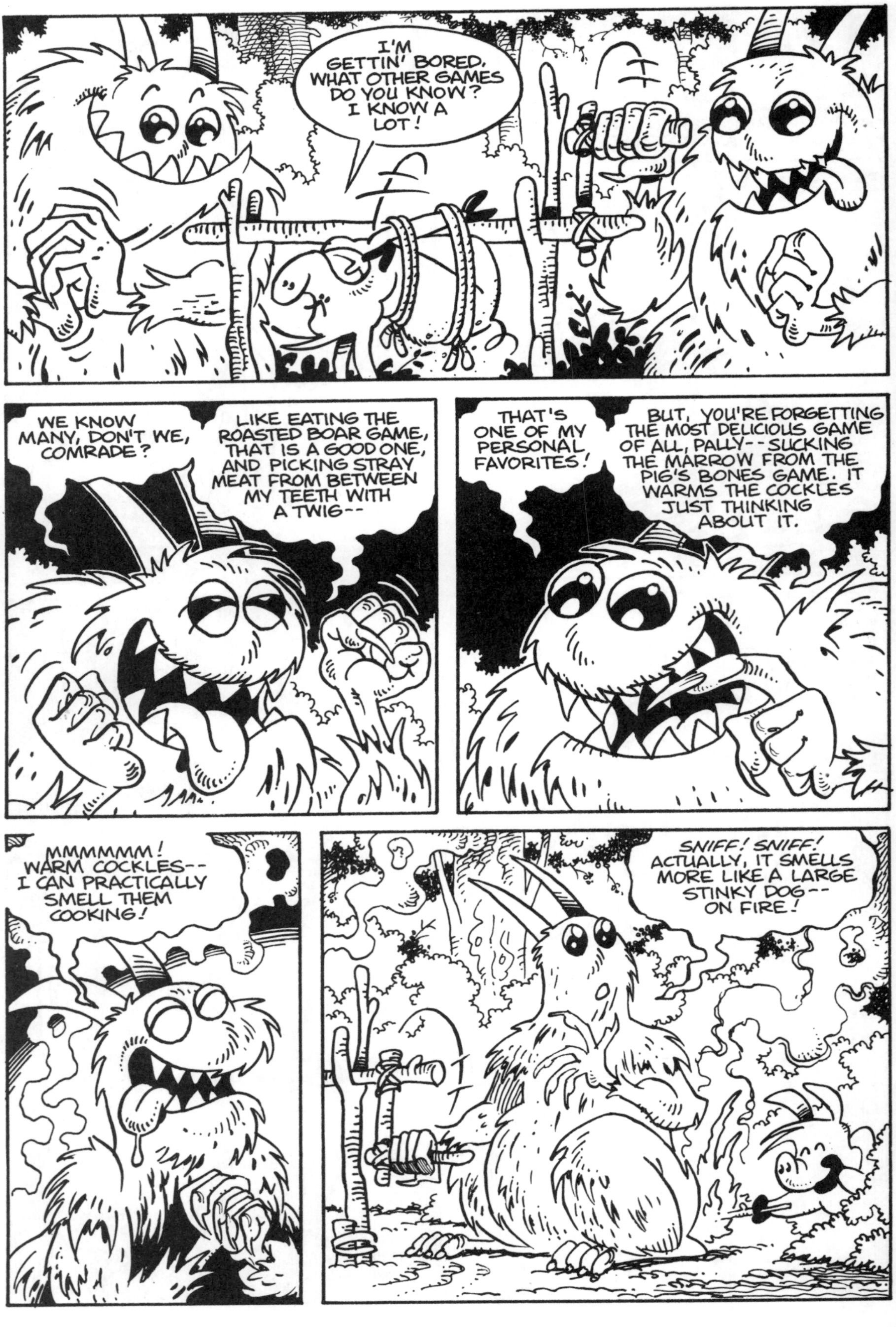
I'M GETTIN' BORED. WHAT OTHER GAMES DO YOU KNOW? I KNOW A LOT!
WE KNOW MANY, DON'T WE, COMRADE?
LIKE EATING THE ROASTED BOAR GAME, THAT IS A GOOD ONE, AND PICKING STRAY MEAT FROM BETWEEN MY TEETH WITH A TWIG--
THAT'S ONE OF MY PERSONAL FAVORITES!
BUT, YOU'RE FORGETTING THE MOST DELICIOUS GAME OF ALL, PALLY--SUCKING THE MARROW FROM THE PIG'S BONES GAME. IT WARMS THE COCKLES JUST THINKING ABOUT IT.
MMMMMMM! WARM COCKLES-- I CAN PRACTICALLY SMELL THEM COOKING!
SNIFF! SNIFF! ACTUALLY, IT SMELLS MORE LIKE A LARGE STINKY DOG-- ON FIRE!

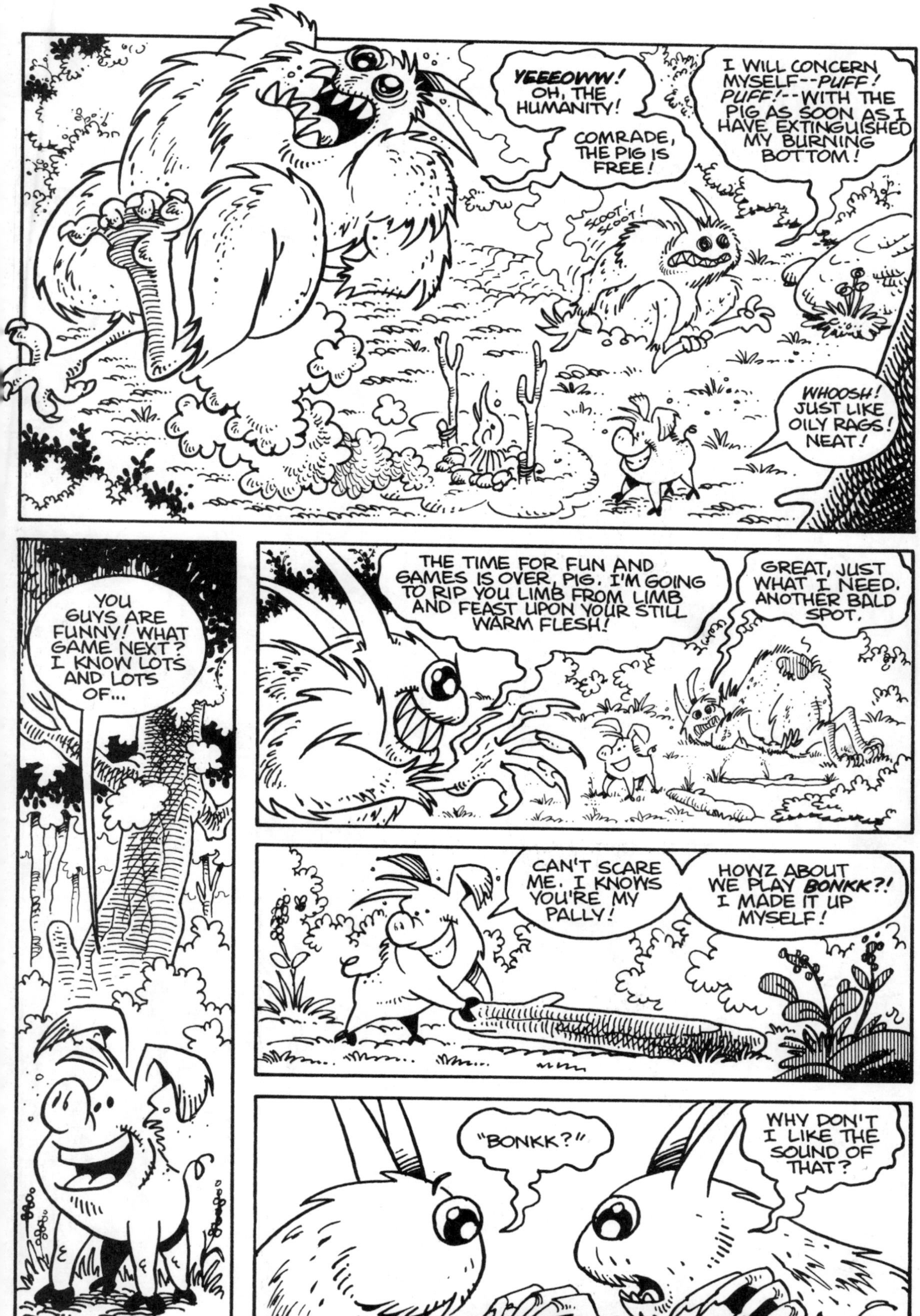
YEEEOWW! OH, THE HUMANITY!
COMRADE, THE PIG IS FREE!
I WILL CONCERN MYSELF--PUFF! PUFF!--WITH THE PIG AS SOON AS I HAVE EXTINGUISHED MY BURNING BOTTOM!
SCOOT! SCOOT!
WHOOSH! JUST LIKE OILY RAGS! NEAT!
YOU GUYS ARE FUNNY! WHAT GAME NEXT? I KNOW LOTS AND LOTS OF...
THE TIME FOR FUN AND GAMES IS OVER, PIG. I'M GOING TO RIP YOU LIMB FROM LIMB AND FEAST UPON YOUR STILL WARM FLESH!
GREAT, JUST WHAT I NEED. ANOTHER BALD SPOT.
CAN'T SCARE ME. I KNOWS YOU'RE MY PALLY!
HOWZ ABOUT WE PLAY BONKK?! I MADE IT UP MYSELF!
"BONKK?"
WHY DON'T I LIKE THE SOUND OF THAT?

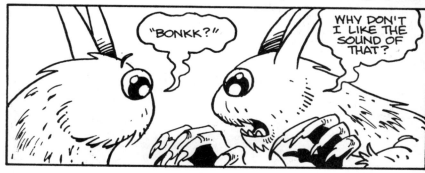

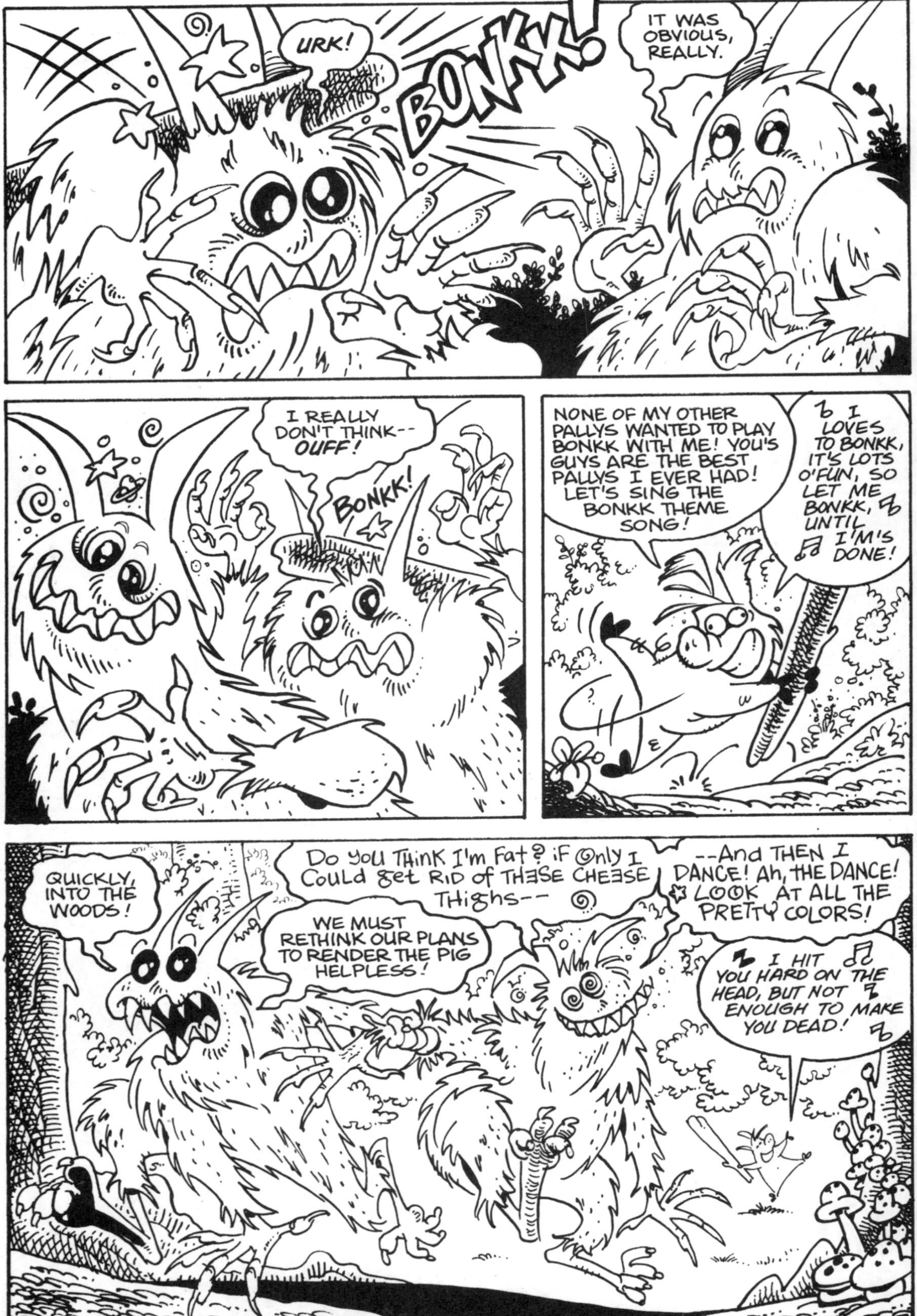
URK!
BONKK!
IT WAS OBVIOUS, REALLY.
I REALLY DON'T THINK-- OUFF!
BONKK!
NONE OF MY OTHER PALLYS WANTED TO PLAY BONKK WITH ME! YOU'S GUYS ARE THE BEST PALLYS I EVER HAD! LET'S SING THE BONKK THEME SONG!
I LOVES TO BONKK, IT'S LOTS O'FUN, SO LET ME BONKK, UNTIL I'M'S DONE!
QUICKLY, INTO THE WOODS!
WE MUST RETHINK OUR PLANS TO RENDER THE PIG HELPLESS!
Do you Think I'm Fat? if Only I Could get Rid of THESE CHEESE Thighs--
--And THEN I DANCE! Ah, THE DANCE! LOOK AT ALL THE PRETTY COLORS!
I HIT YOU HARD ON THE HEAD, BUT NOT ENOUGH TO MAKE YOU DEAD!

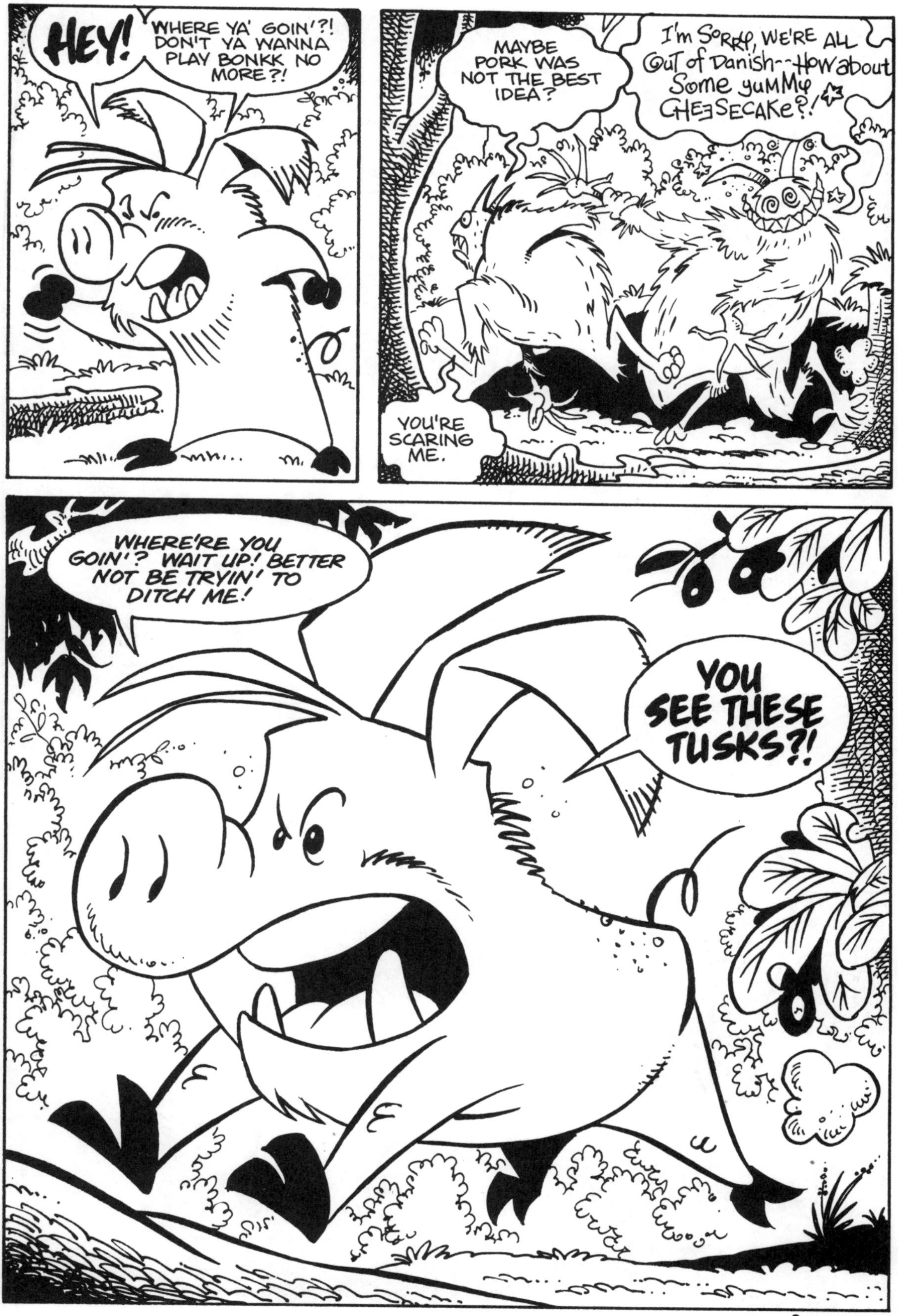
HEY!
WHERE YA' GOIN'?! DON'T YA WANNA PLAY BONKK NO MORE?!
MAYBE PORK WAS NOT THE BEST IDEA?
I'm SoRRY, WE'RE ALL OUT of Danish--How about Some yuMMy CHEESECAKE?!
YOU'RE SCARING ME.
WHERE'RE YOU GOIN'? WAIT UP! BETTER NOT BE TRYIN' TO DITCH ME!
YOU SEE THESE TUSKS?!

END of PART 3

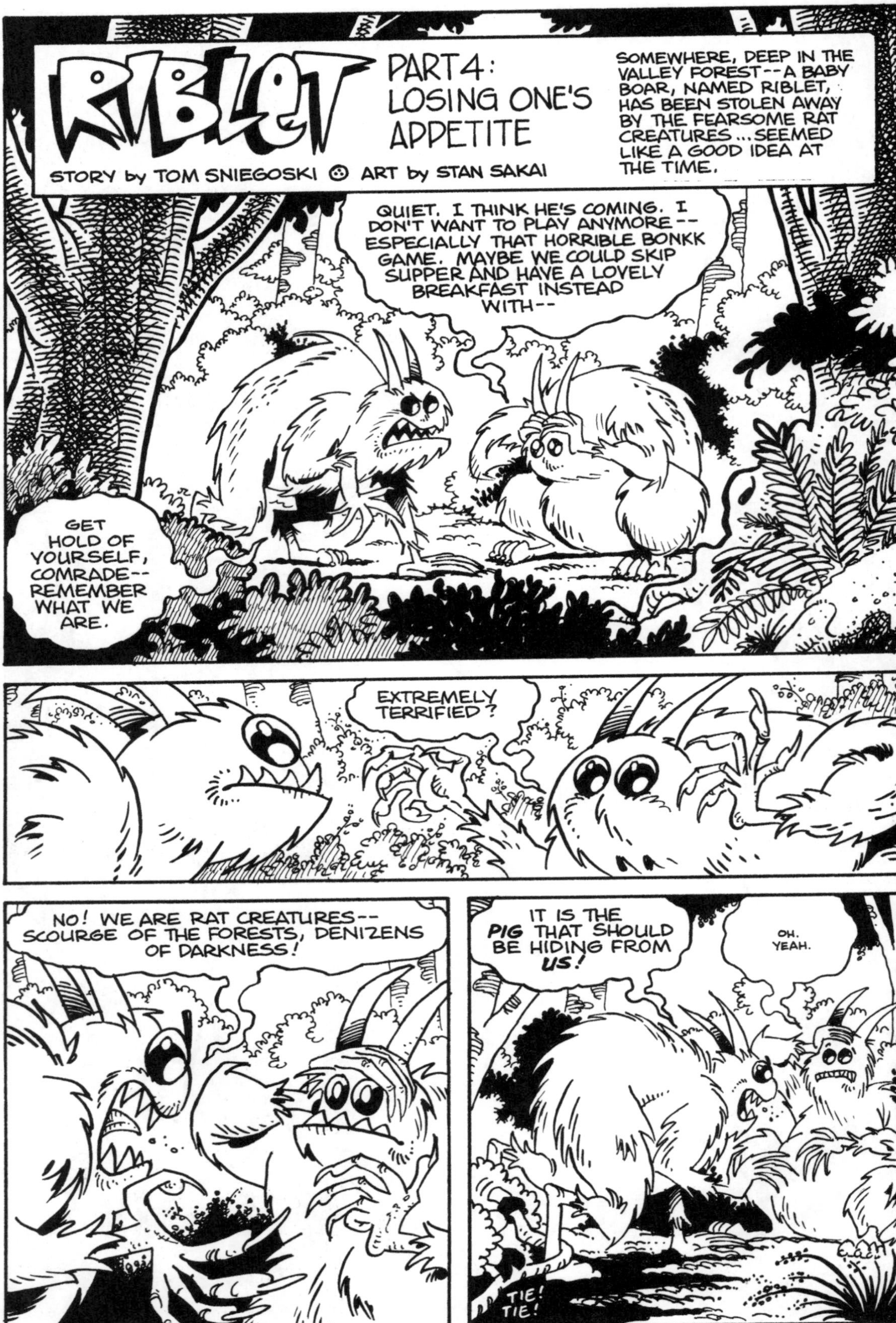
RIBLET
PART 4: LOSING ONE'S APPETITE
SOMEWHERE, DEEP IN THE VALLEY FOREST--A BABY BOAR, NAMED RIBLET, HAS BEEN STOLEN AWAY BY THE FEARSOME RAT CREATURES...SEEMED LIKE A GOOD IDEA AT THE TIME.
STORY by TOM SNIEGOSKI ☺ ART by STAN SAKAI
QUIET. I THINK HE'S COMING. I DON'T WANT TO PLAY ANYMORE -- ESPECIALLY THAT HORRIBLE BONKK GAME. MAYBE WE COULD SKIP SUPPER AND HAVE A LOVELY BREAKFAST INSTEAD WITH--
GET HOLD OF YOURSELF, COMRADE-- REMEMBER WHAT WE ARE.
EXTREMELY TERRIFIED?
NO! WE ARE RAT CREATURES-- SCOURGE OF THE FORESTS, DENIZENS OF DARKNESS!
IT IS THE PIG THAT SHOULD BE HIDING FROM US!
OH. YEAH.
TIE! TIE!

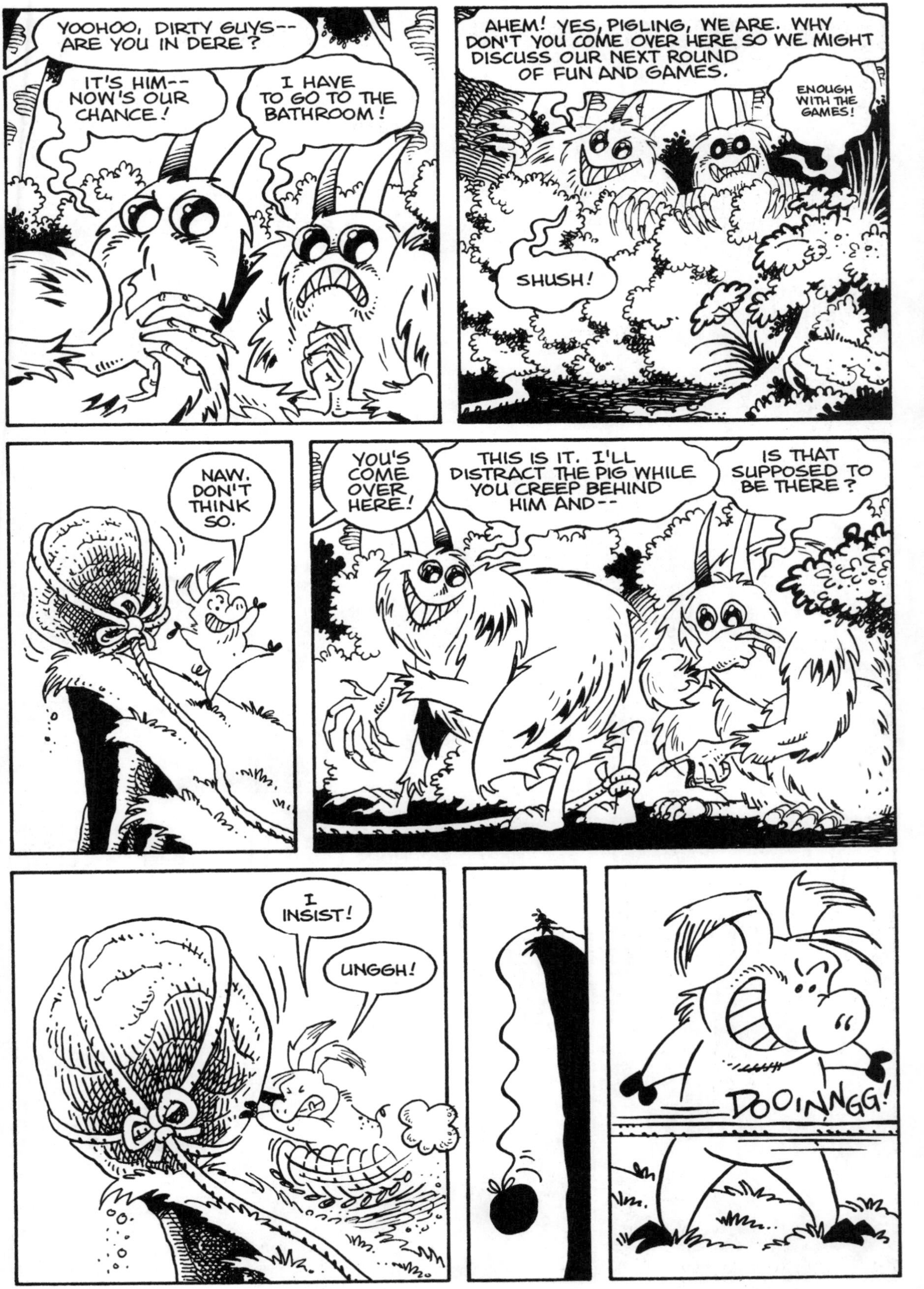
YOOHOO, DIRTY GUYS-- ARE YOU IN DERE?
IT'S HIM-- NOW'S OUR CHANCE!
I HAVE TO GO TO THE BATHROOM!
AHEM! YES, PIGLING, WE ARE. WHY DON'T YOU COME OVER HERE SO WE MIGHT DISCUSS OUR NEXT ROUND OF FUN AND GAMES.
ENOUGH WITH THE GAMES!
SHUSH!
NAW. DON'T THINK SO.
YOU'S COME OVER HERE!
THIS IS IT. I'LL DISTRACT THE PIG WHILE YOU CREEP BEHIND HIM AND--
IS THAT SUPPOSED TO BE THERE?
I INSIST!
UNGGH!
DOOINNGG!

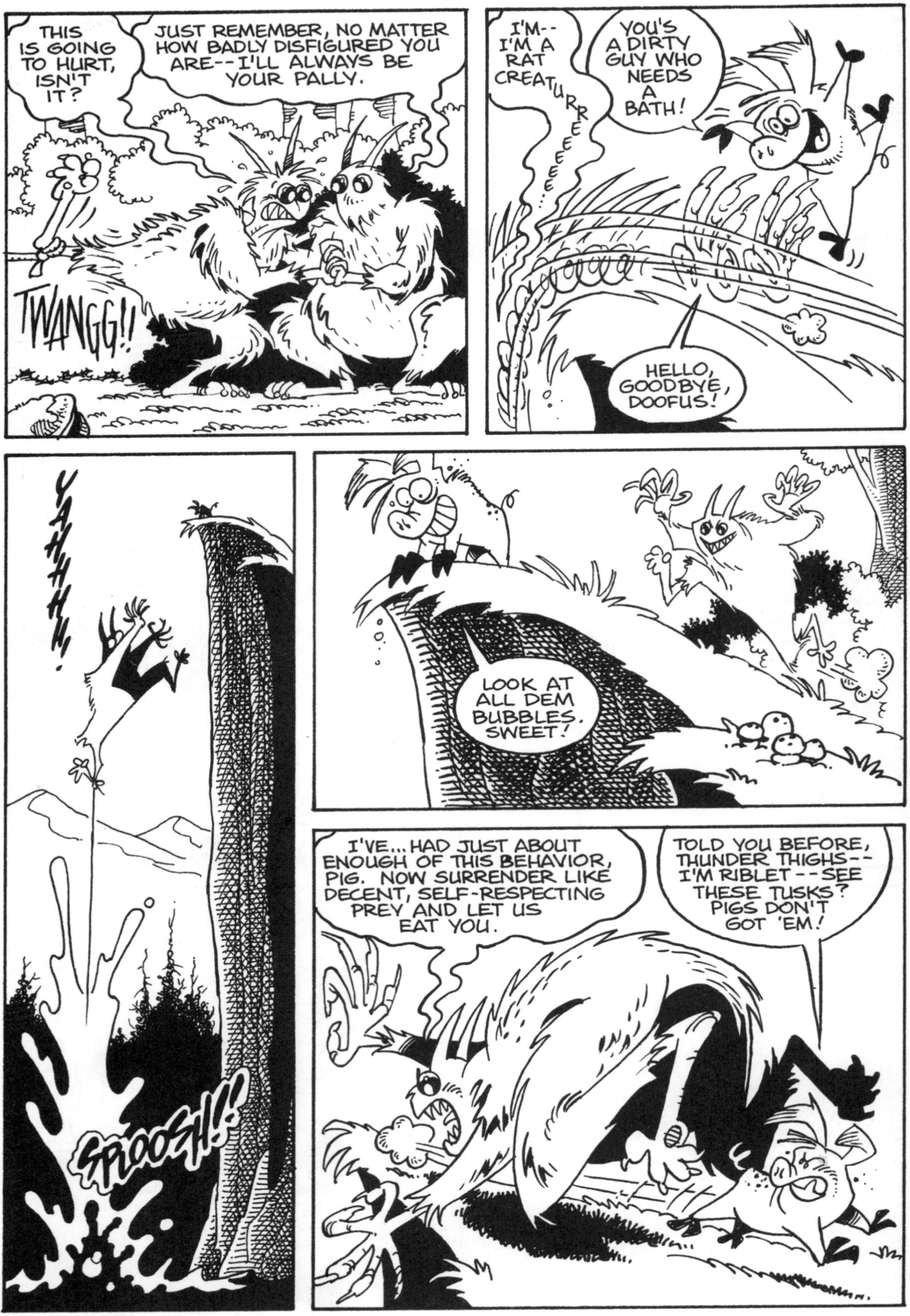
THIS IS GOING TO HURT, ISN'T IT?
JUST REMEMBER, NO MATTER HOW BADLY DISFIGURED YOU ARE--I'LL ALWAYS BE YOUR PALLY.
TWANGG!!
I'M--I'M A RAT CREATURREEEEEEE...
YOU'S A DIRTY GUY WHO NEEDS A BATH!
HELLO, GOODBYE, DOOFUS!
YAHHHH!
SPLOOSH!!
LOOK AT ALL DEM BUBBLES. SWEET!
I'VE... HAD JUST ABOUT ENOUGH OF THIS BEHAVIOR, PIG. NOW SURRENDER LIKE DECENT, SELF-RESPECTING PREY AND LET US EAT YOU.
TOLD YOU BEFORE, THUNDER THIGHS--I'M RIBLET--SEE THESE TUSKS? PIGS DON'T GOT 'EM!

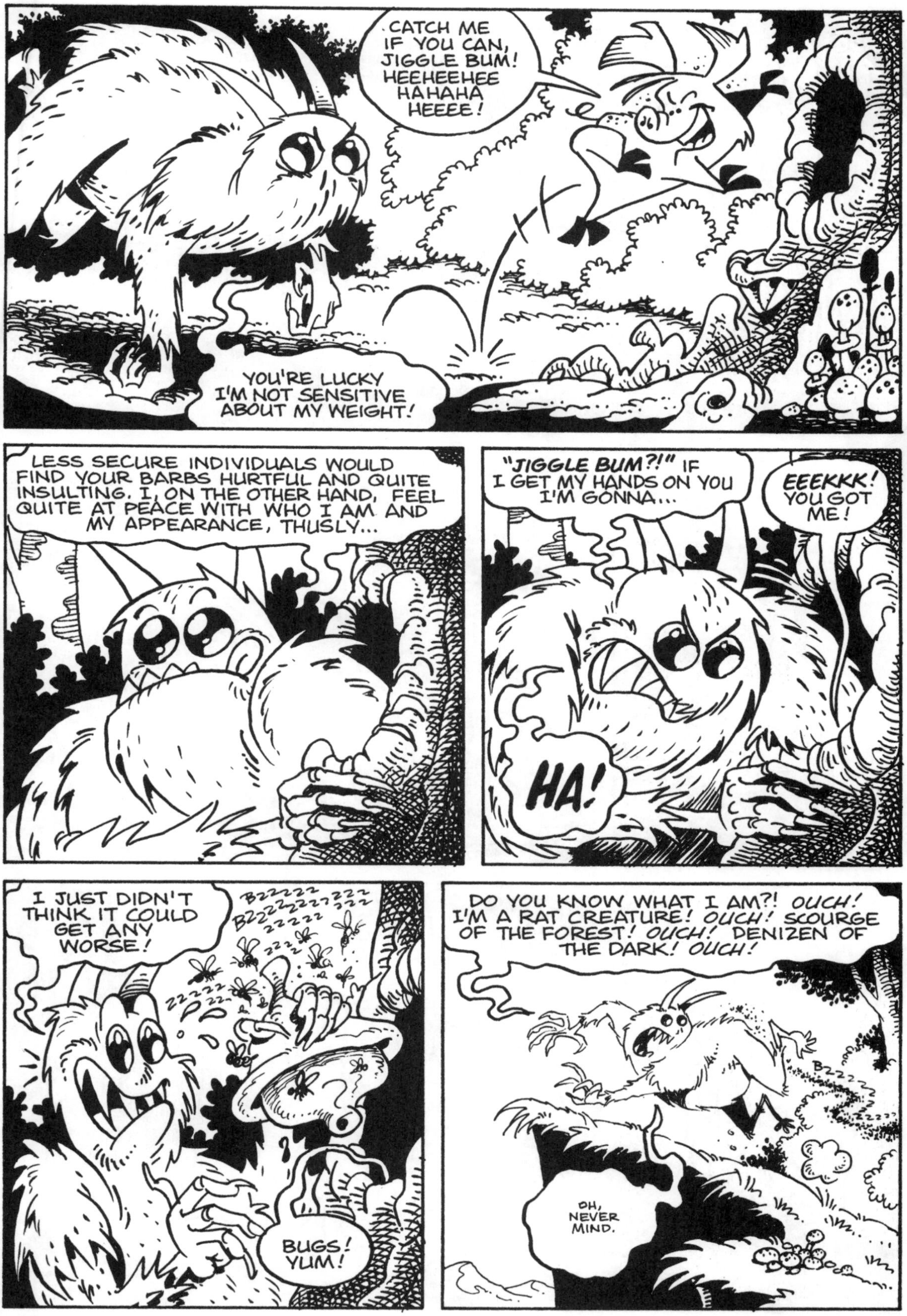

CATCH ME IF YOU CAN, JIGGLE BUM! HEEHEEHEE HAHAHA HEEEE!
YOU'RE LUCKY I'M NOT SENSITIVE ABOUT MY WEIGHT!
LESS SECURE INDIVIDUALS WOULD FIND YOUR BARBS HURTFUL AND QUITE INSULTING. I, ON THE OTHER HAND, FEEL QUITE AT PEACE WITH WHO I AM AND MY APPEARANCE, THUSLY...
"JIGGLE BUM?!" IF I GET MY HANDS ON YOU I'M GONNA...
EEEKKK! YOU GOT ME!
HA!
I JUST DIDN'T THINK IT COULD GET ANY WORSE!
BZZZZZ
BUGS! YUM!
DO YOU KNOW WHAT I AM?! OUCH! I'M A RAT CREATURE! OUCH! SCOURGE OF THE FOREST! OUCH! DENIZEN OF THE DARK! OUCH!
OH, NEVER MIND.

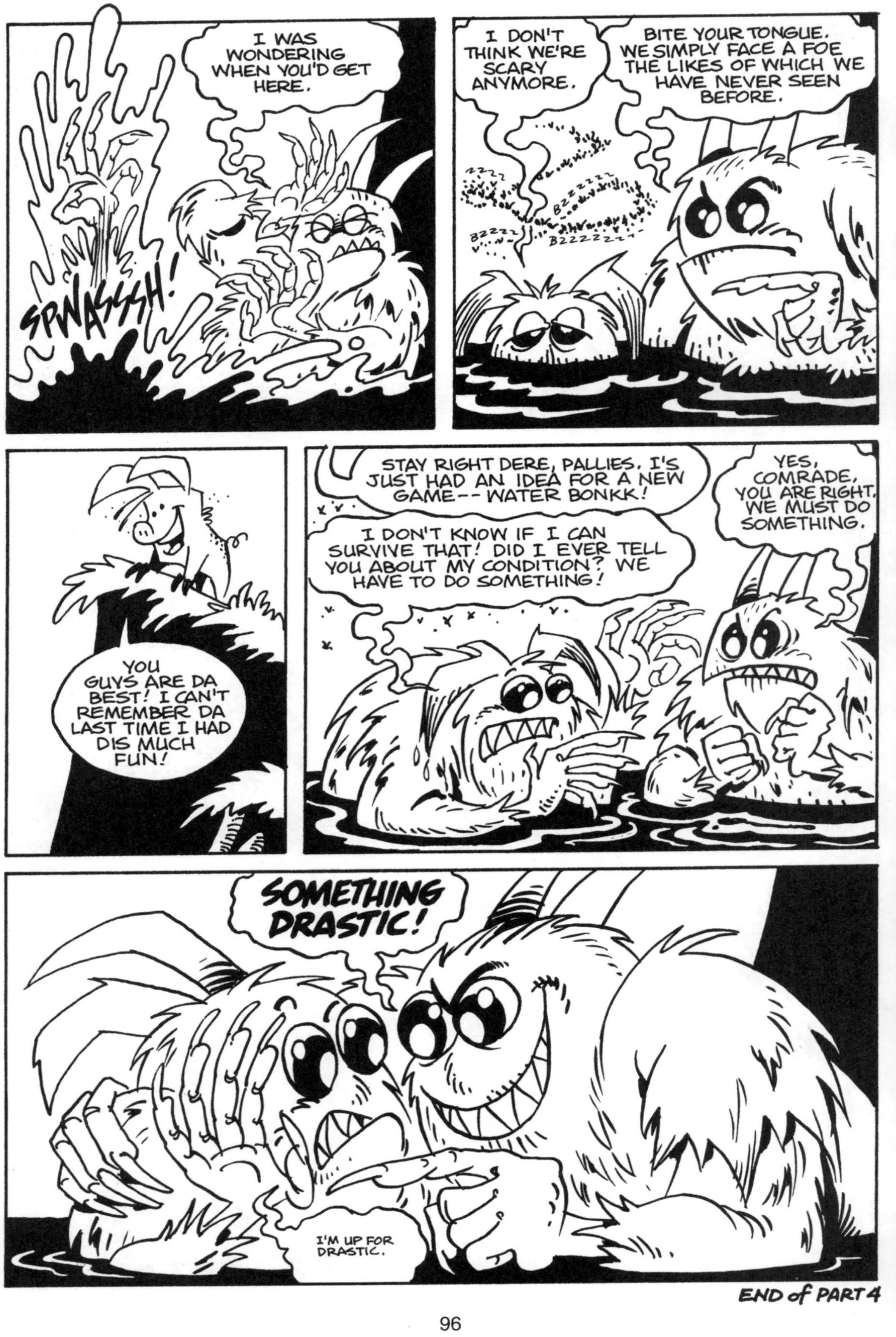
I WAS WONDERING WHEN YOU'D GET HERE.
SPWASSSH!
I DON'T THINK WE'RE SCARY ANYMORE.
BITE YOUR TONGUE. WE SIMPLY FACE A FOE THE LIKES OF WHICH WE HAVE NEVER SEEN BEFORE.
YOU GUYS ARE DA BEST! I CAN'T REMEMBER DA LAST TIME I HAD DIS MUCH FUN!
STAY RIGHT DERE, PALLIES. I'S JUST HAD AN IDEA FOR A NEW GAME-- WATER BONKK!
I DON'T KNOW IF I CAN SURVIVE THAT! DID I EVER TELL YOU ABOUT MY CONDITION? WE HAVE TO DO SOMETHING!
YES, COMRADE, YOU ARE RIGHT. WE MUST DO SOMETHING.
SOMETHING DRASTIC!
I'M UP FOR DRASTIC.

END of PART 4

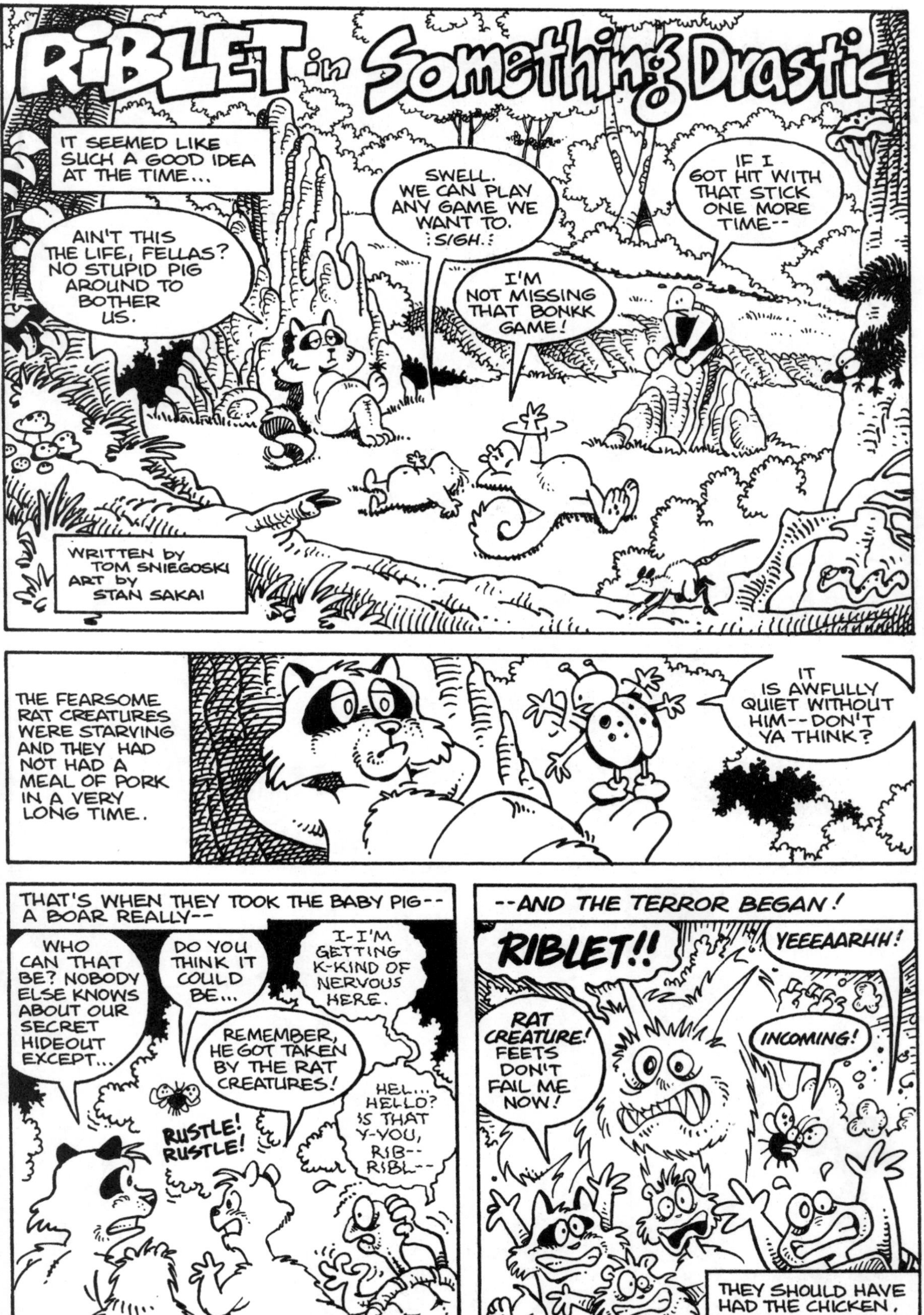
RIBLET in Something Drastic
IT SEEMED LIKE SUCH A GOOD IDEA AT THE TIME...
AIN'T THIS THE LIFE, FELLAS? NO STUPID PIG AROUND TO BOTHER US.
SWELL. WE CAN PLAY ANY GAME WE WANT TO. :SIGH.:
I'M NOT MISSING THAT BONKK GAME!
IF I GOT HIT WITH THAT STICK ONE MORE TIME--
WRITTEN BY TOM SNIEGOSKI ART BY STAN SAKAI
THE FEARSOME RAT CREATURES WERE STARVING AND THEY HAD NOT HAD A MEAL OF PORK IN A VERY LONG TIME.
IT IS AWFULLY QUIET WITHOUT HIM--DON'T YA THINK?
THAT'S WHEN THEY TOOK THE BABY PIG-- A BOAR REALLY--
WHO CAN THAT BE? NOBODY ELSE KNOWS ABOUT OUR SECRET HIDEOUT EXCEPT...
DO YOU THINK IT COULD BE...
I-I'M GETTING K-KIND OF NERVOUS HERE.
REMEMBER, HE GOT TAKEN BY THE RAT CREATURES!
RUSTLE! RUSTLE!
HEL... HELLO? IS THAT Y-YOU, RIB-- RIBL--
--AND THE TERROR BEGAN!
RIBLET!!
YEEEAARHH!
RAT CREATURE! FEETS DON'T FAIL ME NOW!
INCOMING!
THEY SHOULD HAVE HAD THE CHICKEN.

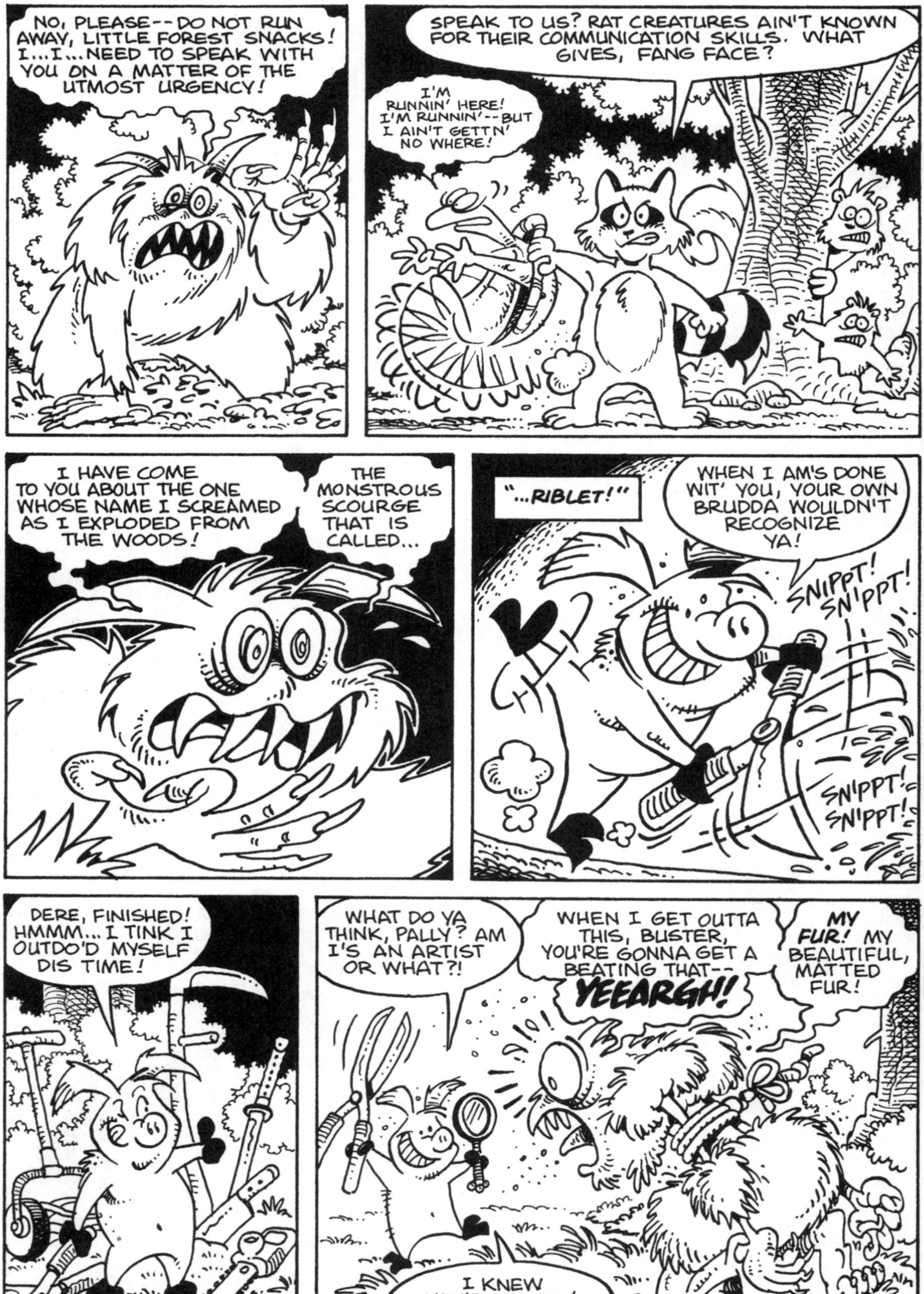
NO, PLEASE--DO NOT RUN AWAY, LITTLE FOREST SNACKS! I...I...NEED TO SPEAK WITH YOU ON A MATTER OF THE UTMOST URGENCY!
SPEAK TO US? RAT CREATURES AIN'T KNOWN FOR THEIR COMMUNICATION SKILLS. WHAT GIVES, FANG FACE?
I'M RUNNIN' HERE! I'M RUNNIN'--BUT I AIN'T GETTN' NO WHERE!
I HAVE COME TO YOU ABOUT THE ONE WHOSE NAME I SCREAMED AS I EXPLODED FROM THE WOODS!
THE MONSTROUS SCOURGE THAT IS CALLED...
"...RIBLET!"
WHEN I AM'S DONE WIT' YOU, YOUR OWN BRUDDA WOULDN'T RECOGNIZE YA!
SNIPPT! SNIPPT!
SNIPPT! SNIPPT!
DERE, FINISHED! HMMM... I TINK I OUTDO'D MYSELF DIS TIME!
WHAT DO YA THINK, PALLY? AM I'S AN ARTIST OR WHAT?!
WHEN I GET OUTTA THIS, BUSTER, YOU'RE GONNA GET A BEATING THAT-- YEEARGH!
MY FUR! MY BEAUTIFUL, MATTED FUR!
I KNEW YOU'D LIKE IT! YOU'RE WELCOME!

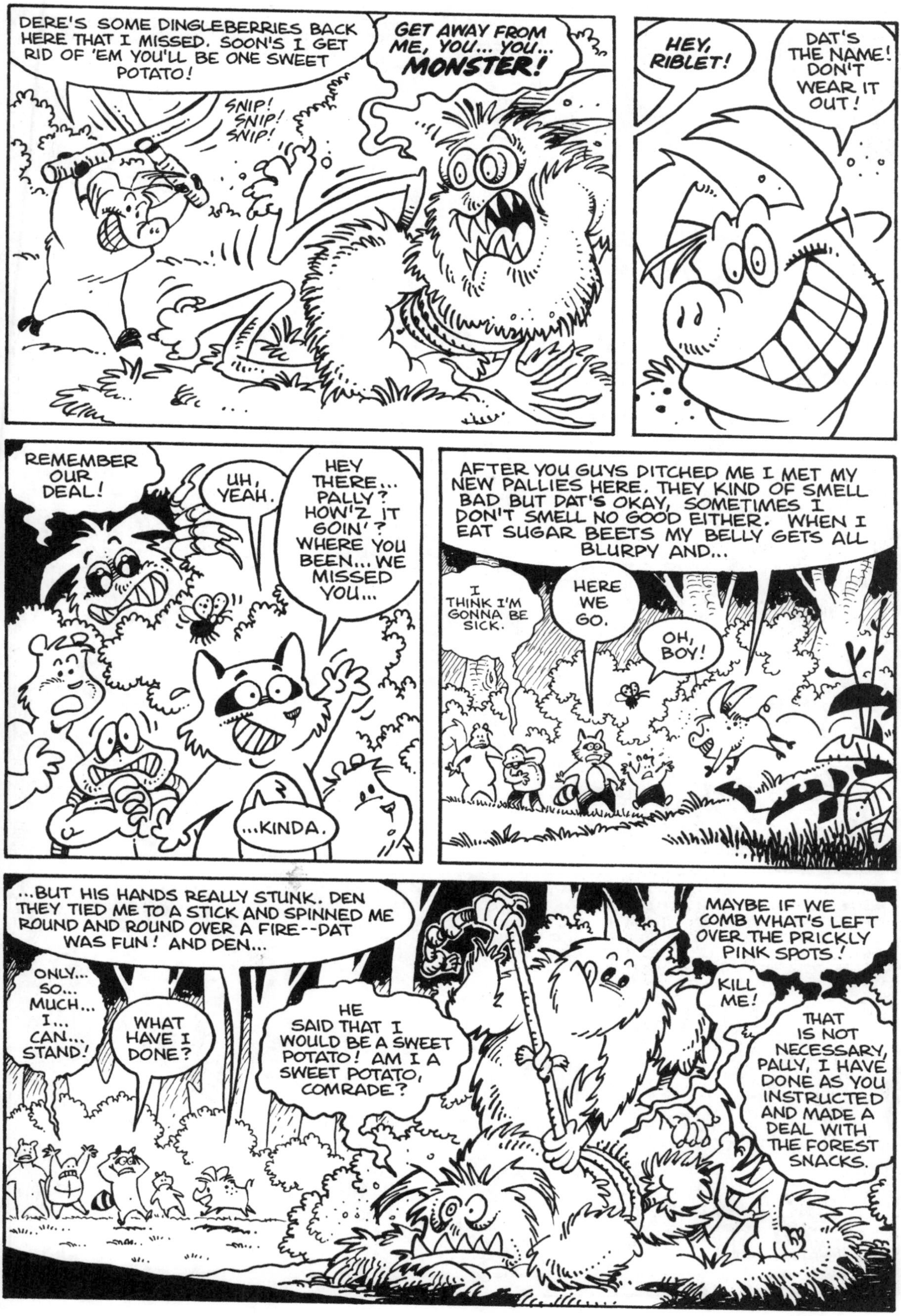
DERE'S SOME DINGLEBERRIES BACK HERE THAT I MISSED. SOON'S I GET RID OF 'EM YOU'LL BE ONE SWEET POTATO!
SNIP! SNIP! SNIP!
GET AWAY FROM ME, YOU... YOU... MONSTER!
HEY, RIBLET!
DAT'S THE NAME! DON'T WEAR IT OUT!
REMEMBER OUR DEAL!
UH, YEAH.
HEY THERE... PALLY? HOW'Z IT GOIN'? WHERE YOU BEEN... WE MISSED YOU...
...KINDA.
AFTER YOU GUYS DITCHED ME I MET MY NEW PALLIES HERE. THEY KIND OF SMELL BAD BUT DAT'S OKAY, SOMETIMES I DON'T SMELL NO GOOD EITHER. WHEN I EAT SUGAR BEETS MY BELLY GETS ALL BLURPY AND...
I THINK I'M GONNA BE SICK.
HERE WE GO.
OH, BOY!
...BUT HIS HANDS REALLY STUNK. DEN THEY TIED ME TO A STICK AND SPINNED ME ROUND AND ROUND OVER A FIRE--DAT WAS FUN! AND DEN...
ONLY... SO... MUCH... I... CAN... STAND!
WHAT HAVE I DONE?
HE SAID THAT I WOULD BE A SWEET POTATO! AM I A SWEET POTATO, COMRADE?
MAYBE IF WE COMB WHAT'S LEFT OVER THE PRICKLY PINK SPOTS!
KILL ME!
THAT IS NOT NECESSARY, PALLY, I HAVE DONE AS YOU INSTRUCTED AND MADE A DEAL WITH THE FOREST SNACKS.

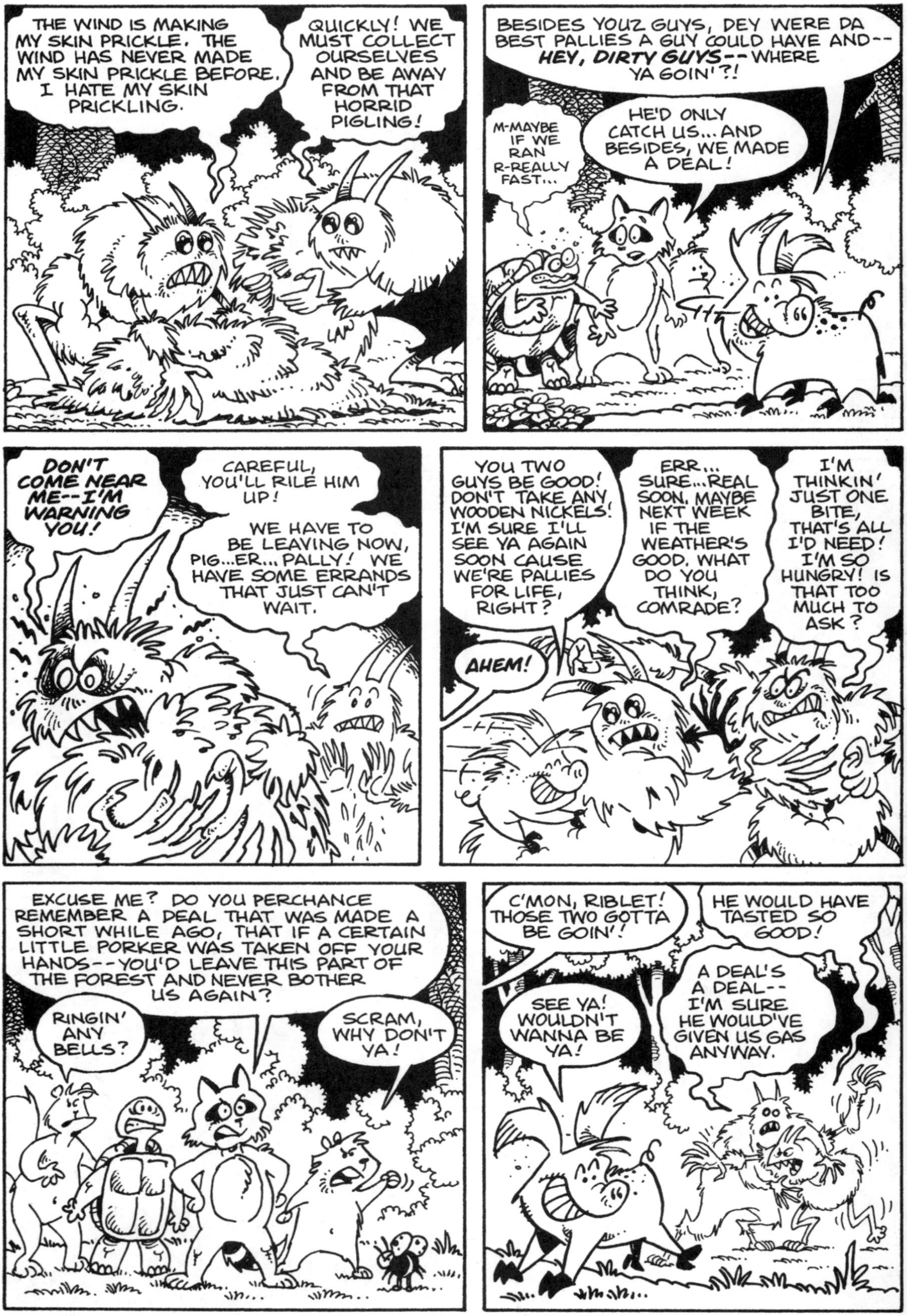
THE WIND IS MAKING MY SKIN PRICKLE. THE WIND HAS NEVER MADE MY SKIN PRICKLE BEFORE. I HATE MY SKIN PRICKLING.
QUICKLY! WE MUST COLLECT OURSELVES AND BE AWAY FROM THAT HORRID PIGLING!
BESIDES YOUZ GUYS, DEY WERE DA BEST PALLIES A GUY COULD HAVE AND-- HEY, DIRTY GUYS-- WHERE YA GOIN'?!
M-MAYBE IF WE RAN R-REALLY FAST...
HE'D ONLY CATCH US... AND BESIDES, WE MADE A DEAL!
DON'T COME NEAR ME--I'M WARNING YOU!
CAREFUL, YOU'LL RILE HIM UP!
WE HAVE TO BE LEAVING NOW, PIG...ER... PALLY! WE HAVE SOME ERRANDS THAT JUST CAN'T WAIT.
YOU TWO GUYS BE GOOD! DON'T TAKE ANY WOODEN NICKELS! I'M SURE I'LL SEE YA AGAIN SOON CAUSE WE'RE PALLIES FOR LIFE, RIGHT?
AHEM!
ERR... SURE... REAL SOON. MAYBE NEXT WEEK IF THE WEATHER'S GOOD. WHAT DO YOU THINK, COMRADE?
I'M THINKIN' JUST ONE BITE, THAT'S ALL I'D NEED! I'M SO HUNGRY! IS THAT TOO MUCH TO ASK?
EXCUSE ME? DO YOU PERCHANCE REMEMBER A DEAL THAT WAS MADE A SHORT WHILE AGO, THAT IF A CERTAIN LITTLE PORKER WAS TAKEN OFF YOUR HANDS--YOU'D LEAVE THIS PART OF THE FOREST AND NEVER BOTHER US AGAIN?
RINGIN' ANY BELLS?
SCRAM, WHY DON'T YA!
C'MON, RIBLET! THOSE TWO GOTTA BE GOIN'!
HE WOULD HAVE TASTED SO GOOD!
SEE YA! WOULDN'T WANNA BE YA!
A DEAL'S A DEAL-- I'M SURE HE WOULD'VE GIVEN US GAS ANYWAY.

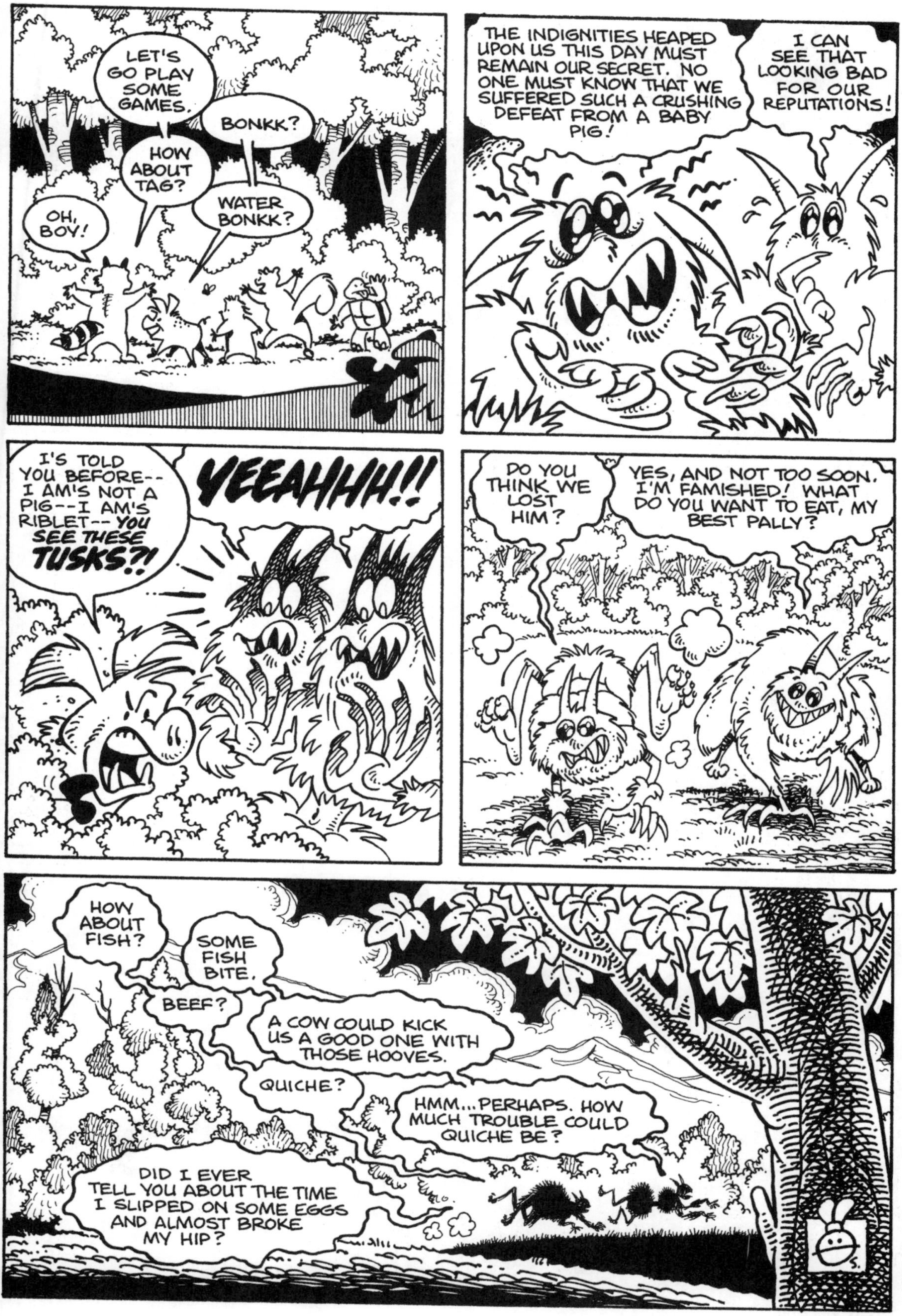
LET'S GO PLAY SOME GAMES.
HOW ABOUT TAG?
BONKK?
WATER BONKK?
OH, BOY!
THE INDIGNITIES HEAPED UPON US THIS DAY MUST REMAIN OUR SECRET. NO ONE MUST KNOW THAT WE SUFFERED SUCH A CRUSHING DEFEAT FROM A BABY PIG!
I CAN SEE THAT LOOKING BAD FOR OUR REPUTATIONS!
I'S TOLD YOU BEFORE-- I AM'S NOT A PIG--I AM'S RIBLET--YOU SEE THESE TUSKS?!
YEEAHHH!!
DO YOU THINK WE LOST HIM?
YES, AND NOT TOO SOON. I'M FAMISHED! WHAT DO YOU WANT TO EAT, MY BEST PALLY?
HOW ABOUT FISH?
SOME FISH BITE.
BEEF?
A COW COULD KICK US A GOOD ONE WITH THOSE HOOVES.
QUICHE?
HMM...PERHAPS. HOW MUCH TROUBLE COULD QUICHE BE?
DID I EVER TELL YOU ABOUT THE TIME I SLIPPED ON SOME EGGS AND ALMOST BROKE MY HIP?
S.

THE END